The La Follettes
AND THE WISCONSIN IDEA

Robert La Follette, Jr. and the statue of his father in
Statuary Hall, Capitol Building, Washington, D.C.

The La Follettes

AND THE
WISCONSIN IDEA

EDWARD N. DOAN

RINEHART & COMPANY, INC.
NEW YORK   TORONTO

92
L165d

Contents

Acknowledgments

Acknowledgments

NEVER, to paraphrase a famous remark, has one person owed so much to so many people. To the many busy men and women who were so generous in volunteering their time and knowledge that this book might be more complete, I can only repeat my grateful thanks.

Had it not been for the wholehearted assistance of the staff of the Wisconsin Legislative Reference Library, Mr. Howard Ohm and his assistants, Mrs. Hazel Kuehn, Miss Jane Lester, Miss Eleanore Laurant, and Miss Alice Fosse, who made the drudgery of research a real pleasure, preparation of the manuscript for this book would have been much more difficult. The foresighted policy of the Library has made available not only a voluminous collection of data concerning the Senators La Follette, but a rich source of carefully catalogued information on the whole Progressive movement in Wisconsin.

I appreciate the courtesy of the staff of the Wisconsin State Historical Society in making available for study materials in the manuscript division of the Society.

Mr. and Mrs. Wilbur Voigt and Miss Grace Lynch of Washington, D. C., saved me from many egregious errors of fact and interpretation, for which I am grateful.

My indebtedness to Morris H. Rubin for his courtesy in permitting me to quote from *The Progressive*, his unbounded interest in my efforts, and his patience and good humor in the face of my sometimes unduly thoughtless demands on his time and energies is especially deep.

To the Editors of *Life* my thanks for their courtesy in granting me the privilege of quoting from various editorials.

To Walter Davenport, editor of *Collier's*, my thanks for his cordial co-operation in permitting me access to material published in that magazine.

E. N. D.

The La Follettes
AND THE WISCONSIN IDEA

CHAPTER I

Introduction

IN THE RELIGIOUS FIELD they are called Seekers—those who forsake formal religious dogma in their search for direct knowledge of God. Roger Williams, Thomas Jefferson, Ralph Waldo Emerson are perhaps the outstanding examples in American history. All three, Williams and Jefferson directly and Emerson more indirectly, played important roles in the political development of this nation.

In politics they are called radicals, insurgents, destroyers of society, and subversive elements. They call themselves Progressives. They seek in the political field to develop a direct, responsive government in which each citizen is accorded the full dignity of sovereignty. In short, the essence of the progressive idea as it has developed in the United States is the simple demand for fair dealing, for exact justice between man and man.

Both the religious Seekers and the political Progressives have in common an unshakable belief in the democratic principle of self-government. They are the liberals who have fought to establish the principle that governmental machinery, because of its nature, must be as concerned for the rights of the inarticulate mass of citizens as for the rights of the articulate and economically powerful few. These champions of democracy, like the Disciples at the beginning of the Christian era, have sprung from all parties and all groups of society.

To claim, as all political parties in the United States have on occasion, that one particular group is *the* progressive and liberal party is arrant nonsense. An urbane cosmopolite like Thomas Jefferson risked the censure of the group he presumably represented to strike down religious intolerances and to establish the principle of universal education. Andrew Jackson came from the rough frontier to shock the smug and comfortable people of the seaboard into knowledge of the lively and real interest of the citizens beyond the Alleghenies in a truly political democracy. He fought against the power of entrenched wealth and struck down the Bank of the United States.

Perhaps no more radical document was ever written than Abraham Lincoln's Proclamation of Emancipation. It was a breath-taking denial of property rights and struck down another institution that was inimical to political and economic democracy.

In the shift from a predominantly agrarian economy to an industrial economy and the comparative centralization of wealth that followed the Civil War some of the fundamentals of political and economic democracy were temporarily neglected. Not for long, however, for the laboring man began to waken to the truth of strength in organization. The farmer in the Midwest, by nature and force of circumstance a rugged individual, began to stir and populism swept over the prairies.

During the 1890's and even earlier, individual voices could be heard denouncing morally and socially irresponsible industrial monopolies. Eugene Debs frightened the forces of entrenched industrial power by preaching socialism. His movement was put down with brute force. William Jennings Bryan frightened the banking powers of the nation by his denunciation of the cross of gold that was being forced upon the work-weary shoulders of laborers in every field.

Robert Marion La Follette, in Wisconsin, sought to bring about changes through the orderly procedures of a government dedicated to secure the greatest good to the greatest number. Like other progressive thinkers, La Follette, during the 1890's, was more a teacher than he was a political agitator. For ten years he preached the doctrine that government was established for the good of all—not just a few. His fighting leadership brought renown to Wisconsin as a truly progressive state. He helped to establish once more in men's minds the fact that political and economic democracy can work.

At the beginning of the twentieth century, however, people were still skeptical of the solutions worked out in Wisconsin. But Robert M. La Follette and his associates in Wisconsin had laid solid foundations and the legislative structure was sound. Soon Governor Albert B. Cummins was proposing similar progressive legislation in Iowa. Governor Woodrow Wilson in New Jersey wrought many progressive changes and paid tribute to the pioneering work of La Follette and the Wisconsin progressives. Governor James M. Cox of Ohio sent delegations to Wisconsin to find out how to put into effect the new social and economic legislation. He borrowed experts from Wisconsin to help him. Governor Hiram Johnson of California told fearful conservatives that he looked to Wisconsin as the fount of his Republicanism and not to William Howard Taft and the standpat conservatives of the party. Within recent years Governor Ellis Arnall has sponsored and put into effect many progressive changes in Georgia.

There is an exciting parallel between the fight Governor Arnall has carried on to get a state government responsive to the needs of all its citizens and the battles of Robert M. La Follette with the railroads, entrenched political bossism, and often heartbreaking lack of interest on the part of people who should have been most concerned.

Just as the Seekers caused embarrassment to formalized religious groups from which they came, so did the progressives cause acute pain to the formalized political organizations. Although it caused chagrin among the regulars and they gave the worst possible interpretation to the action, it was natural for progressives to step across party lines and assist each other. William Jennings Bryan was glad to go to Madison on Governor La Follette's invitation to address a joint session of the Wisconsin legislature to urge it to pass legislation regulating the railroads. It mattered not to the Democratic governor of Ohio, James M. Cox, that the progressive legislation he wanted to adopt in his state had been developed by a progressive Republican administration in Wisconsin.

Such situations have raised the query: Why not a realignment of party elements in order to present completely liberal and completely conservative parties in the United States? Or, Why not a liberal third party? At times of political or economic crisis, third parties have arisen in this country. But they were short-lived and never succeeded in welding together the dissident elements of the two major parties. In the long run, the presence of both liberal and conservative elements within the two major parties in this country has ensured a balance that has served the nation well. Both groups remind each other that democracy does not lie either at the extreme left or at the extreme right. The true liberals have been willing to take temporary defeat, even at the hands of their own party, in order that their ideas might be given a hearing. Asked why he did not start a third party, Robert M. La Follette once said that a third party would do him no good. "People listen to me because I am a Republican." Only the knowledge that the Republican party had reached such a low moral ebb and would not, or could not, meet the challenge of the domestic troubles of the early 1920's forced La Follette to run as an independent in the campaign for the presidency in 1924.

In a sharp reply to Speaker Nicholas Longsworth and the House Republican caucus for refusing Wisconsin Republican members their rightful places on committees because they had supported La Follette's candidacy for the presidency in 1924, Representative Joseph D. Beck of Wisconsin answered the taunting question as to why they remained in the Republican party.

"The best answer," Beck told the House of Representatives, "is that no state in this Union has a better claim to the Republican label than the people of Wisconsin. It was in Wisconsin in 1854 that a little band of farmers and common folks—radicals, if you wish—met in a convention, formed the Republican party, gave it its name, and devoted themselves, under the leadership of Lincoln and Schurz and Seward, in waging uncompromising warfare against the slave system and for the rights of the common people. We have remained in the Republican party for the simple reason that in Lincoln's principles of free representative government, and in his denunciation of the Supreme Court for its subservience to a vicious economic system, and in the original principles of the party as fashioned in Wisconsin, we have found abundant warrant for every principle of government we have advocated."

As a Republican Robert M. La Follette carried his unyielding fight for democracy into the Senate of the United States. He lost engagements in the battles over principles he stood for. But as the years have rolled by, the causes for which he literally gave his lifeblood have become established in our law. The soundness of those "radical" doctrines which La Follette championed and for which he was often reviled is questioned today only by the foolish and unwise. Death ended twenty years of distinguished service to democracy and the American people.

To the older of his two sons, Robert M. La Follette, Jr., was granted the opportunity to carry on in the United States Senate. One of the youngest men ever elected by popular vote to that distinguished body, Robert M. La Follette, Jr., possessed a knowledge and understanding of the inner workings of politics and government seldom at the command of a freshman senator. He had served for six years as his father's private secretary and had been at his side as manager during the 1924 presidential campaign.

The twenty-one-year record of Senator Robert M. La Follette, Jr., testifies to the fact that, like his father, he believes that if we have the courage to make American democracy work, not only politically but economically as well, we need have no fears for the future. So firm is his belief that he literally sacrificed his seat in the Senate to take advantage of the opportunity to secure passage of the bill reorganizing Congress during the summer of 1946. To him it was more important to help make Congress more responsive to present-day needs and better able and equipped to carry out the desires of a democratic society than to absent himself to enter the campaign for nomination and re-election.

With his background and training, it is not surprising to find Senator Robert M. La Follette, Jr., looking ahead to see what kind of social and economic troubles the nation might be headed for. He warned the Hoover administration of the approaching crash in 1929. He foresaw widespread unemployment and sought to set up the machinery of government to soften the blow of economic depression. Another administration came to power and adopted the ideas.

His services as chairman of a subcommittee of the Senate Education and Labor Committee to investigate violations of free speech and the rights of labor stopped cold hysterical demands for repressive labor legislation. Instead, the La Follette Civil Liberties Committee, as it was popularly called, awakened citizens to the dangers inherent in the lawlessness of a minority of industrialists. It was in effect, a re-examination of the fundamentals of democracy and the work of groups who have always waged bitter war against the efforts to make democracy work.

As the record shows, Senator Robert M. La Follette, Jr., has never been satisfied with mere patchwork to settle the persistent problems that trouble our nation. He has always wanted to know *why* they have appeared. He has sought always to prevent a recurrence. In his view, amelioration was never the answer. The answer lay in devising social and economic instruments that not only cured, but prevented a return of the disease.

He fought peacetime conscription and literally shamed the Congress of the United States into making provisions for better pay for men in the armed services. Events have proved his argument that better pay and more attractive inducements for voluntary enlistment would eliminate any necessity for peacetime conscription. He was, like his father during the first World War, severely criticized for his position.

A stanch and determined spokesman for the voiceless majority of citizens, Senator Robert M. La Follette, Jr., always insisted that taxes be levied on the principle of ability to pay. He opposed lowering of income tax exemptions to include more wage earners unless those able to pay shared their portion of the burden.

When the nation was preparing for defense and ultimately war during 1940 and 1941, Senator La Follette constantly tried to keep before the American public the fact that merely getting ready to defend ourselves was not enough. He called attention to the serious dislocation caused by the change-over from normal peacetime economy and living to "defense economy" as he characterized it. Long before others seemed to be aware of the problems of housing, the problem of migration of workers to defense centers, Senator Robert M. La Follette, Jr., was calling attention to such matters.

So, it is understandable that when the citizens of Wisconsin snapped off their radios after the night news summary at ten o'clock on August 13, 1945, they shook their heads in bewilderment. They went to bed with a feeling that, although he would be nominated in his bid for re-election to the United States Senate, Bob La Follette would not have too many votes to spare.

Those same citizens were surprised next morning to hear that Senator La Follette had been defeated. Citizens in other states in the nation were not surprised—they were shocked. An outstanding liberal leader of the Senate had been rejected by the people of his own state.

During his twenty-one years of service in the Senate, Robert M. La Follette, Jr., demonstrated the fact that he believes democracy can work. He gave expression to his basic philosophy in a talk delivered over a state-wide radio network during the 1946 campaign. He said:

"The basic issue looming up urgently is the issue of freedom versus absolutism, democracy versus dictatorship. Our form of government and our democracy are under serious attack today.

"The war dramatized the issue between democracy and dictatorship but did not resolve the fundamental conflict. The issue will ultimately be settled and determined in peacetime by the success with which the two competing ideologies provide their people with opportunities for a richer, fuller, more abundant and significant life.

"The challenge to America is this: Make our democracy strong enough so that it becomes a dynamic force for world-wide reconstruction along democratic lines. A program to meet this challenge must be an affirmative program to strengthen the social and economic welfare of our citizens and at the same time guard their liberties."

La Follette declared that freedom does not mean the freedom to starve in the midst of plenty nor the freedom to live in a squalid slum. It does not mean freedom to spend one's old age as a charity ward nor the freedom to die of a curable disease

because of lack of funds. It does not mean freedom to squeeze
the farmer and independent businessman. It does not mean freedom for returning veterans to join a breadline when the boom
ends.

"Freedom, as I understand its fullest and richest meaning,"
La Follette told his listeners, "is the preservation by the people
of their individual liberties—civil, political, and religious—while
banding together as a free people to elect a government of their
own choosing for the purpose of providing for the common welfare
of all."

It was simply the restatement of a basic political and social
philosophy that had been hammered out and tested through the
centuries of man's search for democracy and expressed in terms
of the issues with which we are confronted in this age.

The chapters that follow tell something of the story of the
two Senators La Follette and their role in helping to shape constructively the destinies of this nation. In a real sense, as the
record shows, these two men, father and son, are direct political
descendants of the early Seekers who, from Roger Williams on,
have striven to make democracy work. With son succeeding
father, the Senators La Follette have a unique 41-year record in
the Senate of the United States. Each in his own way has made
mighty contributions to American government and the American
ideal of democracy.

CHAPTER II

The Wisconsin Idea and
Robert M. La Follette

WISCONSIN has a reputation among the states as being "a bit queer" both politically and governmentally. The reputation was acquired because of the movement that culminated in the election of Robert M. La Follette as governor in 1900 and the coming to political power of the progressive Republican faction. Those reformers sponsored and passed legislation of enormous social and economic importance. In Wisconsin, government was re-shaped to respond better to the needs and hopes of the citizens.

Wisconsin pointed the way for other states to follow in their groping after ways and means of meeting and solving the difficult problems of the period. The effects of the work initiated in the state were eventually felt even in the national administration which accepted and put into law the "experiments" of the progressive Wisconsin administration.

Efforts to explain Wisconsin's pre-eminence among the states generally boiled down to use of the phrase "the Wisconsin Idea." It was used to explain a new technique in public administration. It was used to smear anything new that might upset the status quo. The term has come to mean so many things to so many people that it seems pertinent to examine its true meaning at this point. It will help to explain the emergence in national affairs of the La Follettes and why they are significant.

Fundamentally the so-called Wisconsin Idea involves a number of factors. The last decade of the nineteenth century witnessed many social, economic, and political developments. It was the period of emerging big business, of political machines attached to business in a manner that boded little good for the average citizen. It was the period of rampant rugged individualism that held government in scorn and contempt except when it could use government to further its own ends—to help pile up greater aggregations of wealth and economic power in the hands of fewer individuals and smaller groups.

At the same time a serious note of protest arose against such developments. Labor began to stir and to attempt to organize effectively. Farmers were in revolt. There were a few leaders in Wisconsin, as in other states as well, who believed, strangely enough, in the doctrine of democracy and who could and did lead the political fight against the "robber barons."

These leaders talked in terms not only of political democracy, but of economic and social democracy as well. They were vitally interested in the struggles of the lowly for a richer, fuller individual life. They believed in the dignity of the individual and his right to share in the good things of life. Perhaps, too, there was a fear that independent and democratic political processes might be swallowed up by failure to challenge the continued growth of the centralization of wealth and economic power.

The leaders in Wisconsin were thinking in terms of bringing under control for the public good the privately owned utilities— the railroads which by their callous indifference to the welfare of their own customers manipulated legislatures and their rates to the point where farmers and consumers were stranded in an economic slough out of which they could not climb. They were thinking also, terrible heresy, about distributing the tax burden in terms of ability to pay.

The leaders in Wisconsin were thinking in terms of serving the common interests of all the people rather than the special interest of particular groups. Monopoly and special privilege were the dragons those leaders went out to destroy.

Robert M. La Follette, among others, went out to the citizens of the state and expounded his ideas. With evangelistic zeal he patiently talked to the citizens of the state. But, unlike most evangelists, Robert M. La Follette was practical. He was able, with the help of others, to translate ideals into reality. He aroused the people by "reading the record." The railroads operating in Wisconsin were brought under control. Wisconsin legislators passed measures that startled the rest of the nation. The fight was not easy by any means but by 1914, the Republican party of Wisconsin could look back over ten years of reform and boast, as it did in its platform of that year:

"Its achievements have been the beacon lights of legislation and human advancement, and among the many of recent years the following are a few:

"A stringent corrupt practices act; a railroad commission; a strict dairy and food law which protects both the producer and the consumer.

"Wise legislation for the better protection of health and sanitation, which, with the aid of medical science, has confined contagious diseases to isolated cases, and has made epidemics a thing of the past.

"A two-cent passenger fare on railroads; a law providing shorter hours for railroad employees; an eight-hour labor law on public buildings and on public works; a reasonable child labor law.

"A law which makes it mandatory for minors engaged in manual labor to receive a certain amount of educational instruction; a public utility law, which regulates the rate and manner of service of gas and electric companies, and other similar agencies; a workman's compensation law, and an industrial commission to enforce and carry out its provisions."

There were other reforms about which that 1914 Republican platform boasted. In their day they were considered as bold advances, yet today we accept them as a matter of course. But such positive results were won only after terrific battle in the first decade of the twentieth century. It was amazing enough that such legislation should have been passed but what was more amazing was that the people in Wisconsin really made them work. They were effective measures.

What made those economic and social reforms possible?

First, those Wisconsin "radicals" asked themselves a number of questions and in seeking the answers ultimately found the solution. What are we trying to do? What has caused the trouble? Has anyone else worked out a solution? How can this problem be handled through the instrumentalities of representative government to provide for the best interests of all the citizens? These were searching questions and required careful study and plain hard work to answer. Unlike many reformers, the men of Wisconsin were patient. Robert M. La Follette expressed the philosophy of Wisconsin's political reform movement by declaring that the principle of any matter worth fighting for not only had to be comprehended but fully established in government. He disdained halfway measures and believed it better to lose rather than to get a weak and indefinite statute passed.

Wisconsin was fortunate in that it not only had among its citizens the men of vision who saw and recognized the needs, but counted among its population the men of disciplined mind who were willing and eager to put to the test the results of their study and experimentation. The University of Wisconsin had on its faculty a number of men who not only taught but disregarded the academic amenities by actually going to see what the world of reality was like. Chamberlain in geology, Adams and Van Hise, all of whom served the university as president, Richard T. Ely and John R. Commons in economics, Paul Reinsch in political science, who later served as American minister to China, were among those who contributed to the development of the Wisconsin Idea.

These teachers and their students were acutely aware of the world they could view from their ivory towers on top of Bascom Hill. In 1894 Professor Ely, seeking the economic facts of the labor war, shocked the community by participating in a strike picket line. Charged with economic radicalism, a regents' investigation exonerated Ely and President Adams issued the report that carried the now famous declaration for academic freedom:

"Whatever may be the limitations which trammel inquiry elsewhere we believe the great State University of Wisconsin should ever encourage that continual and fearless sifting and winnowing by which alone the truth can be found."

University faculty members accepted the challenge of that statement. They continued their probing researches into the social and economic problems of the day. They gave freely of their talent and time to the state and its citizens. After he became governor, La Follette never hesitated to get advice from the experts who were members of the university faculty. It was a matter of pride to him that he appointed, whenever possible, faculty men to the various state boards and commissions. He recounts in his *Autobiography* how an informal group of state officials, legislators, and faculty members met regularly for lunch on Saturdays to discuss the problems of the state. La Follette and the progressives anticipated the "brain trust" by thirty years!

An acute observer and keen student of Wisconsin affairs has suggested that this interplay between the university and the state capitol was the heart of the Wisconsin Idea. It was a joining of the soil and the seminar. The seminar provided the background of fact and theory while the men of the soil provided the opportunity to test pragmatically those findings.

The Wisconsin Idea was "that continual sifting and winnowing" carried on not only in the classroom and laboratory but jointly in the classroom and government administrative office. It was the joint effort of the politician and the professor to serve the common interest of all the people rather than the special interest of particular groups.

It was the application of intelligence, knowledge, and an open mind to the circumstances of each situation as it arose. The method produced enduring results for, although nearly every bit of the legislation listed in the Republican state platform of 1914 had been challenged in the courts, not one was ever pronounced unconstitutional.

In the larger sense the Wisconsin Idea is the practical embodiment of the theory that it is the duty of the state to promote the general welfare—to serve the common interest of all rather than the special interest of particular groups. It is democratic liberalism in practice.

The vitality of the Wisconsin Idea, attested to by the record of legislation about which the 1914 Republican platform boasted, stemmed from the vigor of its leading exponent, Robert M. La Follette. It was not born full-blown as Minerva from the head of Jupiter. It was the product of years of struggle by La Follette and a group of men devoted to the public service.

Robert Marion La Follette was born June 14, 1855, on a farm in Primrose Township, Dane County, Wisconsin. He was the youngest of the four children of Josiah and Mary La Follette. Robert La Follette's grandfather had been a neighbor of Thomas Lincoln in the Knob Creek country of Kentucky. The La Follette family migrated to Indiana and in 1849 Josiah and his wife settled on a farm in Primrose Township. In Robert M. La Follette was the blood of pioneering Scotch, Irish and Huguenot forebears who had made the long trek from Europe to the American frontier.

Six months after his birth, Robert's father Josiah died. The La Follette family continued on the farm for some time, but when Mrs. La Follette remarried they moved to the nearby village of Argyle where young Robert attended the public schools. In 1873 the family moved to Madison, where Robert entered the University of Wisconsin.

Besides teaching a country school near Madison, to help family finances, Robert La Follette was proprietor of the *University Press,* the bimonthly college paper. He not only did the editorial work but sold the advertising space and subscriptions.

During his university days the germ of insurgency began to develop. He had seen, and reported in his college newspaper, how class elections had been managed to elect Greek-letter fraternity men to the high offices. La Follette decided to do something about the situation and succeeded finally in organizing the so-called "independents" into a machine that ousted the Greek-letter men.

Interested in dramatics and oratory, he represented the university at the Northern Oratorical League contest in Iowa City in his senior year. La Follette won the contest with an analysis of Shakespeare's character Iago. On his return with the coveted prize, he was greeted at the station by a large delegation of enthusiastic students who placed him in a surrey and, manning the shafts, pulled him to Bascom Hill where a royal reception awaited him. That evening a formal reception was given him in the state capitol at which outstanding citizens, faculty members, and others spoke.

Sixty-seven years later—on the evening of September 29, 1946, to be exact—the Madison radio station announced the arrival at the municipal airport of the specially chartered plane that carried members of the university football team returning from Berkeley, California, where the day before they had defeated the University of California 28 to 7. The radio announcer told of about 2,000 jubilant rooters who crowded the landing field to pay homage to the returning victors. Oratorical contest winners these days rate no more than a paragraph on the inside pages of the university daily!

Following his graduation from the university in 1879, young La Follette studied law and was admitted to the Wisconsin bar the next year. He also entered politics. With complete and disarming candor La Follette declared in his *Autobiography* that his only motivation in seeking the office of district attorney of Dane County was the salary and expense money attached to the position. The $800-a-year salary plus $50 for expenses "seemed like a golden opportunity."

Apparently believing in the democratic right of any citizen to seek public office, Robert M. La Follette began his campaign for the post by driving out into the country and talking with the farmers in furtherance of his candidacy. He neglected to inform the Dane County Republican boss, E. W. Keyes, of his intentions. Learning of this unheard-of and flagrant flaunting of the organization and its wishes, Boss Keyes called La Follette to account and told him that another man had been selected for the post. Resenting this highhanded interference with what he considered his rights as a citizen, La Follette told Boss Keyes that he refused to quit and intended to be elected.

Instead of depending on others, La Follette continued his personal campaign among the voters and, to the astonishment of the county organization, he was nominated as the Republican candidate for district attorney at the county convention. This lack of deference to the absolute rule of Boss Keyes prompted the boss to switch his support to the Democratic candidate in the general election. But with the help of friends La Follette was elected by the narrow margin of 93 votes. In January, 1881, he was sworn in as district attorney.

Looking back in later years on that first political fight, La Follette believed his success lay in the fact that he had gone behind the machine to the voters themselves.

On December 31, 1881, La Follette was married to his university classmate, Belle Case, of Baraboo. Mrs. La Follette was part of every political success or failure in which her husband participated. Herself a graduate of the Law School of the university, the first woman to receive a law degree from the State University, she never actively practiced but was a source of constant inspiration to Robert La Follette. Her political sagacity was recognized by the whole group of which La Follette was the leader. Her advice was sought on every point of each campaign.

"If this gets by Belle, we're all right," La Follette is reported to have said to his associates one time as they were gathered in his law office to make plans for one of their campaigns during the 1880's. La Follette served two terms as Dane County district attorney and was elected to Congress in 1884.

Lincoln Steffens once observed that "to judge the staying power of a public man, one must know his wife." Throughout his public career Robert M. La Follette often referred to his wife as "the Counselor." It was no mere jest, for Mrs. La Follette was pre-eminently her husband's counselor.

Mrs. La Follette joined wholeheartedly in her husband's political plans and provided the calm balancing influence that helped him through many difficulties. In addition to being the mother of four children, two sons and two daughters, the wife and gracious hostess of a governor and senator, Mrs. La Follette found time to participate actively in a number of movements of a public character. An advocate of reform of women's dress in the 1890's, Belle Case La Follette was accused of seeking notoriety. When, as the wife of the governor of Wisconsin, she entertained a group of Suffragists at the Executive Mansion she was declared to be "a bit queer."

"When we were Governor" was often used in their conversation with friends by both the La Follettes. It symbolized their togetherness in all things. Mrs. La Follette often declared herself more radical than her husband when politics was the topic of discussion.

Besides serving as her husband's secretary when he first went to Washington as congressman, Mrs. La Follette was active in trying to secure for the Negroes of the District of Columbia some measure of justice. She was in the forefront of the protest against establishment of jim crow streetcars in the nation's capital. When, at the beginning of the first Wilson administration, racial segregation was introduced in the departments at Washington she took up the cudgels in behalf of the Negro civil service employees. She called on the heads of departments to protest and even went to the President himself.

The novelist Zona Gale once wrote of Mrs. La Follette that she was the one woman among such as Jane Adams, Lillian Wald, Mary McDowell, the Abbotts—"women of social passion" —who used politics as her method of helping to "change the bitter conditions under which the majority of the human race support life."

Besides her personal interest in woman suffrage, her opposition to radical intolerance, her interest in dress reform, Mrs. La Follette contributed to the leadership of the Women's Committee for World Disarmament, the League of Women Voters, the Consumer's League, and child welfare activities. She accompanied the senator on his campaign tours and used the opportunity to speak to many women's audiences.

Robert M. La Follette became a well-known lecturer on the Chautauqua circuit. Among women speakers, Mrs. La Follette was no less well known. In 1914, Mrs. La Follette spoke on sixty-four consecutive days at Chautauqua meetings in four midwestern states on the subject of suffrage.

When, at the age of twenty-nine and the youngest member elected to the 49th Congress, Robert M. La Follette went to Washington with his wife and their first-born daughter, they were already a husband and wife team destined to travel far and bring to many people the results of their joint thinking about social and economic problems.

From 1885 to 1891, for three terms, La Follette served in the House of Representatives as a regular Republican and began to appreciate the corrupting influence of great wealth and the concentration of economic power. His first brush with the dominant political and financial group in Wisconsin came during this period. As a member of the House Committee on Indian Affairs he succeeded in killing a measure that provided for the sale to private interests of the pine timber from the Menominee Indian reservation in northern Wisconsin. The bill had been introduced at the request of Senator Philetus Sawyer, who had a personal interest in getting that pine timber. He was one of the biggest lumber operators in Wisconsin.

Another incident involving Indian lands came before the Indian Affairs Committee and brought forcefully to La Follette the alliance between business and politics at work against the best interests of the public. A bill was offered to ratify an agreement between the Sioux Indians and the Northwestern and Milwaukee railroads for rights of way through the reservation. Believing that provisions granting what La Follette believed to be excessive amounts of land to the railroads in addition to the rights of way were all wrong, he prepared and introduced an amendment cutting the grants to reasonable requirements for stations and terminal facilities.

Both the railroads involved were powerful political forces in La Follette's home state of Wisconsin. Upon hearing through Senator Sawyer of La Follette's action, railroad representatives went to Washington to "put the squeeze on" the recalcitrant congressman. Chief among them was Henry C. Payne of Milwaukee, secretary and later chairman of the Republican State Central Committee. Less impassioned testimony than his agreed with La Follette that Payne was "political manager of the Wisconsin machine, lobbyist for the St. Paul Railroad and the Beef Trust, and had the backing of important corporate interests of the state." La Follette would not budge from his position and finally secured adoption of his amendment.

La Follette's position on such matters was apparently dictated more by instinct than real appreciation of the situation. He confessed years later that at the time he was in Congress he was unaware of the trend toward the development of monopoly interests and their impact on government.

As a member of the House Ways and Means Committee during his last term, La Follette developed the beliefs on tariffs that stood out in bold relief twenty years later when as a member of the Senate he led the insurgent fight against the Payne-Aldrich tariff bill. With an "inside view"of the way tariff rates were constructed, the member from Wisconsin confessed in later years that he came to the conclusion that the protective tariff for which the Republican party had traditionally stood did not work to the advantage of the average citizen.

Legislation setting up the Interstate Commerce Commission and the Sherman anti-trust law were passed during the years La Follette was a member of the House. He endorsed and voted for both because he believed they were sound efforts at positive action of government either to prevent or to control monopolies.

The elections of 1890 proved a notable turning point in Wisconsin politics. The results were not immediately felt nor were those most affected really aware of what had happened or why matters had turned out as they had. La Follette was running for a fourth term as congressman and apparently felt so confident of being re-elected that he admittedly neglected the campaign in his own district to appear in other parts of the state. The immediate election result was that the Republican party was swept out of every office in the state and all, including La Follette, but one Republican representative in Congress were retired.

A number of factors—and personalities—were involved. The Republican machine had long been in power. The impact of great wealth had materially altered political life. As a matter of fact, the Republicans, supported by the railroad and lumber interests, had been in undisputed control of the state since the Granger-Democratic reform efforts of the 1870's. At the height of that movement William R. Taylor, a Democratic governor, signed the Potter law, which was the first real attempt in Wisconsin to regulate the railroads. Refusing to obey the law because they claimed it to be unconstitutional, the railroads were confronted by the decision of the state Supreme Court that the state did have the right to regulate them. Railroad interests got busy and the election of 1875 resulted in a return to power of the Republican party. The new legislature immediately took the teeth out of the Potter law.

The convention system of selecting candidates for public office played into the hands of those to whom it was advantageous to control the government. Because of the increased number of local and state elective offices, the nominating machinery became almost unbearably cumbersome. In years of presidential elections at least six caucuses were held in each voting precinct to determine the delegates to the various conventions—the state convention for selecting delegates to the national convention, Congressional district conventions, state senatorial district, assembly district, county, township, and city conventions, not to mention a state convention to nominate candidates for state offices.

Only the railroads and lumber interests, in Wisconsin, commanded the necessary organization and money to control such a sprawling and awkward system of selecting candidates for public office. And the railroads and lumber interests were tied to the Republican party.

It was natural, therefore, that the men who were most influential in the Republican party and who dominated its actions were closely associated with the railroads and the lumber interests of the state. The triumvirate ruling the destinies of the party in Wisconsin included Philetus Sawyer of Oshkosh, a lumberman whose checkbook was always available to the party war chest, John C. Spooner, an able constitutional lawyer and railroad attorney, who served with Sawyer in the Senate of the United States, and Henry C. Payne of Milwaukee. Payne received much of the credit for the election of McKinley in 1896 and was rewarded for his work in the 1900 national campaign by being appointed postmaster-general. Payne was also elected chairman of the Republican National Committee to succeed Mark Hanna. Those three ruled the destinies of the Republican party in Wisconsin with an iron hand and were unalterably opposed to La Follette. By 1890 many citizens had had enough of the Sawyer-Spooner-Payne brand of political control.

Another factor, more immediate in its effect on the election, was the passage by the 1889 legislature of the Bennett law designed to protect the interests of the young people of the state. It prohibited the employment of children under thirteen years of age, required that all children between the ages of seven and fourteen should attend school, and provided that "no school shall be regarded as a school unless there shall be taught therein . . . reading, writing, and arithmetic and United States history in the English language."

Democrats and Republicans alike had voted for the measure in its course through the legislature. Democrats were quick, however, to take advantage of the resentment to the bill shown by supporters of parochial schools. In many school districts the only language used was German or one of the Scandinavian languages and followers of the Roman Catholic faith saw in the measure an effort on the part of the state to interfere with religious matters.

Finally, there was widespread dissatisfaction with the McKinley tariff and the handling of the currency question. There was also a sharp decrease in the Republican vote.

As happened many years later on a national scale when Franklin D. Roosevelt was elected to the presidency, the Democratic party in Wisconsin in 1890 was swept into power on a rising tide of dissatisfaction with Republican rule and discontent rising from economic and social ills.

Because of this political turnover, Robert M. La Follette found himself "gone" from public life. He did not propose, however, to be "forgotten." Sympathetic Wisconsin commentators, writing of the period from 1890 to 1900, refer to it generally as the period of "the holy war"—the period of planning by the insurgents to break the grip of the special interests on the Republican party. La Follette and his small band of associates joined in combat against foes equipped with every piece of armament in the political arsenal to assure their success—money, patronage, and the power that money and patronage provided.

La Follette's own experiences and observations as a member of Congress had given him some understanding of the forces at work. The inspiration and philosophical basis for the struggle against the Sawyer-Spooner-Payne triumvirate that ruled the Wisconsin Republican machine he found in the address to the 1879 graduating class of the University of Wisconsin delivered by the chief justice of the state supreme court, Edward G. Ryan. Ryan admonished the class:

"Money as a political influence is essentially corrupt; is one of the most dangerous to free institutions; by far the most dangerous to the free and just administration of the law. An aristocracy of money is essentially the coarsest and rudest, the most ignoble and demoralizing, of all aristocracies. Here it comes, a competitor for social ascendency. It is entitled to fear, if not respect. The question will arise, and arise in your day, though perhaps not fully in mine, which shall rule—wealth or man; which shall lead—money or intellect; who shall fill public stations—educated and patriotic freemen or the feudal serfs of corporate capital."

As the struggle developed La Follette used this idea until it became the refrain of the battle cry of the Wisconsin insurgents against the machine. At the time, however, La Follette was not so much interested in returning to public life as he was in readjusting to private professional life.

La Follette's unwillingness to take orders from Payne and Sawyer when he was a member of Congress, his flaunting of the desires of the county bosses with respect to his running for office, made him highly suspect in the councils of the party. La Follette, on the other hand, felt no particular personal animus toward the bosses. He believed that they were doing what they honestly thought to be right but he disagreed with them both as to method and ultimate aim. The final, irreconcilable break between La Follette and the Sawyer-Spooner-Payne command did not come until after the so-called "La Follette-Sawyer incident" in the fall of 1891.

When the Democrats under the leadership of Governor George Peck, better known for his humorous sketches of *Peck's Bad Boy*, went into office, they were anxious to make a record for efficiency and at the same time to embarrass the opposition. Suits were brought against former state treasurers and their bondsmen for interest on state moneys for twenty years back.

It had long been the practice of treasurers to deposit money not actually needed in day-to-day transactions and to take the interest received on such deposits as their own. Sawyer and a number of other prominent machine men, as bondsmen for former treasurers, discovered themselves faced with possible judgments totaling approximately three-quarters of a million dollars of which Senator Sawyer was liable for about $300,000.

The cases were scheduled to be tried before Judge Robert G. Siebecker of the Dane County Circuit Court. Much to the amazement of everyone, a day or two before the beginning of the trials, Judge Siebecker announced that because of matters which had come to his attention he could not try the cases. There was much speculation as to the reasons for the announcement. More excitement was added when the Chicago *Times* on October 25 suggested that there was the possibility of attempted bribery in the case.

The Milwaukee *Sentinel* for October 27 carried a prepared statement from Senator Sawyer to the effect that he had asked La Follette to take a retainer in the case but withdrew the offer when he learned that Judge Siebecker and La Follette were brothers-in-law. The statement went to some length to explain that no attempt had been made to influence the court and implied a certain degree of megalomania on the part of both Siebecker and La Follette—Siebecker for refusing to hear the cases and La Follette for refusing to accept a generous retainer fee.

Two days later the *Sentinel* carried a prepared statement by La Follette in which he clearly alleged that Sawyer had attempted to bribe him to speak to Siebecker in order that the decision in the treasury cases would be "right."

It was a curious circumstance, to say the least, that on the heels of a dope story in a Chicago paper Senator Sawyer should rush into print with an explanation of a situation about which only La Follette's intimates knew. He had met with Sawyer in Milwaukee at the senator's request and had refused, after listening to the senator, to accept even expense money for the trip.

The case created a sensation throughout the state. To charge one of the most highly respected men in Wisconsin public life with bribery and to denounce that man's explanation as a lie brought down on La Follette's head the fury of almost unbelievable censure and ostracism. His refusal to protect the secrets and feelings of Senator Sawyer in the treasury cases was looked upon as unpardonable by the party bosses. This action sealed La Follette's doom so far as they were concerned.

Looking back on the incident, La Follette concluded that the incident was the beginning of his career as an insurgent.

CHAPTER III

Ten Years of Struggle

OSTRACIZED by the party leaders, La Follette was marked for political oblivion. He was not even permitted to speak during the 1892 campaign even though he was one of the most popular political speakers in the state. He offered no candidacies and was not himself a candidate for any public office but he did, as a Republican, expect to be called upon to speak in behalf of the party candidates. Nothing but deep silence came from Republican headquarters and La Follette finally wrote suggesting his availability for speaking engagements.

Henry Thom, a personal friend and chairman of the State Central Committee, came to see La Follette and told him that, because of the feeling against him, the leaders of the party were of the opinion that it would be better not to have him speak. La Follette declared that he did not like the prospect of being silenced in that manner and, if that was the feeling of the committee, he would arrange his own speaking tour for the campaign. The committee immediately got busy and saw to it that La Follette was given ample opportunity to speak. At least La Follette kept his ideas before the people of the state. He was not yet ready to battle the machine for control.

Laying his plans carefully during the next two years, La Follette persuaded Nils P. Haugen to run as the antimachine candidate for the governorship in the 1894 campaign. Neither Haugen, La Follette, nor any of the small group of Haugen's

friends who urged him to make the run had any illusions about
the difficulties they faced and the probability of defeat. Nevertheless, it was felt that the time had come to make a showing
against the party machine. Following a spirited fight to control
the Dane County convention, which the La Follette forces won,
the party bosses went to the state convention with the one idea
in mind of stopping the nomination of Haugen at whatever cost.
They succeeded finally in nominating William H. Upham of
Marshfield but at such great effort that La Follette candidates
were nominated to the other state offices.

Announcing himself as a candidate for the governorship in
1896, La Follette was so successful in getting pledged delegates
at the various county conventions that he confronted the bosses
at the state convention with more pledged delegates than any
other candidate. To meet this threat, the machine indulged in
widespread buying of delegates and finally succeeded in nominating Edward Scofield of Oconto as Republican candidate for
the governorship. La Follette's friends and supporters, bitterly
disappointed by the turn of events, begged him to run as an
independent. Realizing that the insurgents would have a better
chance to capture the governorship through the existing party
machinery than by an independent campaign, La Follette urged
his friends to accept defeat and to return again determined to
fight all the harder.

Setting the example for his followers, La Follette spoke in
the 1896 campaign in behalf of both Scofield and McKinley. It
was after this brush with the Republican machine that Senator
Spooner, determined to retire La Follette from state politics, persuaded the newly elected president, William McKinley, to offer
La Follette the appointment as comptroller of the currency. La
Follette refused the proffered position and the Milwaukee
Journal, taking note of the refusal as well as of the calculated
campaign of denouncement against La Follette in the newspapers of the state, said editorially:

"Everybody knows that La Follette is not the aggressor, but
that he was selected for slaughter when he refused to carry out
the wishes of the party boss in the treasury cases. For a time it
appeared that the Madison man's career had been ruined. In

looking over the files of the Republican press of that day, we find that with hardly an exception La Follette was condemned in unmeasured terms by the organs. All kinds of accusations were made against him as if he, instead of the boss, were the guilty one. It was freely charged that the Madison man was getting ready to go over to the Democratic party, and that he had already made his arrangements with the opposition. Hardly a Republican newspaper in the state had one kind word to say of him for his heroic defense of his honor. But the rank and file of the party understood the service La Follette had done them and all the other taxpayers of Wisconsin by refusing a price for trying to unlock the back door of a court of justice, and they did not forget him. It was as certain as the sun would shine that he would sooner or later be called to leadership. The *Journal* warned the organs then that such a time would come. It is here, and the condition of things cannot be changed by alleging that he is making factional warfare. He is but the instrument in the hands of the justice-loving members of the party. The bosses see the handwriting on the wall and that is why they tried to buy him off with the comptrollership of the currency. Twice now La Follette has refused to sell himself. May he continue to fight off infamy."

La Follette put a great deal of thought to the problem of the party caucus and convention as revealed to him by personal experience in 1896. After careful study of the various election systems, he came to the conclusion that the only truly democratic way of assuring proper representation was through the instrument of the direct primary. Several attempts had been made to set up such election machinery in Wisconsin but they had been weak and failed of their purpose.

An invitation from President Harper of the University of Chicago to deliver an address to the faculty and students on February 22, 1897, provided La Follette with the opportunity to present the results of his thinking and research in the field of the direct primary and better representation. He spoke on "The Menace of the Political Machine" and outlined legislation for direct primaries. The speech attracted attention for La Follette supplied copies to every weekly newspaper in the state that would enclose it as a supplement. His purpose was to educate the people, particularly the farmers from whom he received most of his support, to the intricacies of the new direct primary concept. To provide further debate and discussion, La Follette's ideas were incorporated into a bill introduced into the Wisconsin legislature. The bill was finally killed but, with this beginning and sensing that now he had a specific issue to present in his campaign against the bosses, La Follette conducted what amounted to an off-year campaign in behalf of the direct primary.

Beginning with an address before about five thousand citizens at Mineral Point on Independence Day, 1897, La Follette toured the entire state in the next two and a half months. He made essentially the same speech wherever he went, whether before a large audience or before a mere handful of listeners. He made the circuit of the county fairs and was given an enthusiastic hearing wherever he went. The kind of impression he made and the impact of his message on his listeners was described by a citizen of Oshkosh who heard Robert La Follette discuss the direct primary at the Winnebago County Fair. Mr. Daly wrote:

"The speech made a profound and lasting impression on me, and doubtless on most of those who heard it, and convinced me of the man's perfect honesty. I went away in a dazed condition. I could not realize that this man, who scored the Republican party bosses, was himself a Republican, seeking Republican support. And to the everlasting honor of the Republican party in Wisconsin, be it said, he got that support. All the world loves a lover, it is said, and it is equally true that all the world loves a brave man, and certainly none but a brave man would have undertaken the mighty task which La Follette had undertaken and which he was just beginning.

"I was a Democrat, and always before that time I had gone away from a Republican meeting more of a Democrat than ever. But here was a man who spoke to me as a citizen, not as a partisan. He did not attack the other party as a party; he attacked the bad in both parties, especially in his own. Do you wonder men were impressed?

"A most unusual thing about his speech was the bold way

in which he named the leaders of his party who were responsible for the corrupt practices he complained of. No gumshoe methods for La Follette. Everything said was open and aboveboard. No hints or glittering generalities for him."

The bemused Oshkosh Democrat certainly painted a colorful picture of La Follette's effect upon an audience. Today we are liable to forget that modern inventions have altered our habits and even patterns of thought. Any politician who would dare to impose on us for two solid hours to present his exposition of current problems would be given short shrift by his listeners. Political speakers today must take into account the demands and limitations of radio—fifteen minutes, or half an hour at the longest, is the time allotted for discussion of important problems. Radio stations are timid about the matter. Copies of political speeches must be filed forty-eight hours in advance and speakers are warned about libelous matter. Station managers object to the slightest hint of denunciatory vigor. Then, there is the problem of buying the best time available. Net work programs shove the political speaker into either the very early or the very late hours —neither period very desirable from the point of view of getting listeners. Reading habits have been altered and have forced a change in political campaign literature. The news weeklies, and even the daily newspapers, have capsuled the news to such an extent that the reader no longer cares to read a story over a column in length or one that is carried over to an inside page.

The contrast may be appreciated more clearly and the present-day citizen may better understand La Follette's ability to stir his listeners and to get them to think after reading the following article by a Milwaukee *Journal* writer who described the 1897 campaign for the direct primary in these words:

"Ex-Congressman Robert M. La Follette of Madison, as an agricultural fair orator, is far and away ahead of the usual run of speakers who accept invitations to make that sort of address. Whatever purposes he may have had in view in starting in on the tour of county fairs at which he has spoken this fall, his vigorous oratory cannot have failed to have left its impression on his hearers.

"Below the ordinary height, he is compactly built, and has a square, almost massive face, when his stature is considered, and his head is covered with a thick, almost shocky, growth of dark brown hair. He is not a commanding figure by any means, but rather impresses one who sees him for the first time as possessed of a solidity and a bulldog determination. But he is a trained and impressive speaker and knows how to use hands, arms and body as well as words.

"When brought before his audiences he measures at one sweeping glance the entire assemblage. He moves rather sluggishly at first, but is not long in getting warmed up, and he remains warmed up all through his speech even if it covers two hours. This intense and continued display of energy is one of the strong characteristics of the man, as expressed in his work as a public speaker, and it rarely fails to bring his hearers to him and to hold their attention.

"In most speakers such a vast expenditure of energy in the delivery of an oration would become stale and tiresome. But La Follette is infinite in facial expression and gesture. Even much of his solidly knit frame is brought into play. Perhaps the secret of his success as an orator is the fact of the singular appropriateness of each motion intended to emphasize his expressed thought. They harmonize. . . .

"And Mr. La Follette is sometimes sarcastic. His words bite like coals of fire; but his face and gestures are unique. Here, as in other phases, they harmonize, and with his head slightly lowered, his shock of brown hair overtopping the face and the right arm extended, the index finger pointing apparently at the very object of his attack, there is a certain fine frenzy in the man that few public speakers can use to such advantage . . .

"Disgust, hope, honor, avarice, despair, love, anger, all the passions of man, he paints in strong words and still stronger gestures. This may sound like exaggeration—but into the most commonplace of his word paintings he throws the energy of a man apparently fully impressed with the whole force and truth of his statements. He never wearies and he will not allow his audience to weary. He carries his subject and his hearers both, and compels the latter to listen, if he cannot compel them to endorse what he may say.

"There is no joke, nothing frivolous. He is in earnest and gives himself up wholly to the work he is doing . . .

"Mr. La Follette is a study. It may be that you do not agree with him either in premises or conclusions. But it cannot be denied that he impresses even the unbelievers among his hearers that he believes himself and believes in the truth and force of his statements . . .

"Near the conclusion of his speech as he folds his arms across his chest with the air of a man who has done all that can be done, and in a quiet and impressive way delivers his peroration, there is a wonderful change. . . . You realize then that he has been speaking for a long time. He has tired you but you did not know it before. However, he does not seem to have become weary himself. As he bows for the last time and withdraws he seems as fresh as ever. You are impressed with the belief that the man is a sort of steam engine. He is iron in the sense that iron conveys the idea of endurance."

That was the man who electrified the citizens of Wisconsin that warm summer of 1897. That was the man who frightened the bosses of his own political party by taking to the people his proposal for direct primaries. They questioned his motives and accused him of attempting to rig the election laws for the benefit of a small syndicate of Madison lawyers.

It was an enormous educational program that La Follette carried out that fall. The fruits of that campaign—planned and carried out as carefully and vigorously as if he were running for office himself—were not to appear for a number of years. It was the full flowering of his earliest political experience—taking the question to the people to decide rather than abiding by the decisions of party bosses. It was a major contribution to his earlier pledge to destroy the corrupt influences undermining representative government in Wisconsin. The Wisconsin Idea was beginning to emerge.

The 1898 gubernatorial campaign which followed on the heels of La Follette's direct primary campaign was notable in that serious cracks were beginning to show in the walls of the citadel of the regular Republican organization. Governor Scofield won the convention nomination over La Follette but not until after a hard-fought scrap for the uninstructed delegates to that convention. La Follette had come to the convention with more instructed delegates than had the governor. There was, however, a much larger bloc of uninstructed delegates. It was that bloc of delegates which finally helped nominate Scofield. One delegate later told La Follette that, as he recollected it, it cost the Sawyer-Spooner-Payne-Pfister group about $8,300 to buy the necessary votes.

The La Follette insurgents, however, won a major moral victory when one of them forced the convention to adopt the party platform *before* selection of the gubernatorial nominee. The platform adopted was almost wholly written by the progressive group. The platform, for the first time since 1886, concerned itself with state problems. Among other things, it advocated anti-lobby and antipass legislation and demanded equal taxation of all property. The plank referring to the nominating system was admittedly a compromise written in general language that did not specifically mention the direct primary.

Scofield was re-elected along with a legislature dominated by the regulars. Whether more responsive to public demand for reform or hopeful of stemming the tide of the La Follette agitation, the legislature did redeem part of the platform pledges. It killed a proposal for direct primary elections but did establish a permanent tax commission and levied taxes on sleeping-car and express companies. In the dying days of the 1899 session the legislature passed an antipass bill that put an end to an abuse of privileges granted legislators and public officials by the railroads.

The 1900 campaign for the governorship was a far cry from the hammer and tongs fight that had taken place in the two preceding campaigns. It had been presumed, because of his two previous unsuccessful bids for the nomination, that La Follette would not enter the race. Five candidates entered the race early in 1900 and it was freely predicted that the campaign would be close. All five candidates were popular in their own districts but scarcely known in other parts of the state. When La Follette finally declared his candidacy on May 15 in a statement so conciliatory in tone and emphasizing the necessity for party harmony that it amazed everyone, the newspapers were practically unanimous that in view of so many local "favorite sons" he would never win the nomination.

La Follette's previous campaigns and his fight for the direct primary were not without their effect, for as county conventions met to select delegates opposition to La Follette evaporated so completely that he was the only candidate in the field for the Republican nomination! The state convention in Milwaukee nominated him unanimously on August 8.

Sitting on the platform apparently unmoved by the tumultuous ovation given her husband was Mrs. La Follette. Agreeing with the person sitting next to her that it was a "wonderful day" she nevertheless declared that there had been times when she was prouder of him.

"I have been prouder of him when he has suffered defeat," Mrs. La Follette said. "I have always rejoiced at the way in which he has stood firm and undaunted when things went against him."

Another interested but unconcerned spectator was La Follette's five-year-old son Robert Jr. With the insouciant ways of a small boy, his only concern was in increasing the number of convention badges he could wangle from delegates.

That La Follette's victory over the Republican machine was more substantial than a mere whim of political fortune was indicated by the November vote. The successful Republican governor-elect received a net majority of nearly 86,000 votes over all other candidates and received a plurality of 102,000 votes over his nearest rival, the Democratic candidate.

CHAPTER IV

Governor La Follette

On January 7, 1901, Robert M. La Follette, the first native-born citizen of the state to be so elected, became governor of Wisconsin. Just ten years earlier he had been retired to private life from Congress. He had been read out of the Republican party for his revelations concerning the activities of Senator Philetus Sawyer in the treasury cases.

La Follette took office committed to a program of direct primary legislation, tax reform, and railroad control. The legislature of 1901, although called upon by the governor in his message to perform the mandate of the people, as he interpreted the results of the election, passed no laws redeeming any of the party pledges. The bosses had allowed La Follette the empty shell of office but had retained the reality of legislative control. The La Follette faction had enough votes to organize the lower house of the legislature but discovered to their dismay that stalwart votes controlled the Senate.

The legislation that La Follette had promised was presented to the legislature but the pressure of special-interest lobbyists was sufficient to kill off the reform threat. Open bribery and the threat of economic reprisal against possible recalcitrant legislators by the railroads played their part in the failure.

In the midst of the debate on whether or not the legislature should pass a bill taxing railroads on a property valuation basis rather than in terms of a percentage of gross receipts, the legislature passed and sent down for the governor's approval a bill taxing all dogs owned by farmers of Wisconsin. The amount of money thus made available to the state revenue fund was of little consequence, but Governor La Follette was struck by what seemed to him to be the complete cynicism of legislators in passing a bill to add a few dollars to the taxes paid by the farmers while at the same time refusing to take any action on the matter of equitable taxation of the railroads. He used the opportunity to veto the dog tax measure and sent a blistering message to the legislature explaining his action. The veto message so incensed many of the legislators that, although they lacked enough votes to override the veto, they passed a joint resolution of censure. No Wisconsin governor before that time had dared to lecture the lawmakers in such strong language and they smarted under the public castigation.

Governor La Follette did not hesitate to use every opportunity to get his message to the people. He made such effective use of the means available to the governor that many legislators complained that he overstepped the constitutional limitations imposed on the executive and tried to interfere with the legislative branch of the government. At the beginning of the 1901 session, Governor La Follette tossed precedent out the Executive Office window and presented his message to the legislature in person. Previous governors had sent a written message to be read by one of the clerks. The new governor took more than two hours to deliver his message! It was about equally divided between discussion of the need of direct primary legislation and new methods of securing a more equitable tax from the railroads.

The message caused considerable stir because in the campaign of the preceding fall little or nothing had been said about either issue. Most of the campaign oratory had emphasized the theme of party harmony. But La Follette had conducted strong campaigns for both issues. As he analyzed the situation, everyone knew what he stood for and he considered his election a mandate to get those issues into law. The railroad lobbyists were especially upset and raised the cry that La Follette's message was a "stab in the back." They charged that he had broken the pledge of harmony. Despite the failure of the legislature to enact

the La Follette reforms into law, the issues were not allowed to
sink out of sight.

The campaign of 1902 was enlivened by the efforts of the
stalwarts to retire La Follette from politics. They counted on
two factors to regain control of the governor's office: a large war
chest with liberal spending of money to buy the influence of as
many newspapers as possible, and the use of that influence to
spread general dissatisfaction against Governor La Follette on
the score that he hadn't been able to secure approval of one of
his reform measures. But the stalwart group discovered that the
wheel of political fortune had turned full circle. They were on
the outside looking in and the administration forces were lined
up solidly against them. Governor La Follette was nominated
and re-elected. Tactics of the Democratic machine probably
helped the administration forces, for its candidate was a reactionary, David Rose, mayor of Milwaukee. Many disgusted
Democrats voted for La Follette.

Several years later La Follette revealed the fact that William
Jennings Bryan had refused an invitation to come to Wisconsin
to speak in behalf of the party candidates because he had no
sympathy for the state Democratic platform and hoped that
progressive Democrats would support La Follette.

The 1903 session was far different, in terms of legislative
results, than had been the preceding one. Mere recital of the
reforms that had been urged for six years and finally passed into
law fails to tell the story. True, the direct primary election proposal was passed. A railroad tax law replaced the percentage
tax on alleged gross earnings. A graduated inheritance tax law
was enacted, and money was appropriated for an investigation
of railroad earnings to find out if reports on gross earnings had
been honest and fully reported. The resulting investigation brought several hundred thousand dollars into the state
treasury.

The direct primary law was passed only after bitter last-
ditch fighting on the part of the stalwarts. They thought they
had won a victory by forcing adoption of the measure with a
referendum amendment attached providing that the law was to
become effective only if it received a favorable majority at the

November, 1904, elections. The railroad tax measure was passed because administrative forces outmaneuvered the railroad lobbyists.

As in the case of his use of the message to the legislature and the veto to get his ideas across, Governor La Follette made fresh and effective use of the special message during legislative sessions. In his message to the legislature at the beginning of the session La Follette had argued for railroad regulation. To prove his point he presented comparative rates charged by the railroads in Wisconsin and by those in Illinois and Iowa where the carriers were regulated by state law.

The governor's figures were challenged by the railroad lobbyists as being unfair and not presenting the true picture of rates in Wisconsin. The day before public hearings on the railroad regulatory measure were opened, April 28, 1903, Governor La Follette sent a special message on the subject to the legislature. In sheer length it was probably the longest such document ever presented to a Wisconsin legislature—it was 178 printed pages! With the help of a staff of statisticians, the governor had prepared a list of all the stations on the two principal railroads of the state showing the rates for shipping every sort of merchandise and commodity between those stations and the markets. Corresponding rates and distances in Iowa and Illinois were secured and printed side by side with those of Wisconsin. La Follette proved beyond doubt that the railroads were charging from 20 to 69 per cent more in Wisconsin than in the other two states. Despite this devastating evidence for the need of regulation, the bill did not pass. No fight was left to combat the new tax measure after the railroad lobbyists had staved off the threat of regulatory legislation.

Feeling that little of a lasting nature had been accomplished, Governor La Follette appealed to the voters of the state in the 1904 campaign to elect legislators who served them rather than the political machine.

Governor La Follette toured the state by automobile and read to his audiences the legislative records of those seeking re-election. This was the origin of the "look at the record" technique that has proved to be popular in more recent election

campaigns. The method worked, for, as La Follette commented
on the results of that campaign, "I cleaned up the legislature."

The referendum in favor of the direct primary also carried
and, although the total vote had fallen off, Governor La Follette
was given a 50,000 majority and returned to a third term in the
office of chief executive of the state.

Interest in what was going on in Wisconsin was not confined
within the state borders. A popular Chautauqua lecturer, La
Follette spread his message throughout the country. He told
the story of the efforts to secure the direct primary law, the
railroad taxation and regulation program, and the other items on
the reform agenda in Wisconsin.

But Lincoln Steffens, one of the pre-eminent muckrakers-
reporters-social philosophers of the period, freely admitted that
he had no doubt Governor La Follette of Wisconsin was a
charlatan and a crook. He went to Wisconsin early in the summer
of 1904 to prove the charge. What he discovered was published
in *McClure's Magazine* for October. It was a complete and
triumphant vindication of Governor La Follette. After careful
investigation and checking of all the charges, Steffens reported
that so far as he could determine La Follette's great crime was
that under his leadership the Republican party had finally come
to represent the people and through that instrument the governor
was restoring representative government in Wisconsin. The
article helped to clinch the arguments in behalf of the reform
program.

In his message to the 1905 legislature, Governor La Follette
spoke of many things: the need for a corrupt practices act to
control the amount of money spent in campaigns; an antilobby
measure to control "the notorious third house"; a state civil
service based on the merit system; laws protecting workingmen
and working conditions; he asked for a forest conservation program; he discussed the value of the university to the state and
urged that ways and means be provided to make the university
of greater service; he emphasized again the need for laws regulating the railroads and other public utilities.

A Madison newspaper reporter, noting that the message
contained "page on page of comparative rates" and took nearly

three hours to deliver, commented that "few governors can make a long message so interesting in delivery as Governor La Follette and once more the remarkable spectacle of holding a big audience for three hours was enacted."

The first item of legislative business completed by the new session was the election of a United States senator to succeed Joseph V. Quarles, whose term had expired. Quarles, of course, sought re-election. Others sought the office and set up campaign headquarters to dispense cigars, hospitality, and good will to the legislators in the hope of getting the vote. "Back of them all, silent as a sphinx as to giving any intention of his purpose is Governor Robert M. La Follette, of whom his newspaper friends and many of his followers are demanding that he go to the Senate and stand in the nation as he has stood in Wisconsin for certain reforms," wrote "political Observer" of the Madison *Wisconsin State Journal.* The governor was not a candidate, but his friends in the legislature started the move that culminated just four weeks after his inauguration in an overwhelming vote electing La Follette United States senator from Wisconsin. The governor appeared before a joint session of the legislature to thank the members for the honor but in accepting declared that he could not break faith with the voters by resigning the governorship until the reform program he had pledged himself to put through was completed. Elected to the Senate on January 24, 1905, Robert M. La Follette took the oath of his new office a year later, on January 4, 1906.

During that year the regular session under his leadership put through the railroad regulatory measures and much of the rest of the program he had presented. A special session was called in December to complete the legislative work La Follette had promised. The result was that when he resigned as governor at the end of the year, Wisconsin had a state civil service law, a corrupt practices act, an antilobby provision, a railroad commission with full power to regulate not only railroads but other public utilities as well, a forest conservation program, advanced legislation in the field of social services, a workmen's compensation law, and the groundwork was laid for future legislation in such fields as insurance regulation.

The Wisconsin Idea had come to full flower. It was a recognition by men and women of ideals that democracy must be more than a word. It was their search for the tools and techniques to make of democracy "a life" that was the fundamental basis of what happened in Wisconsin under the inspiration of Robert M. La Follette. He, together with a co-operating electorate, revitalized the state government and made all people "equal under the law" in fact. It required patience. It required idealism of a high order and an unshakable faith in humanity to stand up under the discouragement of defeat. It required careful study and research to be sure that the solutions to the evils they were fighting were sound. These qualities the insurgent Republicans of Wisconsin under the leadership of Robert M. La Follette possessed to an extraordinary degree. It was social engineering on a scale that had not before been successful in the United States.

CHAPTER V

Senator La Follette

ROBERT M. LA FOLLETTE was not an unknown when he entered
the Senate in January, 1906. His own prolonged postponement
of final acceptance of the position given him by the overwhelming vote on the first ballot by the Wisconsin legislature—
101 out of a possible 133 votes—in itself focused national attention on him and the program he had put into effect in his own
state. His successes in Wisconsin had been achieved only as the
result of a long campaign. While the individual planks of his
reform platform for Wisconsin seem mild enough today, they
were bitterly opposed by powerful antagonists at the time. The
Payne-Sawyer-Spooner triumvirate and its political inheritors
had wielded tremendous power, not only in the state but in the
councils of the national Republican party. Republican leaders in
Washington were well aware of La Follette's activities. He was
not considered a "regular" and was not given a cordial greeting
by the great men of the Senate—Aldrich, Depew, Hale, Allison,
Quay, and others. Those leaders were not happy at the moment
because David Graham Phillips was exposing "The Treason of
the Senate." Other writers were calling attention to the ways by
which the Senate of the United States was being controlled by
the defenders of privilege.

As William Allen White once observed, La Follette "had a
long line of Wisconsin achievements in his bag," but the Senate
would have none of them. La Follette had asked for assignment

43

on the Senate Committee on Interstate Commerce. He drew the chairmanship of the Committee on the Condition of the Potomac River Front and membership on the committees on Indian Affairs and Pensions. The Republican leadership had thought to keep him so busy with routine detail work that he would be out of the way.

But the memories of senators, even as are those of voters, are short. The Senate leadership had forgotten about La Follette's championship of the Indians when he was in the House of Representatives. A House bill came before the Senate committee providing for the settlement of affairs of Indians in the Indian Territory which provided for continuing the policy of leasing coal lands in the reservations to private companies. With characteristic zeal, the new member of the Indian Affairs Committee dug into the matter and discovered that the railroads running through the territory were being given a virtual monopoly on valuable leases. Defeated in his attempt to change the plan, La Follette's opposition called public attention to it and the plan finally had to be abandoned.

By that action to preserve the public coal lands the freshman member of the Senate served public notice that he was unalterably opposed to the "3-D" doctrine of the special-interest groups interested only in "division, disposition and dividends" without any thought of conserving the natural resources.

At the time the coal leasing bill was pending before the Senate Committee on Indian Affairs, Senator La Follette was waited upon by a group of businessmen from the Indian Territory who were trying to get support for the measure. The senator told the group that he was opposed to such a measure and would fight it with everything at his command.

"But you don't understand, Senator," the spokesman for the group protested.

"I may be dumb," La Follette replied. "Maybe I don't understand this bill, but I do understand the difference between right and wrong."

La Follette's maiden speech in the Senate, however, created widespread interest because it was on a subject about which he knew a great deal and his retort to the studied attempt on the part of other Republican senators to snub him bounced back in their faces. The Hepburn bill to amend the Interstate Commerce Act of 1887 was up for debate and passage. La Follette was interested because as a member of the House he had helped to pass the original measure and the Hepburn bill was an effort to repair the damage that had been done the original act by adverse decisions of the United States Supreme Court. The bill sought to grant to the Interstate Commerce Commission real powers in the regulation of interstate commerce, especially as it concerned railroads. He was interested because as governor of Wisconsin he had led the successful fight to bring railroads under regulation. He criticized the pending measure because, as he believed, it did not go far enough. In his argument he insisted that the Interstate Commerce Commission could not hope to get very far in its regulatory procedures until it possessed power to change rates on a basis of the valuation of the properties. Before rising to speak on the bill, La Follette had spent several weeks in preparation. Shortly after he rose his Republican colleagues discovered, one by one, that matters in the cloakroom required their attention. It was the senatorial hazing of a freshman member. He turned to the presiding officer and said:

"Mr. President, I pause in my remarks to say this. I cannot be wholly indifferent to the fact that senators by their absence at this time indicate their want of interest in what I may have to say upon this subject. The public is interested. Unless this important subject is rightly settled, seats now temporarily vacant may be permanently vacated by those who have the right to occupy them at this time." Approving response from the galleries to this observation brought the senators back to their seats.

La Follette was unable to get acceptance of his amendment giving the Interstate Commerce Commission power to make an independent evaluation of the railroads, but he did gain attention and respect. His arguments in behalf of the property evaluation amendment were persuasive enough to impress Senator Jonathan Dolliver whose committee on interstate commerce had reported the measure for passage without the amendment. Dolliver and La Follette were among the five senators who voted for it.

Halfhearted efforts were made then, as they had been made before, to attach to Robert M. La Follette the opprobrium of destructive opposition. The attempts never fully succeeded, for his record of constructive effort in Wisconsin was too solid and too substantial to be ignored. He was never content with simply being opposed to a measure. He always modified his opposition with constructive legislative proposals. He opposed the leasing and sale of coal deposits in the public domain but offered a positive proposal to use them in the best interest of the public. He did not oppose the Hepburn measure, he hoped to make what he considered an imperfect bill a better one. His intensity of purpose, his deep knowledge of the subjects he battled for, his refusal to compromise, and his complete understanding of the forces opposed to his proposals made it often appear that he was simply a congenital "aginner."

Senator La Follette was most certainly not to be classed in the same category as the Mississippi state senator representing a hill district in the northern part of that state during the governorship of Theodore Bilbo. He slept through most sessions of the legislature and roused only long enough to vote on legislative business. His only criterion in casting his ballot was the answer to his question "Is Bilbo for it?" If his colleagues assured him that Bilbo was for it, "I'm agin it!" He'd cast his "no" vote and go comfortably back to sleep.

La Follette's was an attitude, a point of view that was just beginning to make itself felt in the Senate of the United States. It was an attitude based on refusal to accept a proposal merely because someone in power wanted or ordered it. La Follette had not achieved election to the Senate on a platform of obeisance.

Evidence of La Follette's abilities, even as a "freshman" member from Wisconsin, is to be found in the record of his legislative accomplishments during his first two years in the Senate. Railroad employees were grateful for a new champion. La Follette introduced and secured passage of two measures beneficial to them. One provided for more adequate protection of railroad employees and the other limited by law the number of hours of consecutive service. La Follette carried his fight against corruption of public officials by the utilities to a point where he secured passage of a bill prohibiting use of telegraph franks by federal officials. He anticipated later developments in conservation by getting Congressional approval of a bill to authorize the selective cutting and sale of timber by Indians on the Menominee reservation. That bill laid down a new policy for timber conservation and management of the resources of the Indian reservations.

La Follette watched with close interest how the Republican leadership in the Senate often jammed legislation through. He took note of their strategy in delaying introduction of bills they were personally interested in until near the end of the session when appropriation measures were up for consideration. He learned how, by these tactics, special-interest groups gained their ends without too much scrutiny. In January, 1909, the Naval Appropriations bill was suddenly reported out of committee with the usual request for immediate passage. Objecting that neither he nor other members had been given opportunity to study the bill, La Follette successfully blocked the move for immediate consideration. There was a weekend between then and the time for taking up the bill for final consideration.

Interested naval officers pointed out the logrolling defects in the bill and suggested changes in the interest of a more efficient service. La Follette arranged for a meeting of the Navy men and three of his colleagues. He asked Albert B. Cummins of Iowa, William E. Borah of Idaho, and Joseph Dixon of Montana to attend the meeting. Those men, assisted by the naval officers, spent Sunday going over the bill and deciding which part each senator would take as his responsibility in the debate. They lost their fight but succeeded in attacking and airing the methods used by the Senate bosses in making up the Senate committees. It had been La Follette's thesis that members from states where appropriations were to be expended ought not to be on committees which controlled those expenditures. The argument was basic to his attack on failure of the measure to consider the real advantages to the Navy of harbor developments other than those located in certain Congressional districts. To emphasize his point, La Follette introduced an amendment to the bill for appointment of a commission to study Navy needs. The Republican

majority defeated it by a parliamentary ruling that the amendment was not germane! But that fight against the hurried passage
of appropriations measures helped put a stop to the practice.

Later in the summer of 1909, constituents of Senator Robert
M. La Follette were reading the following estimate of their sena-
tor in the Milwaukee *Journal* as written by Gilson Gardner,
Scripps-McRae correspondent in Washington:

"For three years and six months the Senate of the United
States has had a consistent and aggressive minority of one. The
minority's name is Robert M. La Follette.

"The government of the United States is a 'representative
government.'

"The majority of the Senate represents $.

"La Follette represents the people.

"La Follette has performed a very valuable public service
during the three and a half years he has been a member of the
Senate. He has not made a tomtom war. His blows have been
real blows. He has dealt in facts rather than in personalities. He
has studied much and ranted little. But he has been everlastingly
on the job.

"The country owes a debt of gratitude to Wisconsin. La
Follette is only nominally a Senator from that state; he is in
fact our representative-at-large."

In the latter months of 1908 Senator La Follette began turning over in his mind the possibilities of establishing a new
journal or magazine to serve as a vehicle for progressive thought.
He had been impressed with the interest shown in William
Jennings Bryan's paper, the *Commoner*, and believed that there
was a place for a publication that would reflect his own ideas
as well as those of other progressives. He was also thinking in
terms of the newspaper situation in his own state of Wisconsin.
The press of that state was solidly regular, or stalwart, in its
editorial interpretation and news presentation of political events.
Nationally, the proposed publication could provide a rallying
point for the group of insurgent congressmen and senators who
were beginning to make their presence and ideas felt in the national legislature. Finally, as associates of the senator at that
time have stated, perhaps Senator La Follette was beginning to

look toward 1912 and the possibility of a presidential nomination.

On January 9, 1909, the first number of *La Follette's Magazine* made its appearance. As editor, Senator La Follette declared in his salute to the readers:

"*La Follette's* will be a magazine of progress, social, intellectual, institutional. Moreover, it will be Progressive in the more distinctly political sense.

"It is founded in the belief that it can aid in making our government represent with more fidelity the will of the people. . . .

"We shall have no strife with individuals as *individuals*. If they serve special interests, to the injury of the public, they are enemies of the public. Against them as enemies of the public we shall make war.

"With the political fortunes of officials and candidates we shall have no concern except as they affect the public welfare. *Who* represents the people in public affairs is not important. *How* they are represented is vital. . . .

"*La Follette's* will speak the truth. No eminence of position in party or government shall protect a servant of the people from deserved criticism; and its approval will be gladly given to all who commend themselves to it by brave and right action in any party or place.

"Men and measures are both important. This magazine will discuss measures and political parties and policies impartially and fearlessly. It will not shrink from making estimates of men and will from time to time call the roll in order to disclose the exact position of those who are true and those who are false to public interest."

With that statement of policy, and the editorial motto "Ye shall know the truth and the truth shall make you free," *La Follette's Magazine* with Senator Robert M. La Follette as editor was launched. For a publication with avowed political purposes, an unusual and highly interesting department made its appearance with the first issue—a department headed "Women and Education" conducted by Mrs. La Follette. In her foreword she wrote:

"This department will discuss the subjects of health, children,

home, education, life in Washington, and other topics of everyday interest to women. . . . The department will report the
work of women's organizations. Its policy will be particularly to
promote the cooperation of women for the welfare of home and
school."

Published as a weekly for the first three years of its existence
and without the benefit of much advertising revenue, *La Follette's* was dependent on circulation for income. The senator for
many years turned over his not inconsiderable earnings as a
Chautauqua lecturer to the publication. In 1912 the magazine
became a monthly and changed its format from the 9 x 12-inch
size to what is now called tabloid form. Senator La Follette
continued actively as editor until his death and penciled notes accompanied his copy to the managing editor in Madison from
wherever he was—on a speaking tour, Washington, or on vaca-
tion—with full instructions as to position and even size of type.

Shortly after *La Follette's* had been established, the senator
astonished his office staff one day by announcing that he had
thought it over and had decided to incorporate the magazine.

"What for?" asked his secretary, Albert O. Barton.

"So we can be sued," the senator laughed in reply.

La Follette did attack "men and measures" in no uncertain
terms in the columns of the magazine but those attacks were
always based on the public record. Readers of the magazine got
not only generous doses of passages from the *Congressional
Record* but record roll calls showing how representatives and
senators voted.

Immediately after his inauguration in 1909, President Taft
called a special session of Congress to pass a tariff bill. Attention was focused on this action because the Republican plaform
had advocated tariff revision and the President, in speeches delivered during the campaign, had advocated revision in words
that were accepted as meaning downward revision. Many citizens were therefore astonished when the President's message to
Congress, taking about two minutes to read, merely called attention to the unsettled and uncertain condition of business because
of the question and requested speedy action. Republican insurgents throughout the Middle West had supported Taft as a

friend because of his speeches in favor of lower tariffs. The Republican party was traditionally the party of protectionism, but midwestern Republicans had for some years been increasingly critical of party orthodoxy with respect to tariffs. They saw in the high tariffs the foundation of the trusts and monopolies. During his service as governor of Iowa, Albert B. Cummins had given impetus to the "Iowa Idea" for destroying trustification. It involved the removal of all duties on competing products coming into this country. So it was that midwestern Republicans listened with interest to Taft's message to the special session and were disappointed. Nothing had been said about downward revision.

The Payne-Aldrich measure, originally a general re-enactment of the Dingley tariff law of 1899, was finally passed by the House after insurgents there had tacked on numerous amendments reducing various schedules. Certain groups, alarmed at the reductions were assured by conservative Republican leaders that "the Senate would take care of them." In the meantime, Senator La Follette and other advocates of reduction had been assured by the President that he would support their fight to secure a "better bill."

Forty-eight hours after it had been referred to the Senate Finance Committee, of which Nelson B. Aldrich of Rhode Island was chairman, the bill was reported out with a request for immediate passage.

Senator La Follette, however, had witnessed such tactics before. He protested immediate consideration of the bill on the same grounds he had blocked the railroading of the naval appropriations measure just a few months earlier. La Follette spoke with some assurance, for word had been passed along to the small group of insurgents that President Taft had meant what he said in the campaign regarding the necessity for lower tariff rates. Senators Albert Beveridge and Jonathan Dolliver, who had also been urging lower tariffs, were encouraged by the turn of events.

A number of standpat eyebrows on the Republican side of the Senate were raised when these two announced their opposition and supported La Follette's position against immediate consideration. Both Beveridge and Dolliver had up to that time been considered regular Republicans. Dolliver, however, had been the victim of Senator Aldrich's tyrannical rule of the Senate when Aldrich refused him the seat on the Finance Committee made vacant by the death of Senator Allison. Dolliver's insurgency was deeper than mere surface irritation. He had admitted to intimate friends that the only thing that had kept him from breaking with the regular Republican leadership long before was a promise to his old colleague, Senator Allison, not to make the break until he was gone.

Albert J. Beveridge of Indiana had been considered among the most regular of the Republican Senate majority. He began to have his doubts, though, as he saw how big business was entrenching itself in power and using its power for completely selfish purposes. As was the case with Senator Dolliver, the debate on the Hepburn bill in 1906 marked the beginning of Beveridge's insurgency. To the dismay of the Old Guard bosses he voted for the measure. During that same year Beveridge began thinking about tariff changes. Not only that, but wherever he spoke he discussed the need for downward revision of the Dingley rates. Against heavy opposition Beveridge led the fight for adoption of a federal meat inspection measure. During the 1907 session of Congress the senator from Indiana aroused further bitterness in the ranks of the Old Guard Republican leadership by sponsoring a federal child labor law.

All three insurgents—La Follette, Dolliver, and Beveridge— were among the most effective public speakers on the Republican side of the Senate. They possessed a common appreciation for facts and none of them ever spared themselves in doing the "homework" necessary to get the facts with which to support their public utterances. These three, together with Albert B. Cummins of Iowa, Joseph L. Bristow of Kansas, and Moses E. Clapp of Minnesota, all Republicans, bore the brunt of the insurgent attack against the Payne-Aldrich tariff bill.

One of the points that must impress all who have read American political history is that the insurgents who led the battle against entrenched and predatory privilege in the national Congress during the first decade of the present century were for the most part Republicans. There were, of course, a number of members on the Democratic side of both the House and the Senate who made common cause with the insurgents and believed just as sincerely as the insurgents in the steps proposed for social and economic justice. The apostasy of the Republican insurgents attracted attention and made enemies because they were Republican. The insurgents looked upon themselves as good Republicans. The late Senator George W. Norris admitted to a belief that the Republican party could do no wrong and he took his faith in it from the "inspired and enlightened leadership of Abraham Lincoln."

All the Republican insurgents of that period could easily accept the same hopes and beliefs that Senator Norris expressed in explaining his Republicanism. He wrote that he hoped to strengthen his party in its position in this country and to free it from influences which in his eyes were lessening its usefulness and destroying its opportunities to be a party of service to the American people. It was the beginning of that collision of aims within the party that challenged and seriously threatened the narrow parochialism and almost insolent refusal of the Old Guard leadership to recognize the needs and hopes of a great group of citizens who up to that time had not been heard. Comfortable and smug in their belief that there were two classes— the exploiters and the exploited—Republican Old Guardmen paid no heed to the warnings of the historian Frederick Jackson Turner that the American frontier in its physical sense had disappeared. The new Republican voices—voices of destruction and protest, they were contemptuously called—sensed the new social and political and economic frontiers. They were trying to realign party politics in terms of the newer and pressing problems, which were not being solved by continued application of the older economic philosophy of frontier days.

These men were respected for their abilities even by their most bitter political foes. Only rarely were they the subject of personal attack in Congress. Their motives were never successfully impugned. Their methods did not give the opposition a chance to descend to such tactics. They were not simply congenital "aginners." They refused to bow to the dictates of others with respect to national legislation of great importance to the mass of American citizens. Like those who fathered the Wisconsin Idea in that state, the insurgents wanted to know why such matters were being pressed by particular groups. They wanted to know what would be the effects of such proposals.

The insurgents spent long weary hours digging out the facts. Their debates were literally scholarly treatises on the subject up for discussion. They rejected the use of emotional appeals to get their points across; nor did they resort to political pull and horsetrading. Instead, they read into the record great masses of statistics and information that demolished the argument of the opposition. They were reviled and read out of the party simply because they dared to lay bare motives and facts embarrassing to the standpatters. They shared a consuming belief that democracy must be made to work, that the Republican party was the vehicle for expressing and shaping that democracy, and a belief in the soundness and integrity of judgment of the American people. The late William Allen White once observed that the appeal of the insurgents had a low emotional content. But the insurgents gave the people a glimpse of how the rich men got their money.

The majority of the Republican membership in the Senate did not, naturally, agree with the results of the re-examination and redefinition of Republicanism that the insurgents had undertaken. With almost Bourbon stubbornness, the standpatters, whose unquestioned boss was Senator Nelson B. Aldrich of Rhode Island, resented and resisted every proposal put forward by the insurgents. Aldrich was ruthless in his exercise of power. Despite their superior seniority in the Senate membership, both Dolliver and Beveridge were refused places on the Finance Committee, of which the Rhode Island senator was chairman. His social philosophy seemed to be based on the simple proposition that mankind is composed of two parts—the rulers and the ruled. Aldrich considered himself a representative of the rulers of America, the economic rulers, and became the recognized representative in public life of big business. He had nothing but contempt for the farmers and workingmen and -women of the nation. He looked upon himself as the representative of the business interests only. He was firmly convinced of the rightness of using the agencies of the government to further the selfish interests of big business. He was brilliant in debate and a master of the studied insult. The Republican plutocrats in the Senate included Henry Cabot Lodge and Murray Crane of Massachusetts, Hale of Maine, Penrose of Pennsylvania, Kean of New Jersey, and Gallinger of New Hampshire, all of whom were able in debate and adept in the art of compromise and vote trading. The tariff bill was to their liking because interest could be played against interest and section against section if dissaffection should rear its ugly head to question what was being done for particular interests.

The Old Guard group had the initial advantage of majority control and was disposed to rush the bill through despite La Follette's successful blocking of immediate consideration. In introducing the new bill, Senator Aldrich had made the statement that as it stood there were many reductions in the tariff schedules incorporated in it. La Follette refuted the statement by proving from Department of Commerce figures that instead of lowering rates the Senate version of the Payne bill actually increased the rates. Senator Beveridge served notice of his opposition in a speech challenging the Republican party to redeem its campaign pledges. He quoted the President's own campaign statements in favor of lowered tariffs.

In the meantime the small group of insurgents headed by Senator La Follette had met to decide their strategy. Faced with an almost impossible task of mastering all the details of highly technical and even obscure material, they divided the labor, as had been done on the naval appropriations bill. Dolliver took the cotton schedule; Bristow, the lead and sugar schedules; Cummins the metal, glass, and other less involved schedules; La Follette took the wool schedule and helped Dolliver with the cotton schedule. Both Clapp and Beveridge helped in co-ordinating the work with Beveridge taking the responsibility for the parliamentary moves of the group.

Further to embarrass the insurgents and make it physically more difficult, Senator Aldrich secured a rule requiring the Senate to meet each day from ten in the morning until eleven at night until the tariff measure was passed. The insurgent group often met at either La Follette's home or Beveridge's apartment after a long day in the Senate to go over details and lay plans for the following days.

Senator Dolliver led the attack with a searching analysis of the cotton schedule. Then followed Bristow's arraignment of the lead and sugar schedules, La Follette on wool, Cummins on metal and glass. Beveridge completed the exposé of the concerted attack on the consumer's pocketbook with sensational disclosures of the methods used by the tobacco trust to enrich itself at the expense of the consumer.

The Payne-Aldrich tariff bill became law but it was an embarrassment to the victors because the public had finally been given the secret of the power of big business. The President also lost any hope for further progressive support when he failed to fulfill his pledge by vetoing the measure. In fact, he lost all hope of support from the Middle West in the 1912 presidential campaign when shortly after passage of the tariff measure, which boosted many rates above even the old Dingley rates, he declared it to be the best tariff bill ever passed by any Congress. A wide split was developing in the Republican party.

La Follette admitted later that as the battle lines were drawn the progressives realized that they could not force any important changes in the bill. That knowledge did not deter them. In his analysis of the progressive position at that time, La Follette warned reformers that to be successful they must have complete mastery of all pertinent facts. He spoke from the experience of long, heartbreaking campaigns in his own state, where he had had ample opportunity to test and develop the techniques used so effectively by the insurgent senators to expose the Payne-Aldrich tariff grab. Not one of the insurgents ever expressed the least regret for his stand even though it resulted in defeat.

The break between the progressive insurgents and the Old Guard standpatters reached a pitched-battle stage in the Congressional campaign of 1910. President Taft had deserted the progressives for Aldrich and the standpatters. The President was determined to smash once and for all time the progressive group that had, as he saw it, sabotaged his administration. He even used the lever of federal patronage to bludgeon the recalcitrant members of his party. Aldrich collected funds from high-tariff beneficiaries to finance a terrific campaign of oratory and literature in those states where progressivism was on the march. "Taft Clubs" were financed to spearhead the attack against the insurgents in the various states.

Theodore Roosevelt played an important although, in progressive thought, somewhat equivocal part. Absent on his big-game hunt in Africa during the stirring period of the Payne-Aldrich debates, when the progressive movement coalesced, Roosevelt's reaction to the intraparty strife was a subject of much conjecture. He was apparently not so much concerned over the fact that Taft had embraced the standpat element of the party as he was over the factionalism that had developed. The former President campaigned to bring the two elements together. He was disappointed in Taft's administration for he had chosen Taft as his successor because he believed the man would continue the broad outlines of the program that had been laid down in the seven and a half years of "trust busting" and a "square deal" regime.

Roosevelt aligned himself with neither faction in the 1910 campaign but did his best to bring them into the semblance of a working agreement. In the course of a nation-wide lecture tour Roosevelt brought comfort and cheer to the standpatters on the eastern seaboard by his endorsement of the Payne-Aldrich law. He caused acute alarm among the eastern Brahmins when he enunciated his "radical" concept of the New Nationalism at Osawatomie, Kansas, where he declared that "the man who wrongly holds that every human right is secondary to his profit must now give way to the advocate of human welfare, who rightly maintains that every man holds his property subject to the general right of the community to regulate its use to whatever degree the public welfare may require it."

Many progressive Republicans were disturbed by the apparent ease with which Roosevelt donned or cast off the mantle of progressive leadership. La Follette would have none of Roosevelt's "progressivism." He always looked upon the former President as simply a political opportunist.

Whatever suspicion or alarm he engendered among the politicians, Roosevelt did capture the imagination of many citizens who considered him a progressive leader. The factional fight for party control was of such proportions during that summer of 1910 that it took on the aspect of a presidential campaign. Events of that campaign in Wisconsin were typical of what occurred in the Dakotas, Iowa, Nebraska, Kansas, Illinois, Indiana, Ohio; on the West Coast in California and Washington; and in the East in New York, New Hampshire, and Pennsylvania—the states where the two factions fought most bitterly.

Months before, shortly after the end of the special session of Congress in 1909 in fact, Wisconsin stalwarts had been given to understand that they would get financial aid from eastern businessmen and the support of the national party officers in an effort to defeat La Follette. There was no secret about the matter. The Milwaukee *News* observed editorially on September 30, 1909:

"Politicians at the national capital are expressing the opinion that 'the bitterest fight ever witnessed in Wisconsin will be fought next year to defeat United States Senator Robert M. La Follette.' The Wisconsin senator has made many enemies among the leading and influential politicians the country over and the powerful financial interests are arrayed against him. It is probable that the administration will take a hand in the fight because of La Follette's opposition to President Taft on the tariff."

Early in April S. A. Cook announced his candidacy against La Follette and the stalwart press opened an attack against the senator in language that, as one commentator observed, "savored more of a tavern brawl than a political campaign." Progressive supporters of Senator La Follette were called all the impolite names that could be printed—"factional rats," "party wreckers," "elephadonks." In defiance of the legal Republican organization in the state, twenty-five "Taft Republican" leaders met in Milwaukee and issued a call for a state conference to be held June 8. The convention call demanded consideration of ways and means of redefining and purging Republicanism in the state. The matter was of urgent importance because of certain Republican representatives in the national Congress who were "persistently voting with the Democratic minority in that body to delay enactment of Republican measures, to embarrass the Republican administration, and to defeat or make difficult the redemption of Republican pledges."

Vice-President Sherman came to Milwaukee to bestow the White House blessing on the deliberations. Sherman set the tone of the speeches by denouncing progressives for arraying "class against class and interest against interest." He demanded that such apostles of unrest be unceremoniously expelled from the party ranks. Other speakers inveighed against those who had hoisted "the black flag of politics" and preached "the gospel of pessimism and despair." According to another conference orator, "optimism and brotherhood" were not to be found in the vocabulary of the progressives.

The philosophy of complete reactionism was stated to the conference by Levi Bancroft, who branded as "treasonable and revolutionary, unconstitutional and irreligious, progressive appeals to the passions and prejudices of the masses. God's patient poor have made no contribution to world progress. Without energy or inspiration they constitute a drag on the wheels of progress."

That was the tone of the stalwart opposition to the Wisconsin progressives. Serious illness prevented La Follette from taking an active part in the campaign into which the down-East friends of the stalwarts poured nearly $150,000. But progressives from all over the nation went to call on La Follette in Madison and to tour the state in his behalf. Jonathan Dolliver and Albert Cummins from Iowa, Moses Clapp from Minnesota, Joseph Bristow from Kansas, William Borah from Idaho, Gifford Pinchot from Pennsylvania, James R. Garfield from Ohio, Judge Ben Lindsey from Denver, George W. Norris from Nebraska, all spoke for La Follette and the progressive candidates. The Wisconsin campaign closed in Madison, where Francis J. Heney, the San Francisco graft prosecutor, spoke to an overflow audience in the university gymnasium. "California," he told that Madison crowd, "is represented in the United States Senate by Robert M. La Follette. By that I mean the people of California. The railroads of California have two senators of their own." Earlier in the campaign, Hiram Johnson, running for Republican nomination for the governorship of California, had hurled defiance at the standpat Republicans of that state by declaring that he went to Wisconsin and Iowa for his Republicanism and not to Washington.

The Wisconsin stalwarts lost in their attempt to carry the state "for Taft and Republicanism over La Follette and Insurgency." The Old Guard standpatters fared no better in other states. Not only did they fail to stop the progressive onslaught, but the Democrats succeeded in winning the governorships of a number of states. Maine elected a Democrat as governor, and a Princeton University professor of government, Woodrow Wilson, was elected governor of New Jersey!

As events turned out, the 1910 campaign and Roosevelt's activities in trying to bring the two elements of the party together only complicated the situation within Republican ranks. Democratic and progressive Republican victories had changed the Congressional situation. Democrats were in the majority in the House and the progressives found that they held the balance of power in the Senate. Against the most fervent pleas of stalwarts not to do it, President Taft called a special session of the new Sixty-second Congress in April, 1911, to consider passage of the Canadian Reciprocity bill. Taft had urged passage to the old Congress but a combination of progressives and Democrats, who opposed the measure on the ground that it gave more protection to already overprotected manufacturers at the expense of farm products, and high-tariff standpat Republicans, who feared that the bill would lead to new questions about the Payne-Aldrich tariff schedules, defeated the measure. Taft insisted that it be approved by the new Congress.

That session was notable for a number of reasons. The Democrats were in control of the House. In the Senate a group of thirteen progressive Republicans was numerically strong enough to make matters embarrassing for the Old Guard. A progressive demand for representation on the Senate committees in proportion to their numbers, a demand which meant that one-fifth of the Republican membership of each committee be composed of progressives, was refused. In return, standpat Republicans were thwarted in their effort to elect Senator Gallinger of New Hamp-

shire as president pro tempore. Progressives led by Senator La
Follette had met separately and had not taken part in the regular Republican caucus. La Follette led the skirmish against election of Gallinger and was denounced by the regulars for party-
wrecking activity. The Wisconsin senator retorted that he did
not recognize the right of any senator to read him out of the
party because of his opposition to plans that had been made in
secret.

The reciprocity bill was finally passed, but Taft's sense of
victory was short-lived because the Laurier government, which
had proposed the action, was repudiated and the Canadian
Parliament refused its approval. Just as high-tariff Republicans
had feared, La Follette and his group of progressives took the
opportunity to force through several bills providing for drastic
downward revision of some of the Payne-Aldrich schedules. One
measure, the Farmers' Free List bill, placed on the free list
articles purchased by agricultural producers. The wool and cotton schedules were revised downward in other bills. Taft vetoed
all the bills. He announced that he did so because they were
political bills; that the reductions were not based upon scientific
findings. The progressive Republican retort was that if President
Taft was so impressed with scientific fact finding as the basis
for tariff determination, why had he not used the method for his
reciprocity measure.

On the constructive side, La Follette carried on a continuing
battle to secure amendments to the Interstate Commerce Act to
empower the commission to make a physical evaluation of railroads which could be used as the basis for rate making. He supported and helped secure passage of legislation setting up the
Commission on Industrial Relations, the Children's Bureau, and
a federal corrupt practices act.

In this same session, Senator La Follette tried to get approval
of a bill defining "restraint of trade." It was the legislative expression of the basic political and economic philosophy to which
he often gave utterance. As he viewed it, the troubles of national
society were caused by the development within a democratic
framework of an economic oligarchy that denied both political
and economic democracy to citizens. The trusts and monopolies

had taken over the government to protect themselves against the intrusion of popular democracy. La Follette's many battles against the party bosses in Wisconsin had been the opening salvos against this oppression. His direct primary proposals were a successful effort to bring government closer to the people. He had proved, at least in Wisconsin, that government regulation of big business had not meant its destruction.

La Follette maintained that the trust had stifled individual initiative and crippled competition. He denounced price fixing and production limitation agreements. His bill defined "restraint of trade" and provided for dissolution of all such combinations. The bill was not passed.

CHAPTER VI

La Follette and the 1912 Campaign

PROGRESSIVE REPUBLICANS in Congress had been encouraged by the results of the 1910 elections. Looking forward to the 1912 presidential campaign, Senators La Follette and Jonathan Bourne, of Oregon, met in December, 1910, with their Congressional colleagues and drew up a statement of progressive principles.

The Wisconsin senator declared that it had become apparent to the progressives that Taft had lost any chance of being re-elected in 1912 and that pressure for the candidacy of an outstanding progressive to oppose Taft had developed. The National Progressive Republican League was organized at a meeting in La Follette's home on January 21, 1911. The declaration of principles of the new league gave its object to be the promotion of popular government and progressive legislation. It advocated direct election of United States senators, direct primaries, direct election of delegates to national party conventions, adoption by the states of constitutional amendments providing for the initiative, referendum, and recall, and thoroughgoing corrupt practices laws.

Headed by Senator Bourne as president, and with Frederic C. Howe as secretary and Charles R. Crane of Chicago as treasurer, the national league had a distinguished list of Progressives on its rolls. William Allen White, James R. Garfield, Louis D. Brandeis, Ray Stannard Baker, Gifford and Amos Pinchot, and

Francis J. Heney were among the outstanding men. Associated with them were the governors of California, Michigan, Wisconsin, Nebraska, Kansas, and Wyoming. The list did not include the name of Theodore Roosevelt. He had been asked to join the effort but had declined. He expressed qualified approval to his progressive friends and even went so far as to say nice things editorially in the *Outlook* about it. As he interpreted the results of the 1910 elections, Roosevelt could find no suggestion of Republican victory in 1912. In the early months of 1911 he believed that Taft would be beaten. He felt, however, that it would be disastrous for the party to split on the question of a nominee. He continued the role he had outlined for himself in the 1910 campaign. He wanted a united party, and it has been suggested that he was looking forward to 1916 and another chance at the presidency.

To Washington political observers, the new National Progressive Republican League was a nominating machine. They admitted in their dispatches to midwestern newspapers that there was no confirmation of their suspicions, but immediately after announcement of the formation of the league the political reporters stated definitely that La Follette would be a candidate in 1912. The league grew rapidly and state organizations were set up in Minnesota, Wisconsin, Michigan, Nebraska, South Dakota, and Washington. These organizations, together with the national headquarters staff, released quantities of anti-Taft material and spearheaded discussion of a truly progressive candidate for 1912. That campaign technique was the same as used and perfected by the Democratic National Committee between 1928 and 1932. Charles Michelson, for the committee, kept up a constant barrage of anti-Hoover publicity that eventually, with the help of the depression, proved highly effective.

Both La Follette and Roosevelt were prominently mentioned as presidential candidates. Roosevelt's refusal to signify whether or not he would be a candidate shifted the emphasis to La Follette. Not sure of Roosevelt's ultimate course of action, La Follette made every effort to find out. Despite the former President's laudatory articles in the *Outlook*, the Wisconsin senator was reluctant to declare himself a candidate.

The two men never completely trusted each other. It was a profound clash of personalities grounded on the differences in their basic philosophies. All who knew both Roosevelt and La Follette agreed on this point. Even such a warm admirer of both men as Lincoln Steffens stated that, of the two, La Follette was the real progressive. William Allen White expressed the highest admiration for the two men but refused to permit himself to be used as a go-between because he knew that sooner or later he would lose the friendship of one of them. White was quite frank in his belief that of all the men who might have been chosen president in 1912 La Follette would have been the best.

During the early months of 1911 La Follette made every effort to find out what Roosevelt would do. Illness at one time prevented the Wisconsin senator from going to Roosevelt's home for a personal discussion. Those who did talk with the former President reported to La Follette that Roosevelt was convinced Taft could not win in 1912 but that the party ought not to split by offering a progressive candidate. Roosevelt made a lecture tour of the country in the spring. Interviewed by Gilson Gardner, Scripps-McRae Washington correspondent, Roosevelt was reported to have said that he had changed his mind about putting a progressive candidate in the field against Taft. Another mutual friend of the two men also went to Roosevelt about the same time to find out what his intentions were. John R. Commons, one of the pioneer labor economists in the United States, reported to La Follette that Roosevelt had been emphatically in favor of the Wisconsin senator in his reply to a direct question about his support of La Follette's possible candidacy.

La Follette, however, did not announce his candidacy until June 17, 1911, after he had been assured of adequate financial support for the campaign by the Pinchots, William Kent of California, Charles R. Crane, and Alfred L. Baker. A busy summer of campaigning, with mounting interest in the La Follette candidacy, caused political commentators to suggest that there might be a possibility of defeating Taft for the nomination. Favorable reaction to an article written by Roosevelt outlining a plan for complete regulation of the trusts brought forth the suggestion that possibly the former President might be induced to make the run again.

Many progressives hesitated in their headlong support of La Follette. Organizations in Ohio, Michigan, Illinois, Kansas, California, and other progressive states began to turn toward the possibility of a Roosevelt boom. A national gathering of progressive leaders in Chicago in the latter part of October had endorsed La Follette for the presidency but the doubt was spread that he was being used as a stalking horse for Roosevelt. The latter, by his refusal to say he would not be a candidate, complicated the situation. Honest Progressives who held both men in high esteem were bewildered. The more practical political Progressives were convinced they had a better chance in the 1912 elections with Roosevelt than with La Follette.

Plans for La Follette's candidacy had developed so far, however, that arrangements had already been made for the publication of the senator's autobiography in the *American Magazine*. Publication began serially in the October, 1911, issue and continued through the March, 1912, issue. With the title *A Personal Narrative of Political Experiences*, the autobiography was subsequently published by Doubleday, Page with additional chapters on the 1912 campaign.

During December and January of 1911–1912 Senator La Follette toured through Ohio, Michigan, and Illinois. He spoke to overflow audiences wherever he went. Enthusiasm mounted for La Follette as the Progressive Republican candidate to oppose Taft. Plans had been made for the Ohio Progressives to endorse La Follette in Columbus on January 1, 1912. James R. Garfield, Walter Brown of Toledo, and Dan Hanna of Cleveland, leading the Progressive movement in Ohio, had other plans. They opposed a frank endorsement, hoping to leave the way open to Roosevelt should he, as seemed likely, become an avowed candidate. The conference in Columbus finally adopted a resolution of a general nature without naming a specific candidate.

Two other events of importance to the undeclared candidacy of Theodore Roosevelt occurred in January. Representatives of big business and high finance let it be known that they believed the election of a Progressive could not be avoided and that they felt that Roosevelt, of all the Progressives, would be the safest. On January 16 a Roosevelt National Committee was formed in Chicago. Attempts were made by the Pinchots and other Progressives who had up to that time supported him to persuade La Follette to withdraw from the race. La Follette, however, refused. He refused to countenance any action that might be interpreted as a compromise between himself and Roosevelt. He felt that he had gone too far to turn back at that juncture. So long as Roosevelt was not an avowed candidate and so long as La Follette continued, those Progressives who hoped Roosevelt would eventually announce his intentions were embarrassed. Having supported La Follette from the beginning and having provided financial support, they would have opened themselves to charges of desertion and political opportunism had they made the break.

At a conference in the La Follette Washington headquarters, called by Gifford Pinchot on January 29, the Roosevelt sympathizers tried to force La Follette into withdrawing either in favor of Roosevelt or simply to leave the field open for the group to choose whomever they favored as individuals. Informed by the Associated Press that Chicago papers were printing a story that afternoon announcing the conference and reporting that as a result of the meeting La Follette would issue a statement withdrawing from the race, La Follette issued an emphatic denial of any such action on his part.

Hard on the heels of the physically debilitating tour of the Midwest came the badgering by Roosevelt supporters to force La Follette to withdraw. Worrisome details of running the Washington headquarters further sapped the senator's vitality. The serious illness of his youngest daughter weighed heavily upon him. With those burdens and following a particularly heavy day in the Senate, La Follette spoke at the annual banquet of the Periodical Publishers' Association in Philadelphia on February 2. It was an unfortunate circumstance for the Progressive candidate. Physically and mentally weary, sick at heart over the turn of events among those he had considered his stanchest supporters, Robert La Follette delivered the poorest public address of his entire career. He was not sure of himself. He fumbled. He dropped his prepared speech to harangue. He spoke too long. When he finished, he sank exhausted to his chair. The speech he attempted to deliver to that gathering of periodical publishers was a terrific indictment of the commercial and financial despotism under which the nation had fallen. He came close to indicting the press of the country as the tool of the special interests in their efforts to control the political and economic life of the nation. Press comment the next day was highly critical and carried comments of his "collapse."

With almost indecent haste the Pinchots, William Flinn, Medill McCormick, and others deserted La Follette. Gifford Pinchot announced that because of the physical incapacity of La Follette he was transferring his support to Roosevelt. A simple announcement from La Follette's headquarters in Washington to the effect that illness due to overwork required the cancellation of the candidate's engagements for the next two weeks was distorted to mean that La Follette had withdrawn. Gilson Gardner wrote a dispatch from Washington flatly stating:

"Senator Robert M. La Follette has been sacrificed to the Progressive cause.

"He led the first charge. He took command of a forlorn hope."

In effect, wrote Gardner, it was too bad that such things had to happen to Senator La Follette but the sad fact was that Progressives could not hope to win under the leadership of the senator from Wisconsin. The correspondent had acted as liaison man between the La Follette headquarters and Oyster Bay. He had stood with the Pinchots and others who had urged La Follette to quit the race. Gardner's dispatch paved the way, evidently, for a formal statement issued by Gifford Pinchot the middle of February in which he said, among other things:

"Senator La Follette's candidacy was undertaken for two clear and specific purposes: first to hold the Progressives together as an effective fighting force, and second, to prevent the nomination of a reactionary Republican for the Presidency."

Pinchot even telegraphed the Minnesota Republican League that "La Follette's condition makes further serious candidacy impossible." It was an effort to swing that group to Roosevelt. It failed. Events moved rapidly in February. As if by prearranged signal, Roosevelt clubs came into being all over the Midwest and on the 26th of that month Roosevelt announced in Columbus, Ohio, that "my hat is in the ring."

A hectic campaign followed to secure as many pledged delegates as possible to the national Republican convention. Despite the heartbreaking defection of many he had counted on as last-ditch supporters, La Follette stayed in the race. William Allen White and others had shifted their support to Roosevelt and did so, as they testified in later years, because of the reaction to La Follette's speech at the Periodical Publishers' Association banquet. But what happened in Kansas happened in many other up-to-that-time-La Follette strongholds. White himself declared that when three county conventions had met and refused to name La Follette delegates, "we let nature take its course."

Local politicians in Kansas, faced with an alternative, chose Roosevelt because they were surer of winning locally with the former President at the head of the ticket than with La Follette. William Flinn, the political boss of western Pennsylvania, was engaged in a fight for supremacy in the Keystone State with the eastern Pennsylvania machine headed by Boise Penrose. Senator Penrose supported Taft and Flinn was interested, not because he was in any way a Progressive, but because he wanted a candidate who stood a chance of defeating Taft. He rode along with La Follette until Roosevelt became an avowed candidate.

Roosevelt supporters got a bad jolt on March 19 when citizens of North Dakota gave Robert M. La Follette a 10,000 majority in their presidential preference primary. He lost in every other state where he campaigned except Wisconsin. La Follette went to the national convention with thirty-six pledged delegates. As a result of the terrific fight between Roosevelt and Taft for delegates in a number of states, neither had a clear majority of uncontested delegates to the convention. Nearly a third of the seats were contested by the Roosevelt forces but, with the Republican National Committee dominated by Taft supporters, the contests were resolved in favor of the President's candidacy. The charges and countercharges of theft, fraud, graft, and other

forms of raw crime changed an otherwise tumultuous convention
into an uproar.

Roosevelt lost his first test of strength over selection of temporary chairman. He had entered Governor Francis E. McGovern
of Wisconsin as his candidate apparently in the hope of uniting
the Progressive elements. Senator La Follette objected strenuously
to McGovern's candidacy as temporary chairman on the ground
that it would be accepted as evidence of a compromise between
himself and Roosevelt. La Follette's campaign manager, Walter
Houser, denounced the move from the convention platform.

Elihu Root, Taft's candidate for both temporary and permanent chairman, was given the post by a 558-to-502 vote.

Roosevelt had already paved the way for a break when he
addressed his followers at the Chicago Auditorium the night before the convention. He served notice that he would not be
bound by the convention if the delegates whose seats were contested were permitted to take part in organizing the convention.
That was the speech which he ended with the famous words,
"We stand at Armageddon, and we battle for the Lord." When
the convention, on June 22, nominated Taft on the first ballot
by a vote of 561 for the President, 107 for Roosevelt, and 41 for
La Follette, Roosevelt men announced a convention to meet that
night to form a new party. With Hiram Johnson of California as
his running mate, the Progressive party nominated Theodore
Roosevelt by acclamation. Senator Robert La Follette, however,
refused to join the Progressive party. He believed it more important, in view of the historical development of the two major
parties, to stay in the Republican party and do all he could to
make it the vehicle of public interest—to restore it to the high
place it held when it was the party of Abraham Lincoln.

The political situation was further complicated for the development of a third party that summer of 1912; first, by the
nomination of Governor Woodrow Wilson of New Jersey as
the Democratic party nominee and, second, by the refusal of a
number of Progressive Republicans to affiliate with the new
party.

As governor of New Jersey the former Princeton University
president sponsored much progressive legislation. His progres-

sivism was the more impressive because as a teacher of government and a writer of textbooks on the subject, Wilson had been a thoroughgoing exponent of the theory that the best government was one that did as little governing as possible. As governor he was confronted with new problems of the relationships between business and labor and of public welfare. An honest intellectual, he was forced by circumstances to change his philosophy. In the *New Freedom,* Wilson argued that life had become so complicated that the law had to help create the conditions of life tolerable for the masses. Like La Follette, Wilson was suspicious of the growth of trusts and large business combinations. He agreed with La Follette that it was the duty of government to eliminate artificial barriers to free competition. Unfair trade methods that stifled competition and permitted monopoly must come under the purview of government. Wilson believed the relationship between employer and employee to be wholly antiquated. New rules had to be devised to equalize bargaining power. The obligations and responsibilities and rights of both labor and capital had to be revised to provide real equality. These were principles for which Progressive Republicans had long been fighting.

Democrats went into the campaign united behind a liberal candidate. Republicans were split over the issue of progressivism versus standpatism. Roosevelt's candidacy received another blow when the Progressive Republican support he had received for the nomination at the Chicago convention refused to follow him into the new party. Some Progressive Republicans openly supported Wilson.

La Follette's first public statement about his position came in an address at La Crosse. He told his audience: "I do not propose to vote for any of the three candidates for president." The tone of his remarks suggested a friendly attitude toward Wilson's candidacy but he told the citizens of La Crosse that he had some reservation about johnny-come-latelies into the Progressive movement. At Superior a few days later he declared that he wouldn't be much surprised if Wilson was elected and "if he shows himself a Progressive, I not only intend to support his policies but to influence such as I can in the Senate to do likewise." At Wausau, La Follette delivered his final judgment on the matter:

"I would like to talk to you about Wilson. Wilson is a Progressive. He has made a splendid record as governor of New Jersey. In this election, vote after you have thought it over very carefully. I have nothing up my sleeve. . . . It goes without saying that I am not supporting Taft nor Roosevelt. Neither will I vote for Wilson.

"I think the Republican party must be preserved. I have no sympathy with Roosevelt's attempt to destroy it. The Republican party is a Progressive party. The Democrats have only one Progressive state, New Jersey. Its laws are copied from Wisconsin but that does not detract from Governor Wilson. I believe that if Wilson is elected he will try to give a Progressive administration. . . . I want to maintain my influence with the Progressive Republican group of senators and members of the House. This Progressive Republican strength has developed until it enables us to rewrite and reframe much legislation. If Wilson proves to be a Progressive, as his splendid record, in New Jersey entitles us to believe he will be, this independent group of men may assist him. When I turn to scorch him as I surely will do if he fails, I do not want anyone to say: 'You voted for him.'"

The election result in Wisconsin was in itself testimony to La Follette's strong position with the voters. Wilson received 164,000 votes, with Taft getting 130,000 and Roosevelt only 62,000. The Progressive Republican candidate for governor, Francis E. McGovern, received 179,000 votes while the Democratic candidate received 167,000.

Of course, La Follette was criticized by Roosevelt Progressives for his stand. One of the bitterest denunciations came from Governor Hiram Johnson of California, who wrote William R. Nelson, publisher of the Kansas City Star, to beware of "pseudo-Progressives like La Follette, Cummins, and Borah." In Johnson's view they were not "legitimate Progressives." The letter was published in the Star.

"Our chief danger in the next year," Johnson wrote to Nelson, "will be this Congressional group, and particularly La Follette who showed not only a dastardly streak in the recent campaign, but who showed himself lacking in real courage when with all his mendacity and hatred he did not dare openly to come out for Wilson, but pretended he was still a Republican who preserved his party regularity, while all the time he was beseeching his friends and satellites to get into the open for Wilson."

Within two weeks after the inauguration of Woodrow Wilson as president, Senator Robert La Follette had been invited to a White House conference. Purpose of the visit was to discuss plans for uniting Progressives in both parties to obtain passage of tariff and other legislation. The Republican minority in the Senate also named the Wisconsin senator to the steering committee. Political writers wondered if the action of the stand-patters in naming La Follette to that committee might be a subtle way of taking him into camp. As a matter of cold, political fact, standpat elements in the Senate had little choice in the matter. Boise Penrose had been badly beaten in Pennsylvania by the Flinn machine's support of Roosevelt. The situation in such Old Guard citadels as Massachusetts was almost as bad. La Follette had to be accorded recognition—the Progressive Republican movement could no longer be turned aside by the Old Guard.

CHAPTER VII

Prelude to War

DEMOCRATIC LEADERS were busy putting together their tariff bill in the summer of 1913. A great deal of editorial speculation was printed about Senator La Follette's probable reaction. Newspaper correspondents noted that there appeared to be some sort of working agreement between the Wisconsin Progressive Republican and the Democratic members of the Finance Committee. Several of La Follette's suggestions about rates were adopted by the Democratic majority. His ideas for higher rates of taxation on the larger incomes were incorporated into the bill. The final vote on passage of the Underwood-Simmons tariff measure, cast on strict party lines, disclosed La Follette as the lone Republican voting for it.

On another major legislative matter the Wisconsin senator did not agree at all with the Democratic administration. La Follette objected strenuously to the Federal Reserve Act. He frankly admitted the need for providing greater elasticity for the currency in the United States. But he did not like giving bankers the right to acquire stock in the reserve bank, which action, he said, "establishes a bankers' control and a bankers' ownership at the vital point of the whole plan—to provide elasticity for the currency system. It sets up a system that legalizes the monopoly of banking power."

La Follette took a parting shot at the new Federal Reserve Act in his magazine on January 3, 1914, by observing editorially:

"Having turned the Money Power over to the unrestrained fury of the Big Banking Interests and thus provided the people with 'protection from the control or domination by what is known as the Money Trust,' to quote the Baltimore platform, the Administration can now give its attention to other monopolistic trusts."

Other problems engaged La Follette's attention. He sponsored a bill, passed by the Senate, for the 8-hour day for women employed in the District of Columbia. It was killed in the House. He asked the Congress to pass a bill setting up standards of safety and protection for seagoing passengers and providing for better wages and working conditions for seamen on American-owned ships. The proposal had been before Congress for nearly twenty years and La Follette pressed for passage. It took another two years of work before the La Follette Seaman's Act became law.

His experience as governor had made La Follette a thoroughgoing believer in the use of the expert in government and he tried to secure approval of a measure setting up a legislative reference bureau in the Library of Congress to assist congressmen in bill drafting and in getting facts about problems up for legislative action. His bill failed, but a year later this aspect of the Wisconsin Idea was established in the national government when La Follette secured adoption of an amendment to a departmental appropriation granting $25,000 annually to the Library of Congress for setting up the Legislative Reference Division.

La Follette had been urged by many people to take the lead in reorganizing and revitalizing the Republican party. He warned, however, that "unless it advances under such tried progressive leadership as will insure a vitally sound and thoroughgoing government, it cannot hope to win and ought not to win the national election of 1916."

The new National Progressive party under the leadership of Theodore Roosevelt had not caught on. Elements in the group were divided over two problems. The first was the influential position in party affairs of George W. Perkins, the Morgan partner. The anti-Perkins group demanded his ouster. Then, a considerable number of Progressives accepted La Follette's argument that the only way to gain political victory was to work as Progressive Republicans. Roosevelt, however, kept the party alive but the 1914 elections sounded the death knell of the new third party under his leadership.

Amos Pinchot had been one of the most articulate Progressives in the fight against Perkins. He finally made the break from Roosevelt's leadership and charged that Perkins had betrayed the Progressive party. Senator La Follette gave Pinchot space in his magazine to air the charges! In the 1914 campaign La Follette was generous to those Progressives who had deserted him in 1912. He announced his support of nearly all his old friends. In *La Follette's Magazine* he was warm in his praise for Senator Bristow of Kansas, Governor Hiram Johnson and Francis Heney of California, and others who had deserted him in 1912.

La Follette faced a problem in his own state, where five Progressive Republicans were in the race for nomination as governor. With the vote so badly split, the Stalwart Republican candidate, Emanuel Philipp, was nominated. Philipp was one of the stalwarts who had given Lincoln Steffens "evidence" of Governor La Follette's mishandling of state affairs in 1904 which Steffens investigated and found groundless. La Follette himself was urged to run for the governorship but another Progressive Republican, John J. Blaine, was finally put forward as an independent candidate. Philipp won the election. Of the result in Wisconsin, Theodore Roosevelt wrote friends that even in that state people were tired of progress—the dog "had returned to its vomit!" As he analyzed the political scene, the former President dourly observed that progressivism had run its course.

War clouds of a far more sinister nature began to form. Trouble with Mexico had been inherited by the Wilson administration. Armed conflict between various factions trying to get control of the government had paralyzed the normal functioning of affairs in that unhappy country.

President Wilson addressed a message to Congress on the Mexican situation in the late summer of 1913. He reviewed the steps taken by the United States and declared that efforts of this country to settle the trouble had failed because of misunderstanding. He urged Americans not to get impatient and to observe true neutrality. Wilson also asked all American nationals not urgently needed there to get out of Mexico. Finally, the President announced an embargo on all shipments of munitions to Mexico from the United States.

La Follette had anticipated President Wilson's position by urging, the week before the presidential message was read to Congress, that "intervention for the protection of private property interests is upon all authority to be condemned.

"Those who invested their capital in Mexico," La Follette pointed out, "did so with full knowledge of the hazard. Property rights were obviously insecure. The big American financiers who coveted control of transportation and the timber and mineral wealth of Mexico invested at their peril. The losses which they may suffer, while a proper subject for settlement in the usual way between nations, will not be made the excuse for forcing recognition of the Huerta government."

Throughout the Mexican trouble, La Follette supported every effort of the President to bring about peaceful settlement between the two nations. As he interpreted events, establishment of a government in Mexico in the interests of citizens of that nation was opposed by powerful American corporations with heavy investments there. Thus, as he saw it, the demands for intervention were motivated solely by selfish economic interests and not based on any humane desire to help Mexico get back on its feet. In short, Senator La Follette valued human rights above corporate rights. He warned against governmental secrecy in any negotiations between the two countries and called upon President Wilson to keep the people of the country informed of all the facts concerning the United States in its relations with Mexico.

La Follette deplored the landing of troops at Veracruz but believed that argument over what ought to have been done was futile. "It's done," La Follette wrote in his magazine. "Let it be known in every capital of the world that the President has the support of a united nation . . .

"Make it plain to Mexico and to all mankind that we will not, under any circumstances, exercise any measure of sovereignty, jurisdiction, or control over Mexico or any portion of her territory.

"Proclaim our fixed purpose to withdraw the armed forces at the earliest possible moment consistent with national honor."

La Follette hailed the acceptance by the United States of an offer by Argentina, Brazil, and Chile to mediate the trouble. As it developed in the argument over the Mexican trouble, La Follette's opposition to war was based on two factors. The first was his humanitarian concern for the "little man." He shuddered at the waste of human resources exacted by war.

"It is well for us to remember," La Follette told readers of his magazine, "that war is always cruel; that its iron tread means destruction and devastation, whether its march is across Europe or from Atlanta to the sea; that war arouses all the fiercest human passions; that there are always cases of brutality and outrage—and that usually there is quite as much of it on one side as upon the other."

The second important factor in La Follette's opposition to war was his belief that the breeders of international misunderstanding were the economic interests who, having exploited the people of a nation to the limit, were turning to other nations and newer fields to exploit for their own gain. The only difference between Robert M. La Follette and many of his contemporary fellow Americans was that he was willing to sacrifice his whole public career for his stand.

Shortly after the beginning of the war in Europe, President Wilson addressed the nation. He urged all citizens to maintain a spirit of impartiality and friendliness. "The United States must be neutral in fact as well as in name during these days that are to try men's souls," Wilson said. La Follette characterized the statement as "high statesmanship and splendid patriotism." He applauded the efforts of the President and his secretary of state, William Jennings Bryan, to set up by treaty the machinery for international arbitration. Impressed by those efforts and the success of the A.B.C. mediation of our difficulties with Mexico, La Follette introduced a resolution in the Senate on February 8, 1915, which provided that the United States call a conference of all neutral nations to promote early cessation of hostilities; limitation of armaments and nationalization of the manufacture of munitions; promulgation of rules and regulations to prohibit export from one country to another of munitions of war; establishment of an international tribunal; provision, by neutral nations, for neutralization of certain waters and maritime trade routes; action to lead to establishment of permanent world peace.

In support of the resolution La Follette said:

"We do not want to see the map of Europe changed by might of conquest. We cannot believe that it is in the interest of human progress that any one nation should be wiped off the face of the earth . . .

"It is a mistaken policy that assumes a community of nations can prosper any more than can a community of individuals by one or more tyrannizing over others and monopolizing the world's markets. The world's greatest progress must be best served by the largest possible development of the national life of each country. We believe there is still room for all in the vast and undeveloped areas of the earth."

Disappointed by failure of the Senate to take action on his peace proposal, La Follette soon found comfort in pushing to a successful conclusion a campaign in which he became interested in 1909. On March 4, 1915, President Wilson attached his signature to the La Follette Seaman's Act. The act freed American seamen from a bondage that made them virtual slaves, provided for better working conditions, hours of labor, and higher wages. It also set up new standards for safety of passengers and cargo on lake- and oceangoing vessels flying the American flag.

"I shall always remember that Senate debate on the Seaman's Act," Edward Keating, editor of *Labor*, said in recalling the incident. "I went into the Senate to talk to Senator La Follette about something that must have been awfully important at the time because I used my prerogative as a former member of Congress to get onto the floor.

"When I entered, the senator was discussing the provision in the proposed law relating to the requirement that both master and crew of the ship speak the same language. To make his point clear, La Follette described a ship at sea in a storm. The ship was about to be engulfed by the high seas and no one knew exactly what to do. The captain spoke one language and the crew another. The interpreter had been swept overboard by the high seas.

"The seas grew angrier. First the prow of the ship was lifted almost out of the water. Then a great dip and the stern rose toward the heavens. The senator was so dramatic in his presentation that two-thirds of us who were listening were about half seasick from the motions of that hypothetical ship!"

Robert M. La Follette, however, virtually apologized because the act bore his name. He felt that he was but an instrument in bringing about safer sea travel and liberating seamen from bondage.

"In all the years of this historic struggle for human liberty, which finally culminated with President Wilson's signing of the Seaman's law," La Follette editorialized in his magazine a month after the measure was signed, "Andrew Furuseth was the one man who had the faith, the vision and the courage necessary to sustain the contest. He launched the movement. He kept it afloat. Every moment of the 21 years he was at the helm. Through legislative storms and calms, over the sunken reefs of privilege, across every treacherous shoal and past all dangers, he held his cause true to its course and brought it safely into port."

Senator La Follette watched with anxiety the mounting tide of the war spirit. Wherever he went, wherever he spoke, he urged his fellow citizens to maintain a strict neutrality. The German U-boat campaign, the British declaration of a blockade against Germany and the Central Powers, financing more and bigger loans to the Allies by American banks, all made La Follette apprehensive of the future. He unhesitatingly opposed demands of the Administration for appropriations to increase the armed forces. Such action, he insisted, could only lead to war.

In the spring of 1916 La Follette made himself unpopular with the Administration by his sharp criticism of Wilson's efforts to kill a resolution before Congress warning American citizens to keep off armed merchant ships. Senator La Follette termed it "interference" and declared that the President's action in demanding, in effect, that Congress keep silent about foreign affairs was unprecedented.

"Democratic control of foreign policies is a basic principle of all organized effort looking for the future establishment of permanent world peace," La Follette declared on the Senate floor.

Supporting this statement of the right of citizens in a democracy to take part in forming foreign policy, La Follette introduced a bill calling for a referendum on war. "Why not," he asked in presenting the bill for consideration, "let the people themselves on whom the burden of war falls, have a voice . . . along with finance and diplomacy, in determining whether there shall be war?" He called attention to the need, as he saw it, for Congress to know public sentiment on pressing and vital issues. The Wisconsin senator anticipated by a number of years public opinion poll techniques by suggesting machinery by which the Congress might get public opinion reaction.

In an address at Madison on February 22, 1916, La Follette told his audience that the "preparedness fever" then sweeping the country was inspired by those who stood to profit from government spending for supplies and munitions. He declared himself in favor of an act placing an embargo on exportation of arms and ammunition. He also suggested that there would be less incentive for war if the profits were eliminated by nationalization of munitions manufacture. La Follette expressed his abhorrence of secret diplomacy by saying that "it is obsolete. It is a survival of the past when nations were separate entities. Today the world is a commercial unit . . . the prosperity of each is the prosperity of all."

At the national Republican convention in Chicago that summer, the Wisconsin delegation offered a platform containing the popular referendum vote measure, the neutral nations peace proposal, and planks providing for government manufacture of munitions, an excess profits tax on all manufacture of munitions, and a federal inheritance tax. The Chicago *Tribune* brushed aside both the suggestion of La Follette's availability as presidential candidate and the "Wisconsin platform" editorially by saying:

"Senator La Follette of Wisconsin furnishes the energy behind a resolution to be offered to the Republican convention for an embargo upon arms and ammunition. La Follette is acting as a German because there is a large German vote in the Wisconsin constituency. He is also acting like a Democrat to make trouble for the Republican party. La Follette, in his disappointed ambitions, is a Democrat. He is not a Republican."

Disappointed by refusal of the convention to adopt any of the Wisconsin planks, La Follette pointed out that neither the 1908 nor the 1912 convention had accepted any of the proposals made by the Wisconsin delegation. He noted, however, that of thirty-one proposals made to the Republican convention since 1908, twenty-five had been enacted into law. So far as the nomination of Charles Evans Hughes was concerned, the senator admitted that there was probably no other man upon whom so many Republicans of all elements could have been joined in support.

La Follette's intransigent attitude against war, his insistence upon true neutrality, and his opposition to big appropriations for the preparedness program, all of which he expressed freely during his own campaign for nomination and re-election to the Senate, finally got under the skin of the New York *Times*. That newspaper testily observed:

"Wisconsin has one American Senator. She needs another. Mr. La Follette, beside his multifarious crankeries and orotundities, has not spoken or voted as an American . . . Wisconsin should get rid at last of this noisy 'reformer' . . . this miscellaneous agitator, this fetterer of American shipping. Let the Badgers give him back to the tents of Chautauqua and La Follette's Magazine. He has ceased to be even amusing."

La Follette's support and defense of the Adamson Act did nothing to endear him to the New York *Times* or any of the rest of the majority of American newspapers. The law had been passed to head off a threatened general strike on American railroads. It established an 8-hour day for rail employees and was regarded by most editorial writers as a "force bill" granted at pistol point and without due consideration. They did not like La Follette's reminder that when he had urged passage of a 16-hour workday nearly ten years earlier he had been confronted with the same arguments as used against the Adamson law.

In the meantime he campaigned throughout the state in behalf of his own senatorial candidacy. In contrast to the 1912 campaign, La Follette said nothing about the comparative merits of either Hughes or Wilson. On the eve of the November election, in reply to a direct question, La Follette told a Milwaukee audience that "so much hangs upon the result of the election . . . so much hangs upon every vote . . . that I believe you should settle it between your consciences and your God."

On that advice from their Progressive leader, Wisconsin voters cast 221,000 votes for Charles Evans Hughes and 192,000 for President Wilson. At the same time voters in the Badger State were not even polite to the request of the New York *Times* to retire La Follette "to the Chautauqua tents." The senator received the biggest majority he had ever received. With 251,000 votes, La Follette was an almost 2-to-1 winner over his Democratic opponent, who received 135,000 votes.

CHAPTER VIII

The War Years

With a declaration by Germany of unrestricted submarine warfare on neutral shipping and the oft-repeated propaganda tales of the horrors perpetrated by the armies of the Central Powers to catch the unwary, the warmongers were in full cry in the early months of 1917. Newspapers fanned the flames of jingoism by publishing smear articles purporting to tell of the un-American activities of those members of Congress who had declared their opposition to war. Perhaps because editorial interpreters thought they saw a sinister link between the number of Wisconsin citizens of German descent and his opposition to preparedness, Senator La Follette was singled out for special treatment. Scurrilous articles impuging his motives and patriotism began to appear in newspapers throughout the East. Well-known authors, publicists, and professional men and women added their voices to the swelling chorus of denunciation with letters to the editor.

Disregarding the public clamor against him, Senator La Follette denounced with all the vigor at his command the Armed Ship bill that had been introduced into Congress in the dying days of the Sixty-fourth Congress. The bill was President Wilson's answer to Germany's declaration of unrestricted submarine warfare on all shipping that sought to run the blockade imposed by the Central Powers. Popular support was behind the measure as it came to the Senate for final action in the last few hours of the session. Twelve senators, six Republicans and six Democrats, organized swiftly behind the leadership of La Follette, George Norris of Nebraska, and William V. Stone of Missouri. They planned the filibuster that killed the Armed Ship bill.

The majority of American citizens had accepted President Wilson's argument that only by arming American merchant ships could the neutrality of this nation be maintained. It was a drama-packed moment in the history of the United States Senate when the filibuster against the bill and apparently against overwhelming public sentiment began its course.

Senator Norris organized the speakers against the measure. By common consent, Senator La Follette was allotted the last three hours of the session for the concluding argument against arming of American merchant ships.

As the opposition to passage held and it finally dawned upon those in favor of the bill that the filibuster would succeed, friends of the measure began to speak in favor of passage. They held the floor and prevented Senator La Follette from delivering his speech in the last hours. La Follette was furious. The presiding officer, Senator Joe Robinson of Arkansas, openly ignored the Wisconsin senator's efforts to get the floor. The filibuster was succeeding and Senator Norris went over to La Follette's side to caution him to do nothing that would upset the situation.

"If I have to," La Follette told Norris in a whisper, "I'll toss a spittoon at Robinson to get his attention."

The spittoon was not tossed and La Follette did not get the floor, but the filibuster succeeded. Reaction was immediate and explosive. President Wilson expressed popular feeling when he angrily denounced the opponents to the bill as "a little band of willful men who represent no opinion except their own."

La Follette and his little group of "willful men" had opposed the Armed Ship bill as an unconstitutional delegation of power in that it left solely to the President's discretion the use of methods to maintain neutrality which in themselves were an automatic declaration of war. As they saw the problem, it was exactly the kind of one-man power that had led to the war in Europe. Besides, they argued, it was at best a futile gesture.

The filibuster against the Armed Ship bill had blocked con-

sideration of a number of appropriations measures and President
Wilson immediately issued the call for a special session of Congress. Public protest against the successful filibuster had been
so bitter that the Senate was forced to adopt the rule of cloture to
limit debate. Confronted with President Wilson's request for a
formal declaration of war, Senator Robert M. La Follette and
five of his colleagues were the only ones to stand by their principles to the bitter end.

The six Senate opponents to war, Gronna, Lane, Stone, La
Follette, Norris, and Vardaman, were treated as pariahs by their
senatorial colleagues. Backs were turned on them when they entered the Senate chamber. When they got on elevators in the
Capitol, passengers already on would get off. They were spied
upon; their office files were tampered with. Members of their
families were harassed.

The height, or depth, of the bitterness against Senator Robert
M. La Follette was not reached until toward the end of 1917. In
the summer of that first war year, La Follette and a few others
made every effort to get adopted what they believed to be a
sound and adequate war revenue measure. As a member of the
Senate Finance Committee, the Wisconsin senator urged his colleagues to support a revenue bill to provide for payment of taxes
on the basis of ability to pay and to establish a fiscal policy that
would meet war costs out of current profits and war incomes.
He opposed passage of the War Revenue Act of 1917 on the
ground that it was wholly inadequate to meet the needs of the
government for funds and that taxation features of the bill were
completely unfair. He warned that the government of the United
States was faced with the problem not only of financing the war
for itself but to a large extent for the Allies as well. He warned
further that the method of financing war costs by flotation of
huge loans could result only in financial disaster after the war.
La Follette ridiculed the bill's provisions for taxes on tea, coffee,
sugar, medicine, freight, passenger fares, and bank checks as
wholly unnecessary and unjustifiable.

"It is monstrously unfair," he said in the minority report submitted to the Senate, "to tax the everyday necessaries of the
average man and woman to pay the expenses of this war, in

addition to commanding their services, and the lives of many of them and their children, so long as . . . swollen and abnormal profits are not taken—profits which the war has created, and which will disappear as soon as the war ends."

That report was considered by economists as one of the ablest statements on the raising of war revenues ever presented to Congress. La Follette distributed copies to his constituents in Wisconsin. The material on the dangers of the bond issues in promoting a possible postwar inflation was later used by his detractors as proof that he took part in a deliberate effort to sabotage the various war bond drives! The War Revenue Act was passed early in September. "The people lost—wealth won" was La Follette's only comment.

On September 20 Senator La Follette was the principal speaker at the final session of a three-day conference of the Non-Partisan League in St. Paul. News of his coming to speak stirred speculation about what he would say. He submitted his speech to the publicity committee of the conference, who reported that their meeting had been harassed by the presence of secret service operatives. The committee felt that the speech as prepared might cause trouble. La Follette offered to withdraw from the program but finally agreed to speak extemporaneously. For thirty minutes the senator discussed informally his stand on the war and his voting record on various issues. He talked about the War Revenue Act and what he considered its weaknesses. Among other things, La Follette pointed out that President Wilson had known, as had many others, four days before the ship sailed that the *Lusitania* carried munitions.

In response to a question from the floor Senator La Follette declared at one point in his remarks:

"For my part I was not in favor of beginning the war. I don't mean to say that we hadn't suffered grievances; we had—at the hands of Germany. Serious grievances!"

The Associated Press service picked up the report of the speech and sent to its nearly 1,200 member clients a different version of the statement:

"I wasn't in favor of beginning the war. We had no grievances" was the statement the Associated Press attributed to the speaker.

It was on the basis of that erroneous report that the Minnesota Commission of Public Safety, through Senator Frank B. Kellogg, petitioned the Senate to expel La Follette on the grounds of disloyalty and making seditious utterances. The petition was referred to the Senate Committee on Privileges and Elections. There followed a deluge of petitions demanding La Follette's expulsion. They came from Maryland, the state of Washington, New York City, the Kiwanis Club of St. Paul, California, and from many citizens and groups in his own state. The Alumni Association of the University of Wisconsin called for drastic action against La Follette. Students at the university burned him in effigy. The state legislature addressed a memorial to Congress asking that Senator La Follette and all others guilty of spreading sedition and disloyalty be expelled from that body. Members of the university faculty, headed by the various deans, signed a round robin letter denouncing the senator. One club in Madison to which La Follette had belonged for years expelled him from membership even though the by-laws had to be hastily changed to do it. Two Madison newspapers incautiously and openly charged the senator with treason, sedition, disloyalty, and official misconduct. For La Follette, who had never paid the least attention to editorial criticism, that was too much. He began libel action against the papers. Their editors had to apologize.

Concerned and alarmed at the spreading tendency of the superpatriots to intimidate and terrorize citizens to say nothing critical about the war program, Senator La Follette delivered his famous defense of the rights of free speech in wartime in the Senate on October 6.

He noted, in passing, the campaign of vilification and attempted intimidation being pressed not only against himself but against all the fifty members of the House and the five other senators who had voted against the war resolution.

"Neither the clamor of the mob nor the voice of power will ever turn me by the breadth of a hair from the course I mark out for myself, guided by such knowledge as I can obtain and controlled and directed by a solemn conviction of right and duty," La Follette told the Senate and the nation.

He protested against efforts to stifle discussion and criticism.

Then, if ever, he declared in effect, was the time to "discuss freely and openly not only how the war shall be prosecuted, but the conditions upon which it may be terminated." Such discussion, in La Follette's opinion, was necessary to the successful conduct of the war and to establishment of an enduring peace. In closing, La Follette urged every American to support the war.

"There is, and of course can be, no real difference of opinion concerning the duty of the citizen to discharge to the last limit whatever obligation the war lays upon him.

"Our young men are being taken by the hundreds of thousands—to wage this war . . . They must have the best this country can produce. The dependents and relatives they leave at home must be provided for . . . generously.

"I have done some of the hardest work of my life . . . on the revenue bill to raise the largest possible amount of money from surplus incomes and war profits . . . and upon measures to provide for the protection of soldiers and their families . . . I did all I could and I shall continue to fight . . . until wealth is made to bear more of the burden of this war than has been laid upon it by the present Congress."

That was the creed upon which such violent and bitter attack was made. That speech, the senator later told Justice James Kerwin of the Wisconsin Supreme Court, was in large part the same address he had prepared for the audience in St. Paul.

The Senate committee's subsequent action on the petition for expulsion was one of the most incredible "slowdowns" in Congressional history. In response to a letter from the chairman of the Committee on Privileges and Elections, Atlee Pomerene, La Follette wrote that as soon as he could obtain it from the Non-Partisan League, he would supply the committee with an official transcription of the speech. The copy of his purported speech already in possession of the committee he declared to be incorrect. Six days later La Follette forwarded a certified copy of his speech and asked about the purpose and extent of the investigation. He wanted to know what, if anything, in the speech was to be made the subject of the investigation. The next day Senator Pomerene replied that the committee was only authorized to investigate the accuracy of statements made in the speech.

No other statement of charges against him was ever given the accused senator. Notified that the committee would proceed on November 26, La Follette and his counsel, Gilbert E. Roe, appeared ready for the hearing. They were informed that the hearing had been adjourned to a later date about which he would be given due notice. Not until the latter part of May, 1918, did the committee hear an oral argument in behalf of Senator La Follette. At that time, on May 23, Associated Press officials finally admitted in a letter to the committee that the news service had erred in sending a false report of the statement attributed to Senator La Follette.

At that May hearing Mr. Roe stated that in his view of precedents and authorities the charges of the Minnesota committee presented nothing for Senate action. He moved that the charges be dropped and a prompt report be made to the Senate. Nothing else happened until December 2, 1918, nearly a month after the Armistice, when the Committee on Privileges and Elections reported to the Senate that "the speech in question does not justify any action by the Senate." On January 16, 1919, the report was adopted. The final period was put on the record of the attempt to expel Senator La Follette by unanimous Senate adoption of a resolution on August 24, 1921, directing the secretary of the Senate to pay Senator La Follette $5,000 out of the Senate contingent fund to reimburse him for expenses incurred "in defense of his title to his seat."

The sixteen months' delay by the Senate Committee on Privileges and Elections in taking action on the serious charges filed against a member of the Senate appears to have been either the result of rank carelessness or a deliberate campaign to punish a too-vocal critic of the Administration's conduct of the war. The point at issue seemed to be the statement that news dispatches had attributed to Senator La Follette that "we had no grievances." The admission by the Associated Press of its error would seem to have cleared the senator completely. Behind-the-scenes activities, however, put an entirely different construction on the whole action.

Senator La Follette's public statement that the *Lusitania* had carried munitions and that President Wilson knew about it would, if left unchallenged, have seriously indicted a major portion of the Administration's stated reasons for declaring war. It will be recalled that at the time of the sinking both American and British officials stoutly denied that the *Lusitania* improperly carried munitions. The incident was built up as an unprovoked attack on innocent men and women and a violation of American neutrality rights in that Americans lost their lives.

Dudley Field Malone, collector of the Port of New York at the time of the *Lusitania* sinking, informed Senator La Follette that he could corroborate his statement by getting a copy of the report of the ship's cargo from the Treasury Department. The Treasury Department informed La Follette that the report had been sent to the State Department. The State Department upon the senator's request for a copy of the report, indicated that it had been made part of the secret archives and could not be divulged. Malone then provided La Follette with a copy of the report and offered to testify to its accuracy.

The committee could not have been unaware of La Follette's activity in seeking confirmation of his statement regarding the *Lusitania*. Apparently it also discovered that the Wisconsin senator was prepared to prove the truth of his assertion. When the committee finally learned of these things all charges were dropped but it took nearly sixteen months for vindication to come to Robert M. La Follette. In the meantime he was forced to undergo the most vicious vituperation and calumny for daring to state his position on the war issue.

The public reaction to the false report of his St. Paul address obscured La Follette's record in behalf of legislation to support the war effort. He opposed, it is true, passage of the Conscription Act. In place of conscription, La Follette urged the building of an adequately paid volunteer army. He opposed the Espionage Act, believing that the law would be used for the persecution of loyal citizens. He believed that the censorship provisions would curtail the rights of free speech, free press, and free assemblage as guaranteed by the Constitution. As has already been noted, La Follette labored to get Congress to adopt a fiscal policy of paying for the war effort out of current revenues. Even though his ideas did not prevail, the Badger senator did not hesitate to vote in favor of the huge sums necessary to prosecute the war. He continually warned, however, of the day of reckoning to come.

About the middle of January, 1918, Senator La Follette dropped out of Senate deliberations on the war problems. He did not reappear until the December session of Congress convened. No attempt was made to keep secret the reason for his protracted absence. There were those whose cynical smiles announced that "they knew" but they were just as wrong as was a certain member of the Elks Club in Madison. Four of the members were playing a postluncheon game of rummy, with three or four others watching. One of the players suddenly remarked that he hadn't heard of La Follette in a long time.

"And you won't, either," another player grunted with a vicious snap. "After what's happened, he hasn't got the courage to show his face. It's a good thing, too."

Another player, patriarchal in appearance with his fine head of white hair and long, well-kept beard, shifted in his chair as he reached for the pile of cards in the center of the table to pick one up.

"I think you ought to know," he said in a quiet voice, "that Bob La Follette will be back in the Senate just as soon as he can possibly get there." The entire group of players and watchers turned to the speaker.

"Bob La Follette has been carrying on the biggest fight of his career," the bearded man went on. "He was called home in the middle of January because of the critical illness of young Robert. It was touch and go for weeks as to whether he would live and Bob La Follette never moved from Robert's bedside. He held Robert in his arms night after night talking to him— telling him not to give up and by sheer force of his own fighting spirit keeping alive the spark of life." The group was hushed. Play had been suspended.

"One of the three doctors in constant attendance told me that Bob's indomitable will alone pulled young Robert through and has given him the strength he'll need to move him out to California to recuperate." The white-bearded man paused, looked at his rummy hand, and drew a card. The player who had

started Madison's favorite indoor sport of saying ugly things
about Senator La Follette cleared his throat as if to say something. Glancing around he noticed the whole group was watching
him. His face reddened and he was silent. The old gentleman's
statement had closed the discussion.

Senator Robert M. La Follette was a constant companion
and nurse to his son during that year of struggle against an
anemia aggravated by a streptococcic infection. He took his son
to California in the search for health. La Follette returned to the
Senate in time to hear the Committee on Privileges and Elections
clear him of the disloyalty and sedition charges that had been
made against him for the St. Paul speech. But even in December,
1918, Robert M. La Follette was still an outcast. When he appeared in the Senate chamber after nearly a year's absence he
was still ignored. No one greeted him as he went to his seat up
front.

"I'll never approve of what he stood for, but I'll always have
a warm spot in my heart for Boise Penrose," declared a former
Wisconsin Progressive Republican member of the House of
Representatives in discussing the incident.

"There Bob sat, no one offering to be friendly, when in came
Senator Penrose. He spotted Bob as soon as he came into the
Chamber and in a voice that could be heard by everyone said,
'Why, there's La Follette.' He strode down the center aisle,
grabbed Bob's hand and asked how his boy was. That broke the
icy reception. Penrose was genuinely glad to see La Follette and
made no bones about it."

Stalwart Republicans in Wisconsin tried to make political
capital of Senator La Follette's long absence from the Senate
when they released a lengthy statement during the 1922 primary
campaign listing every roll call he had missed between the middle
of January and the first of December, 1918. That campaign
document carefully refrained from explaining why the senator
had been absent. It emphasized the fact of his absence and accused La Follette of having shirked his duty at an important
time.

The senator referred to the charge of nonattendance just once
during that campaign. A week before the September primary he

admitted to an Eau Claire audience that he had been absent and briefly explained why. The young man he had nursed back to health was sitting immediately behind the speaker. Robert M. La Follette, Jr., was his father's campaign manager that year and had just been chosen chairman of the Republican State Central Committee.

With the signing of the Armistice in November, everyone's attention was turned to the various peace and treaty proposals. Uppermost was the League of Nations put forward by President Wilson as the basic machinery to ensure permanent international peace. La Follette noted and discussed senatorial opposition to the proposed League. He pointed out that the basic idea the senators were opposing had been stated by the President in speeches given as early as January 22, 1917, when Wilson discussed his "League of Peace." If the idea had been wrong then, La Follette believed the Senate had been remiss in not debating and opposing the plan when it was first announced. He believed it came wiith rather bad grace to say nothing for almost two years, lending approval by silence, and suddenly attacking the plan.

"Do we really want a League of Nations that shall insure an enduring peace?" La Follette asked. 'If we do, let us have done with fine spun sophistries and get down to bedrock fundamentals.

"Embody in the international agreement to be entered into, those terms which the experience of mankind proves will prevent future wars."

Senator La Follette then proposed that the contracting nations to the League bind themselves to abolish enforced military training and declare or make no war, except to repel actual invasion, without first submitting the question of war or no war to a vote of the qualified electors of the country.

"If this really was a war for democracy, let us prove it, by taking the war power out of the hands of the rulers in all countries and putting it into the hands of the people in all countries."

The Badger senator also warned of another possible danger to the survival of a League of Nations. "The naval supremacy of one nation spells defeat for the entire plan," he said.

"The remedy is plain. No nation must be permitted to maintain either an army or navy so formidable that either alone or in combination with other countries likely to be united with it in interest will be able to become a menace to the naval or military strength of the League. This requires a disarmament, especially on the high seas, far below anything that will be suggested by the statesmen soon to gather at the peace conference in Europe."

With those words Senator La Follette awaited the return of President Wilson from the Paris Peace Conference and turned to other matters. One of the senator's major interests, from the time he had served in the House, was the conservation of the natural resources in the public domain. Through the years he had opposed any plan of disposition that might make a practically free gift to private interests of the public coal, timber, and oil lands. The Sixty-fifth Congress rapidly coming to a close had passed two measures disposing of the coal and oil lands. A Senate bill would have granted the lands by patent and a House measure would have disposed of them by leasing agreements. A conference report had not been presented because Senate and House representatives could not agree on the final form of the bill. Congressional friends of conservation were content to leave the problem as it was. They looked forward to the new Congress and an opportunity to frame a thoroughgoing leasing bill.

With but a few days left in the session and appropriations bills having the right of way, a conference report on the public lands bill was suddenly presented for action. Stimulated by messages from President Wilson, then in Paris, to "do something" about the bill, the conferees reported a measure that would eventually have disposed of all federal coal and phosphate lands to private interests. Assisted by Senator Sherman of Illinois and Senator France of Maryland, La Follette began a filibuster against the report. Frightened at the prospect of getting no action on appropriations bills, Administration leaders withdrew the conference report. A short time later, with but hours to the end of the session, the report was once more introduced. La Follette immediately took up the cudgels against the proposal and the Sixty-fifth Congress adjourned March 4, 1919, with a filibuster going full blast. Nine important appropriations measures had failed of passage. The filibuster saved the public lands and ultimately nearly a billion dollars!

When President Wilson returned from Paris with the Treaty of Versailles, he called a special session to pass the needed appropriations bill and to ratify the treaty. The bills were rewritten and scaled downward by the new Congress to a total of $992,000,000 less than appropriations in the original bills stopped by La Follette's filibuster against the public lands bill.

In July, 1919, President Wilson submitted to the Senate for ratification the Treaty of Versailles, which included the League of Nations Covenant. In the debate that followed, Senator La Follette opposed both the treaty and the League. The treaty, as he saw it, was a cynical violation of the pledges given by President Wilson and on which Germany signed the Armistice. The League, he believed, was an instrument binding the United States to an unwarranted support of territorial grabs by the other victorious countries.

La Follette drew a sharp distinction between the League of Nations and a League for Peace. The former, he declared time and again, "would bind us to dishonor, intrigue and secret treaties in which we have no part and of which the people had no knowledge when we entered the war."

The second and third planks of the platform put forward by the La Follette Progressive Republicans as the basis for election of delegates to the 1920 national Republican convention summarized most succinctly the senator's views. The second plank of the platform declared opposition to the League of Nations as "a standing menace to peace" and the treaty as an instrument that "would make us a party to the enslavement of Egypt, India, the rape of China, and the ruthless oppression of Ireland."

The third plank favored a League for Peace, "composed of all the nations of the world, provided they were mutually pledged by binding covenants, with proper guarantees, to abolish compulsory military service, and provided further, that the several nations mutually bind themselves to a speedy disarmament, reducing the land and naval forces of each nation to the strict requirements of a purely police and patrol service."

In support of his efforts to obtain the basis for a real, permanent peace, La Follette offered three reservations to the treaty. One would have abolished conscription in peacetime, the second would have written into international law his 1915 proposal for a popular referendum on war, and the third would have provided for reduction of armaments.

These proposals and his vote against ratification of the Treaty of Versailles placed La Follette among the "irreconcilables" of the Senate. His opposition to the treaty, however, had a higher motivation than mere animosity. He fought hard for a peace settlement that would endure. Some interpreted his contributions as a more subtle means of killing the Treaty of Versailles than outright objection. Others, whose objections were motivated by baser desires, were happy to have the support of Senator La Follette. Thus were the issues muddied. But in 1946 an impressive group of important officials were offering practically the same formula for permanent peace that La Follette had fought for in 1919.

In 1946 a war-wearied world was once more looking hopefully for the formula for peace. Both the Security Council and the Assembly of the United Nations discussed the merits of various proposals. The Republican floor leader of the House of Representatives introduced a resolution calling for the United States to take the lead in working for world-wide abolition of conscription. The secretary of war of the United States came out flatly for "disarmament under the auspices of the United Nations" as a great step forward and pledged that "we will do our part in outlawing weapons of war." Other American statesmen and military men joined in endorsing the proposals. It was 1946. The voice of Senator Robert M. La Follette echoed down the years.

CHAPTER IX

Postwar Activities

THE JEFFERSONIAN principle of the intelligent electorate as the firm foundation of democracy kept recurring in the utterances of Senator La Follette. It was basic to the Wisconsin Idea, to which he had contributed so much. He often used the Senate as a sounding board to echo to the people those ideas about democracy at work which he considered important. He never hesitated to repeat and repeat those ideas. Standpat reactionaries were fearful of his continuing championship of the things they fought against. They knew from experience that La Follette had a way of getting onto the statute books those laws which implemented the progressive program they were so bitterly opposed to. They feared him, too, because he never spared himself to get the facts about those matters he discussed. But they respected La Follette because they knew he was sincere and that his integrity was unassailable.

Senator Robert M. La Follette had offered a plan for Congressional approval by which Congress could know what citizens were thinking about important public problems. He recognized, too, the need of the people for authentic information. He joined enthusiastically in conferences, beginning in December, 1920, to establish the People's Legislative Service.

Progressive congressmen of both parties and representatives of labor and farm organizatons joined forces to set up an information service on matters pending in Congress. Senators

Walsh, Norris, and Ladd and Representatives Edward Voigt, John M. Nelson, James M. Mead, among others, helped in establishing the new service. Herbert Croly, Mrs. Edward Costigan, Jane Addams, Smith W. Brookhart, Gilson Gardner, William Kent, the Rev. John Haynes Holmes, Oswald Garrison Villard, Thorstein Veblen, Edward A. Ross, and other prominent Progressives were counted among the founders of the organization.

The People's Legislative Service was launched at a dinner in Washington on April 16, 1921. As chairman of the executive committee and toastmaster, Robert M. La Follette told the more than three hundred in attendance:

"The great issue before the American people today is the control of their own government.

"A mighty power has been builded up in this country in recent years, so strong, yet so insidious and far-reaching in influence, that men are gravely inquiring whether its iron grip on government and business can ever be broken.

"To meet this intolerable situation, in which representative government cannot long survive, there has come into being a movement which to my mind offers today the best single hope of relief for the people—the People's Legislative Service."

La Follette outlined the organization as falling into three divisions: a legislative division to analyze and keep watch of pending legislation and to warn of "jokers" and parliamentary stratagems; a statistical division to compile information required by members of Congress in their work; a publicity division to keep the people informed regarding pending legislation. The senator insisted that it was not a lobby but a fact service. He answered his own question as to how such an activity could cope with the well-heeled lobbies of special-interest groups.

"Though they have been robbed of constitutional rights and economic freedom, never questioned in this country until the last few years, the people still retain in their hands through the direct primary and the franchise, the nomination and election of candidates for legislative office," La Follette declared.

"Too long we have rested comfortably in this country upon the assumption that because our form of government was democratic, it was therefore producing democratic results. But there is nothing mysteriously potent about the forms and names of democratic institutions that should make them self-operative. Tyranny and oppression are just as possible under democratic forms as any other. We are slow to realize that democracy is a life and involves continual struggle.

"The supreme issue involving all the others is the encroachment of the powerful few upon the rights of the many."

To Edward Keating, editor of *Labor*, one of the group of outstanding Colorado Progressives whose numbers included the Costigans and the farsighted Judge Ben Lindsey, had been given the job of introducing a number of the notables attending the dinner.

"It was a last-minute assignment and I was handed a list of people to be introduced. Some of them I knew nothing about and I didn't realize that one or two of them had been asked to address the group," Keating said. "I almost committed one blunder and did commit another."

As he recalled the situation, Keating had introduced a gentleman from Freeport, Illinois, who, much to the chairman's surprise, rose from a table at the far end of the dining room and began to deliver an address.

"I leaned over and asked Bob who this man from Freeport was and suggested that I'd better break in on him," Keating said.

"Oh, for heaven's sake, Ed, let him talk. He's contributed $10,000 to the organization," La Follette whispered back.

"Then I began to realize that there probably were others there who were being counted on to help get our People's Legislative Service started. That suspicion was confirmed a few minutes later when someone came up behind my chair and whispered that Samuel Untermyer was leaving and that he was peeved because he hadn't been given a chance to give his speech." Keating held a hurried conference with his informant and urged him to get the distinguished New York attorney back but if he had to leave to make his train to be sure to get the manuscript of the address.

"The upshot of it all was that Mr. Untermyer did have to leave but he did leave his manuscript," Keating recalled. "I rose and expressed regret that Mr. Untermyer had had to leave early but that I had a copy of his speech in my hands which I would read. It was a good speech, too, and easy to read. I was sorry that Mr. Untermyer hadn't been given a chance to deliver it himself."

Under the direction of Basil Manly the People's Legislative Service for a number of years provided information about current legislation and served as a research organization for members of Congress who needed special information on the many matters they were called on to legislate about.

One of the postwar problems Senator Robert M. La Follette felt deeply about and on which he worked constantly was the measure to provide adjusted compensation for World War veterans. He denounced Congressional action to vote huge sums for the military establishments without providing for needy veterans. He became particularly incensed when President Harding went before the Senate and asked that body to kill the compensation measure on the ground that the federal treasury could not stand the drain. La Follette pointed out that within a month after he had become president, Harding had called a special session of Congress to repeal excess profits taxes.

"If the condition of the Treasury is so alarming why should he urge the repeal of this tax on the excess profits of big business entailing a loss to the Treasury amounting to hundreds of millions of dollars annually?" he asked. La Follette pointed out acidly that the same Administration that was so anxious about the Treasury and had requested the defeat of adjusted compensation for veterans had also asked for enormous peacetime increases in military budgets.

Senator La Follette was scornful of President Coolidge's veto of the compensation bill that finally passed in the spring of 1924. He characterized it as a "frail, sickly, emaciated veteran of six years' struggle with Congress that finally limped to the White House." He recalled how he had tried, as early as the summer of 1917, to secure an increase in base pay for soldiers on overseas service. The senator had prepared a bill incorporating his ideas of high pay and persuaded Senator Hardwick of Georgia to accept authorship and introduce the measure. It became an amendment to the 1917 War Revenue bill but was rejected.

Both Hardwick and La Follette were assailed by their colleagues for "attempting to spread dissatisfaction in the Army"!

As for the Four-Power Conference in session in Washington, La Follette believed that the Hughes proposal was the "result of the expressed desire upon the part of the great masses of people in this country for genuine disarmament." He could not be persuaded, however, that the results of the conference would amount to more than a short holiday.

When the draft of the Four-Power Pact was made public it evoked caustic comment from Senator La Follette. He said that in his opinion it had all the iniquities of the League of Nations Covenant with none of the virtues claimed for that document by its advocates.

"The League purported to embrace all the nations in the world and protect the boundaries of each of them. The proposed alliance is on the face a coalition of four powers who at this time are best able to dominate by force the rest of the world," the senator said.

He went on to say that the pact did nothing more than support secret agreements between Great Britain and Japan concerning control of the Far East. He promised to do everything in his power to prevent ratification and called on citizens of the nation to speak up and let their congressmen know how they felt about the matter. In a parting shot at the pact, La Follette termed it "the Morgan Four-Power Pact" and said that it was framed by the international bankers to protect their investments.

Meanwhile, events foreshadowed by the 1919 filibuster of the public lands bill had reached a point where the Senate began to take an interest. Senator Albert B. Fall of New Mexico, who had made every effort to get the leasing bill passed, had been appointed secretary of the interior by President Harding. Fall persuaded the President to transfer naval oil reserves in the public lands to the Interior Department. Then came the news of the leasing of Teapot Dome and the Elks Hills reserves to privately owned oil companies. Rumors about the deals reached such a point that Senator Kendrick of Wyoming introduced a Senate resolution on April 15, 1922, requesting information from the secretaries of the interior and the navy about the transfer and leasing of the naval oil reserves. Within two weeks, after preliminary correspondence with former Secretary of the Navy Daniels and others, La Follette introduced Senate Resolution 294 calling for a thorough investigation of the matter. That action opened up the whole sorry mess of the Teapot Dome scandal.

On June 14, 1922, Senator La Follette spoke at the annual convention of the American Federation of Labor in Cincinnati, home of William Howard Taft, chief justice of the United States Supreme Court. The yellow waters of the Ohio River eddied beneath the great suspension toll bridge that carried the main burden of traffic between two cities in two states. The warm summer air was moist with an enervating humidity. The delegates to that labor convention were oblivious to all the signs of summer. They were listening to one of the sharpest attacks against the United States Supreme Court uttered in the twentieth century.

"The actual ruler of the American people is the Supreme Court of the United States," Senator La Follette began.

"The law is what they say it is and not what the people through Congress enacts. Aye, even the Constitution of the United States is not what its plain terms declare, but what these nine men construe it to be.

"In fact, five of these nine men are actually the supreme rulers . . . we are ruled by a judicial oligarchy."

With those words Senator La Follette launched into an attack on the Supreme Court for its recent decisions invalidating the child labor law and the minimum-wage law for women and children employed in the District of Columbia. He protested against the Coronado Coal case decision in which the court held that unions could be sued for damages caused by strikes and that funds collected for strike purposes could be assessed as damages.

The speaker argued that the court had usurped the power to declare legislation unconstitutional. The question was especially timely because until within a few years of the time he was speaking, La Follette pointed out, the Supreme Court had rarely decided against the constitutionality of legislation. But more recently the court had gone to the other extreme and found many measures without sanction within the meaning of the fundamental law. The court not only exercised a veto power over laws passed by Congress, the speaker said, but in the process of interpretation was in a position to declare public policy.

"We are confronted with a situation wherein we must make a choice that will determine the destiny of this nation in all generations to come," Senator La Follette said. "Shall the people rule through their elected representatives or shall they be ruled by a judicial oligarchy? Shall we move forward in our development as a nation, carrying out the will of the people as expressed by their ballots or shall all progress be checked by the arbitrary dictates of five judges until the situation becomes so desperate that it can no longer be endured?

". . . The American nation was founded upon the immortal principle THAT THE WILL OF THE PEOPLE SHALL BE THE LAW OF THE LAND. The courts have forgotten this."

Just fifteen years later President Roosevelt used almost precisely the same argument, which stirred up a national controversy over the same issue. President Roosevelt was ably supported in 1937 by Senator Robert M. La Follette, Jr.

La Follette was not content merely to state the case. He caused acute pain to many defenders of the Supreme Court by suggesting an amendment to the Constitution to prohibit an inferior federal judge from declaring a law of Congress unconstitutional. He suggested that if the Supreme Court were to decide a federal law unconstitutional, "the Congress may by re-enacting the law nullify the action of the court."

From Cincinnati Senator La Follette went on to Madison to begin his campaign for re-election to the Senate. His campaign attracted national attention when standpatters up for re-election in both parties began to taste defeat in the various primaries. Gifford Pinchot, opposed by all the interests and the party organization, won the Republican nomination for governor of Pennsylvania. Lynn Frazier defeated Senator McCumber in the North Dakota primaries. Other upsets occurred to make the Republican majority in both Houses of Congress a very slim one.

Politically, 1922 was not an auspicious year for Republican

politicians. The country was still feeling the effects of the collapse of the war-born boom. People in the cities were jobless. Farmers were burdened by heavy mortgages with which they had financed the purchase of land at inflated prices to produce the food needed in the war. They received deflated prices for their farm produce and had to pay inflated prices for farm machinery, clothing, and other necessaries. Bankruptcy was the order of the day in the great midwestern farm area. It was the beginning of the long agricultural depression.

In the speech at Milwaukee, on July 17 opening his campaign, La Follette said:

"If I am returned to the Senate, I will continue the fight I have been making for the right of the people to control their own government, and to establish and maintain in our economic life exact justice and equal opportunity for all."

He reviewed the economic troubles that beset the country but warned that it was not time for pessimism. He acknowledged that he had no ready-made formula for solving the difficulties.

"I have never believed and do not now believe that progress for us is to be found in revolution or violent or sudden change.

"We must progress slowly but surely, consolidating our gains as we make them, but never sacrificing a principle or compromising with wrong or turning from the straight course merely to reap a temporary advantage." In good Jeffersonian language La Follette warned against apathy and noninterest in political affairs.

"Every generation has to fight to maintain its political liberty. This generation has at least one advantage over the last; it has the direct primary, a weapon forged for the use of the voter in that never-ceasing contest he must wage if he will be free. Direct primaries have not failed because people have sometimes failed to use them. The direct primary is not an automatic guarantee against corruption. Like any piece of machinery, it must be used; disuse will bring rust and ruin."

At this opening meeting of his campaign for re-election, Senator La Follette was subjected to a planned effort to heckle him and throw the meeting into disorder. Shortly after he began his address, several individuals seated in the front rows ostentatiously got up and started to leave the auditorium. When they had got about halfway out, another group noisily followed. La Follette stopped speaking. He watched the men leave. They got about three-fourths of the way out of the hall when he resumed his speech.

"It doesn't take long to shake the chaff out of a fine crowd like this," he said. The crowd responded to the quip with enthusiastic clapping and laughter. The would-be disturbers retreated in confusion and there were no further interruptions.

La Follette faced a determined and well-financed Stalwart Republican organization in his campaign for nomination. The Stalwarts supported a college president, Dr. William Ganfield, and based their appeal for votes on what they considered La Follette's bad war record. Veterans' committees sprang into being to oppose La Follette. They were ultimately grouped into the Loyalty League, which issued a number of pamphlets attacking the senator and serving up all the old charges against him. Accepting the challenge of the Stalwarts, La Follette discussed his war record. He declared that he was proud of it.

In the primary election, Republicans of Wisconsin gave La Follette better than a 3-to-1 vote over his stalwart opponent— 362,000 votes to 139,000 cast for the Carroll College president, Dr. Ganfield.

The primary campaign safely over, Senator La Follette turned his energies to help elect Progressives in other states. He campaigned through Minnesota in behalf of Hendrik Shipstead, who was running against Senator Frank Kellogg. The Kellogg organization tried to stir up the ghosts of the past by getting the Minnesota State Fair Board to refuse use of the State Fair auditorium for La Follette's appearance in St. Paul. They based their action on the ground that the Wisconsin senator had been disloyal during the war! A prompt protest from the governor of Wisconsin to the governor of Minnesota stopped the move and La Follette spoke in the auditorium.

Immediately after that St. Paul address, Senator La Follette's traveling companion protested that the speech, although enthusiastically received by the audience, had broken a fundamental practice of the senator's.

"I never heard a man excoriated in public as you attacked Frank Kellogg," La Follette's companion said. "And I'd like to point out that this is the first time you've ever descended to personalities," Ralph M. Immell told the Senator. La Follette thought a moment.

"I hope I'll be forgiven, but you've got to remember, Cap, that Frank Kellogg tried to have me expelled from the Senate one time."

La Follette went on into North Dakota to campaign for Lynn Frazier. He completed his campaign tour with a two-week swing through his own state. When the votes were counted, Senator La Follette's war record, of which the Stalwarts had tried to make so much, was triumphantly vindicated by the largest majority ever given a candidate for the Senate from Wisconsin. Robert M. La Follette received nearly 380,000 votes. His Democratic opponent received 79,000.

The Republican party majority in the new Congress was so slim that the Progressive Republican blocs in both houses held the balance of power. Headed by Congressmen Nelson and Cooper from Wisconsin, the Progressives joined with Democratic members to force a liberalization of the rules. In the Senate, Progressive insurgents halted the usually smooth majority organization of that body by objecting to naming Senator Albert B. Cummins of Iowa as chairman of the Interstate Commerce Committee. Senator La Follette was ranking majority member of that committee and the insurgent group wanted him to be made chairman. Democrats nominated Ellison ("Cotton Ed") Smith of South Carolina from their side of the Senate. Republicans were helpless in the situation. The impasse was resolved when the Progressives threw their votes to Senator Smith in return for pledges of assistance to get consideration by the committee of measures in which they were interested.

Senator La Follette also held ranking position on the Senate Finance Committee. Two years before, the Republican majority had changed Senate rules to require only two members, the chairman and the ranking majority member, to be named to conference committees. This had been done to prevent the naming of Senator Robert M. La Follette, under the old rule of three members, who was at that time second ranking majority member of the Finance Committee. The chairman of the Finance Committee, Senator McCumber, had been defeated in 1922. Reed Smoot became chairman with La Follette ranking majority member. The Republican Old Guard machine had done all it could to keep the senator from Wisconsin off conference committees.

Another method used by party leaders to discipline the recalcitrant senior senator from Wisconsin was to deny him any voice in matters concerning patronage. During the stirring days of the Payne-Aldrich debate, President Taft had attempted to use the bludgeon of refusing appointments suggested by La Follette. His suggestions for census enumerators in Wisconsin for the 1910 census were not even accorded the courtesy of consideration. At that time Senator La Follette was chairman of the Senate Committee on the Census. He never bothered to protest against the treatment accorded him in patronage matters. A Washington political writer once marveled at La Follette's lack of interest in such "practical" political matters in these words:

"His process of maintaining himself is mysterious and in defiance of all known political laws, for while it is said he maintains the strongest of political machines, he thrives without money, attention or political place; he has never given to any henchman a postmastership, a judgeship, a district attorneyship, or a whatnot." Asked by the reporter to explain the phenomenon, an Old Guard senator of long standing is reported to have said:

"La Follette is an idealist. He doesn't need political pap."

Actually, there was nothing particularly mysterious about La Follette's political campaign methods. They developed out of the circumstances that gave rise to Robert M. La Follette's success in politics. From the beginning he found himself opposed by the party machine. He early found that the enthusiastic support of a few friends equaled, if not always overcame, the large donations of wealthy men who derived a sense of power by distributing largess at campaign time. La Follette never had a continuing organization. Every campaign he ever engaged in had its own original organization. They were built around the comparatively few men and women who, like La Follette himself, were uncompromising and constant in their political principles.

"His was the kind of political organization that could succeed only with a man like Bob La Follette," declared Edward Keating, editor of *Labor* and a key campaigner in the 1924 independent presidential campaign.

"La Follette was the kind of man who attracted people to him. You couldn't help but know, when you got acquainted with him, that he was genuinely interested in you and your problems. He had an uncanny knack of understanding people. He recognized the phonies and didn't waste much time with them," Keating said.

He was always willing to help those who really needed help. He may not have been popular among his Senate colleagues but among the Senate employees La Follette was one of the most popular men ever to serve in that body.

The story is told that during La Follette's service as governor a wealthy manufacturer who had supported him in his efforts at political and economic reform called the Executive Office for an appointment. The man appeared for the appointment on the dot but was told there would be a little delay.

"Seems to me the governor ought to know that my time is valuable," the man of affairs grumbled.

He waited for nearly half an hour and was angrily getting ready to return to Milwaukee when the door to Governor La Follette's office opened and out walked the governor with his arm over the shoulder of a roughly dressed individual who was obviously impressed with his friendliness.

"Good-bye, Henry. And when you get back to Madison be sure to come in," La Follette said to his visitor. He turned to greet the manufacturer and apologized for keeping him so long.

"Good heavens, Bob, do you mean to say you've been in that office all this time with that-that-that farmer?" the Milwaukee man sputtered.

"Well, I'll tell you," the governor said placatingly, "Henry is an old friend who has been campaigning for me down in Argyle ever since I ran for Congress. He's one of the stanchest supporters I've got. In fact, he was campaigning for me before you ever knew me. I'm never too busy to see him."

"Behind the front of that heavy frown many people associated with the name La Follette was one of the softest and warmest hearts in Christendom," declared one man who has watched Congresses come and go in Washington for the past thirty-five years. "He was gentle with everyone. And he always had time to listen to other folks' problems."

"Bob La Follette's interests were universal," another old-time Washingtonian said. "From his debates in the Senate you'd naturally suppose his mind was all cluttered up with dry, dusty statistics. I'll never forget a luncheon in the House restaurant in the spring of 1922. We had already spent some time in his office on a legislative problem and from the way we argued all through the meal, it seemed that we were continuing it. Actually we were arguing whether Jack Dempsey was a better fighter than John L. Sullivan was in his prime!"

It was that real interest in people and what interested them that made others want to help their friend during a political campaign. It engendered in his supporters a zeal that all the money in the coffers of the Stalwart organization could not buy. It surmounted an almost unanimous opposition to the senator on the part of Wisconsin newspapers. It overwhelmed the carefully planned precinct-by-precinct organization built up over the years by the Stalwarts. That was the "mysterious process" by which La Follette maintained himself in office about which the Washington correspondent wrote.

In all probability it was this very trait that made Robert M. La Follette so well hated by certain elements in the state. They openly accused him of nurturing a "La Follette cult." They charged his supporters with being hero worshipers. His opponents warned citizens of the state to beware of La Follette because he was nothing more than a shallow, frustrated actor. By his bitterest political enemies he was contemptuously referred to as "Iago" La Follette—a reference to his oratorical successes as a university student.

CHAPTER X

Independent Candidate for the Presidency

ROBERT M. LA FOLLETTE emerged from the 1922 election campaign as one of the outstanding men in American public life. From 1910 on, the regular Republican organization had done everything it could to retire him to private life. They had him "licked" in 1912. In 1917 he was made the victim of one of the most concerted campaigns of vilification any man had ever borne. He was deserted by friends. He stood alone. In 1920 he was "really licked." But in 1922 Senator La Follette reached the zenith of his political power and influence in the United States. He and his little group of Progressive senators held the balance of power. He was chairman of the important Senate Committee on Manufactures and ranking Republican member of the Finance and Interstate Commerce committees.

Just before the elections of 1922, Paul Y. Anderson of the St. Louis *Post-Dispatch* interviewed the Wisconsin senator about the kind of legislative program he thought ought to be enacted. La Follette was full of ideas and plans. He told the newspaperman that he wanted to see laws enacted pertaining to:

Publicity for all income tax returns.
Reduction of Army and Navy expenditures.
Enactment of an excess profits tax.
Increase of inheritance taxes on great fortunes.
Repeal of excessive tariff rates.

Abolition of the use of the injunction in labor disputes.

Election of federal judges by the people for terms not to exceed ten years.

Referendum vote by the people on declaration of war, except in case of invasion.

A bonus for ex-servicemen, to be paid out of a tax on wealth.

Prosecution of war profiteers.

The repeal of the Esch-Cummins Railroad Act and restoration to the states of rate-making powers in intrastate traffic.

Abolition of the "Pittsburgh plus" charge for steel.

Construction of a deep waterway from the Great Lakes to the sea.

Constitutional amendments abolishing child labor and the Electoral College with provisions for a direct national primary for nomination of president and vice-president.

With the presidential elections only a year away, Senator La Follette's name was mentioned on numerous occasions as the best bet for leadership of a possible new third party. Some credence was given to the notion because La Follette took an active part in the campaign to elect Magnus Johnson as senator from Minnesota. The agrarian revolt in the Northwest was becoming articulate, for Johnson was elected as a Farmer-Laborite.

Just before his departure on a two-month trip through Europe in 1923, La Follette told newsmen that, should reactionaries be nominated by the two major parties for the presidency in 1924, "a third party may result." He was asked point-blank whether he intended to enter the Republican primaries or to become a third party candidate.

"Parties are not organized and made effective by resolutions passed by gentlemen who think there should be new parties. They come in response to public needs and demands; they grow, they are developed. That rule will govern the question of a third party next year," the Senator replied.

Frank R. Kent, the competent, conservative Democratic political writer for the Baltimore *Sun*, toured the Midwest in August and September. He could find little to be enthusiastic about. In a dispatch to his paper from Milwaukee he reported that, as he interpreted the political trends, two factors might be the keys to an understanding of the situation. First, he found an apathy on the part of the people toward political matters. He pointed to lower registration figures and fewer votes cast in 1922 as compared with 1920. Second, the "demagogues" who were in office. It was a rare thing for him during that trip, he reported, to hear a kind word for any public official. The people, he wrote, were disgusted. As for the situation in Wisconsin:

"He [La Follette] is the 'Old Guard' in Wisconsin. He is the boss out here, and his machine, when you scrape off the camouflage, is the old-style political machine, run in the old-style political way and for the old-style political purposes—namely, to keep him and his friends in power.

"He keeps firm control over the Republican primaries, holds fast to the Republican party label and nominates his candidates. From the Governor of the state down the line to the justices of the peace, the jobs in Wisconsin are filled with La Follette machine workers. . . . The fact is that La Follette's grip on the state is a strong one. It is not possible under present circumstances to beat him . . . and his control over the state legislature is supreme.

"It is true there is a great deal of opposition to Senator La Follette in the state. There are thousands of voters who distrust his sincerity, hate him for his demagogic methods and careless handling of the truth, and generally regard him as a dangerous man.

"But they are completely unorganized. They have no leader and no effective way of making themselves felt. . . .

"So, as a matter of fact, there is no alternative to La Follette in Wisconsin."

At the same time William Hard, in an article in *Collier's*, agreed with Kent that no other Republican national leader so dominated the politics of his state as did La Follette. But it was Hard's opinion that the senator's "demagoguery" consisted of "perpetually trying to convert the people from their preference to his."

With the *Outlook* as his forum, John Ballard took sharp issue with Kent about "apathy." In Wisconsin, he wrote, "the whole mass of the people is engaged in a degree not equalled since the state aligned itself against slavery." He noted in Wisconsin a strong attachment to, and faith in, the La Follette doctrines among professional people and the white-collar workers. Ballard diagnosed it as a "middle-class emancipation from old party ties" that was gradually seeping out into other states.

But the gentlemen writing for the periodicals on the eastern seaboard and the national magazines were all wrong, according to the editor of the *Wisconsin Christian Advocate*. Dipping his pen into the kind of ink one would not expect to find in such an editorial office, the editor brought comfort to Stalwart Republicans by writing:

"La Follette is a man who has never done anything either for Wisconsin or the nation—who has never been lined up on the right side of any moral issue in all his life. Whose absentee record in the halls of legislation speaks volumes of duties neglected, on account of time given to ambitious schemes of his own—who is not able to point to any legislation either introduced or effected by him, to remove the evils about which he has raved during every past political campaign—a man who is a Communist at heart, although masquerading as a Republican and using the machinery of this party to perpetuate himself in power. . . .

"If there is a state in the Union that has been more completely bossed and hoodwinked for many years, not by a coterie or ring, but by one single individual, than the state of Wisconsin, we would like to have someone tell what state it is."

But in the opinion of Senator La Follette on his return to the United States after his extended tour of Europe, there were more important matters to consider. The American Debt Commission had submitted its plan for refunding the Allied war debts owing to this country and the Senate was asked to approve. It was approved but over the vigorous objection of the senator from Wisconsin. He characterized the settlement as a "one billion six hundred and sixty-six million dollar gift to Great Britain."

Extension of the loans for sixty-two years at a much reduced rate of interest was, in the senator's opinion, a violation of the stated agreement between the United States and purchasers of Liberty and Victory bonds. As a result of the War Debt Commission's proposal, the United States was in the position of being forced, as La Follette interpreted the plan, to pay out in interest much more than was received in the revised interest rates from the Allied nations. It meant an underwriting of British and French imperialism at the expense of American citizens.

La Follette was especially incensed over the fact that when the proposal was presented to the Senate it was hurried through without what he considered proper consideration. He believed that the Administration had not been fair in refusing to make available to members of the Finance Committee the minutes of the conferences between the War Debt Commission and the representatives of the British government.

'Let no one think the terms agreed upon make a closed incident of the British loan," Senator La Follette warned. "The British government will come again asking still more favorable terms and concessions. For years the whole question of foreign debt is certain to be a most serious and complicated issue, until settled either by payment or cancellation. The American people must be informed. They will directly and indirectly have to pass upon and decide the basis of the terms of settlement."

The American farmer was being squeezed between the millstones of deflated prices for his product and inflated prices for what he had to buy. He also was heavily burdened with an inflated debt that threatened to sink him out of sight. A bill was introduced by Senator George Norris setting up a federally owned and operated commodity corporation to deal directly with producers and consumers, to search out foreign markets using idle government ships, and to buy, build, or lease elevators and warehouses and to lend to co-operative organizations. A measure was finally passed that in effect merely extended farm credits without trying, as Norris, La Follette, and other Progressives insisted should be done, to provide the fundamental remedy—markets and better prices.

Senator La Follette was busy helping Norris to get consideration of his "Lame Duck amendment." Agitation for such a measure had been given impetus by a meeting of the Conference of Progressives held in Washington in December, 1922, under the auspices of the People's Legislative Service. It was out of this meeting that the Conference for Progressive Political Action grew, and which met in St. Louis the following February.

Announcement was made in North Dakota about the middle of January, 1924, that Gerald Nye was leading an effort in that state to secure delegates to the 1924 national Republican convention pledged to Senator La Follette. Insurgent senators and Progressive members of the House of Representatives were comparing notes to find out whether the Wisconsin senator could be elected president as an independent candidate. The St. Louis meeting of the Conference for Progressive Political Action was expected to express a preference for La Follette as presidential candidate. Instead, that conference called a convention of "workers, farmers and Progressives" to be held in Cleveland on July 4. Such a convention, in the opinion of a number of political writers for the daily press, would pave the way for a major third party.

Senator Robert M. La Follette kept his own counsel as to what he would do in the campaign. He did, however, ask his friends and supporters in North Dakota to keep his name off the presidential preference ballot in that state. President Coolidge and Hiram Johnson fought it out there for pledged delegates to the Republican convention.

In the letter requesting that his name be withdrawn from the North Dakota primary La Follette wrote that he could not ask his friends to fight for him "when I am unable to do my share of the fighting." The senator was recuperating from a serious illness at the time. He also put the damper on a movement among admirers in Michigan to secure pledged delegates from that state for him.

That action, however, did not stop discussion. If anything, it only gave added impetus to further discussion. Early in March Robert F. Paine, crusading editor of the Cleveland *Press*, exploded in an editorial excoriating the stench of the oil scandals, the scandals unearthed in the administration of veterans' affairs, and the generally low moral tone of the national administration. As to the remedy, the blunt fighting editor wrote that "La Follette is the one man in Washington who can and will change the condition, make your government come clean and clear.

"He has defied his party, when believing it to be wrong," the editorial continued.

"He has risked impeachment for what he believed to be right, when war hysteria would have gone farther and hanged him.

"He is not a silent man but flays the unmasked scamp . . .

"He is not always a cool man. There is no cover-up, no let-it-go about him. In the presence of outrage of the nation's interests or the individual's rights he does get hot, and he hits . . .

"He is known and respected in Washington as its greatest statesman, to be feared by all who move against the rights and greatest good of the nation, because he is incorruptible, because he studies, digs into, knows and grasps the real issues."

The presidential preference primary in Wisconsin named a full slate of La Follette-pledged delegates to the Republican convention. The Farmer-Labor party scheduled a convention in St. Paul for May 30 with the announced purpose of nominating Senator Robert M. La Follette as its candidate for the presidency. La Follette made it clear to leaders of that party, however, that he would not stand as the candidate of a third party. Those close to the senator freely predicted that he would lead an independent national campaign. A number of such movements had sprung up through the Middle West with the announced purpose of joining with the Farmer-Labor convention to name La Follette as a third-party candidate. The fear was voiced that these activities were part of an attempt to drag a lot of red herrings across the trail to pack such a convention in order to kill off La Follette —to smother him with the third-party tag. The Washington *News* took note of these activities and declared:

"Well may Senator La Follette repeat the prayer, 'God deliver me from my fool friends; I can take care of my enemies myself!'

"La Follette, grim and grizzled veteran of a hundred political battles and skillful strategist of a hundred political campaigns, finds himself pitted against the shrewdest politicians of both old parties . . .

"Now . . . La Follette finds himself surrounded by a chattering and at times gibbering flock of folks who are ready and willing to teach the old master the game of political strategy.

"If La Follette tries to execute an ambush the outfit gets out in the open to chant a battle hymn.

"If he tries a deft and delicate shot, a dozen dumb friends joggle his elbow.

"What with the clack and clatter of forty-eighters and third partyers and Godsakers it is no wonder Senator Bob has gone home and gone to bed.

"It is no joke. It is a serious thing for the common, everyday folks of the country. It is a pity that La Follette can not be let alone during the next 90 days, in order that he may salvage for the people as much as possible from the political debris. . . .

"The next three months will be devoted to the most delicate and skillful political maneuvering on the part of professional politicians and their clients, the campaign contributors who make up the invisible government.

"And while his opponents concentrate on their game, La Follette bids fair to be bedeviled and distracted by amateur brass bands . . .

"His enemies are certainly capitalizing said friends and their foolishness. The one thing that will most surely kill any third party or independent party is its premature birth."

After combing through every public utterance Senator La Follette had made about the 1924 presidential campaign, after weighing all the gossip and rumors, the New York *Times* finally concluded that "Mr. La Follette and his friends are awaiting the action of the two major parties."

Frank Kent of the Baltimore *Sun* was most unhappy over the situation. He could not assure his readers that La Follette would certainly head up a new third-party movement. According to the Baltimore newsman, solution to the "political mystery of the year" could only be found in the answer to the question "Will he run?" As Kent analyzed the matter, the answer was extremely important to the well-being of the nation. He even attributed a slowing down of business and a slump in the stock market to the general uncertainty about the answer to the question he propounded.

In the meantime, a La Follette-for-President committee had been set up in Chicago. With W. T. Rawleigh, the Freeport, Illinois, manufacturer as chairman, the committee included: Dante Pierce, Des Moines farm journal publisher; Julius Kespohl, Quincy, Illinois, merchant; Donald Richberg, Chicago attorney; Alan Bogue, Parker, South Dakota; James McGill, Valparaiso, Indiana; and Zona Gale, the well-known novelist of Portage, Wisconsin. Harry Sauthoff, Madison attorney, served as executive secretary.

Chief object of the committee was to provide a rallying point for the really sincere Progressives throughout the country. It worked quietly, so quietly in fact that when Chicago newspapermen learned of the organization and found that "headquarters" consisted of two adjoining rooms in the Auditorium Hotel they paid no more attention.

"The committee was composed of stanch friends of Bob's," Harry Sauthoff, the secretary explained. "There was a revolt out here in the Middle West within the Republican party and we frankly wanted to find out what sort of support the senator could get if he ran for the presidency.

"We distributed blank petition forms urging the senator to make the run and two or three of us spent quite a bit of time traveling throughout the country interviewing key Progressives."

Sauthoff recalled that the matter of finances was always a problem but they managed to survive.

"I'll always have a warm spot in my heart for Julius Kespohl," Mr. Sauthoff said. "We were clear down to the bottom of the barrel when in walked Julius one day."

"What can I do?" Kespohl asked Sauthoff after the usual preliminary greetings.

"Well—" Sauthoff hesitated—"if you really want to do something you might write us a check for $5,000," he said half hopefully, half laughing.

"And bless my soul if he didn't!" Sauthoff exclaimed. "It didn't take much talking either. I don't have any idea now how much money Mr. Rawleigh contributed but my recollection is that he was about the only La Follette supporter who could afford to make substantial contributions," Sauthoff recounted in describing the early activities of the committee. "We were literally on our own. We had no newspaper support, we had no money and knew very few who had money to contribute, and it was discouraging to talk with the fair-weather Progressives."

On one of his trips into Michigan, Sauthoff discussed the situation with one wealthy man who had offered to contribute $50,-000 to the campaign if La Follette would let him name one member of the Cabinet.

"I told the gentleman that I didn't think Bob would go for that kind of deal but that if he were really serious and wanted me to, I'd go to Washington to tell Bob," Sauthoff said. The result was that the secretary of the struggling La Follette-for-President committee went to Washington.

"Tell the gentleman that I never have made a deal and never will. If he wants to support me, he'll have to accept me as I am and on my record," La Follette instructed Sauthoff.

The committee did have a nucleus of strong support among farmers, labor, and small businessmen. It received more than eight hundred thousand signatures to the petitions asking La Follette to become a candidate for the presidency.

"I'll never forget the day that a Chicago taxi driver walked into our little headquarters. He apologized for not being able to turn in more signed petitions but he said that he only had a few hours off each day. That taxi driver handed us petitions signed by five hundred people," Sauthoff said. "That's the kind of support we got."

The Farmer-Labor party convention in St. Paul had been getting publicity because of the activities of the Communist Workers' Party of America affiliation with the movement. On May 28, in a letter to Herman Ekern, attorney general of Wisconsin, La Follette announced that he would have nothing to do with the St. Paul convention scheduled for June 17. At the same time he made it clear that, unless one or both of the major parties named Progressive candidates, an independent presidential ticket would be offered the voters. Of the St. Paul convention he wrote:

"I have no doubt that many of those who have participated in bringing about the St. Paul convention have been actuated by the purest desire to promote genuine political and economic progress.

"Nevertheless, in my judgment, the June 17 convention will not command the support of farmers, the workers, or other Progressives, because those who have had charge of the arrangements for this convention have committed the fatal error of making the Communists an integral part of their organization.

"The Communists have admittedly entered into this political movement not for the purpose of curing, by means of the ballot, the evils which afflict the American people, but only to divide and confuse the Progressive movement and create a condition of chaos favorable to their ultimate aims. Their real purpose is to establish by revolutionary action a dictatorship of the proletariat, which is absolutely repugnant to democratic ideals and to all American aspirations.

"Not only are the Communists the mortal enemies of the Progressive movement and democratic ideals, but under the cloak of such extremists, the reactionary interests find the best opportunity to plant their spies and provocatory agents for the purpose of confusing and destroying true Progressive movements."

Aside from embarrassing the backers of the St. Paul convention and drawing the denunciation of the Communist members of the executive board of that meeting, the immediate result was to clear the air. Many Republicans who had held aloof because of the St. Paul convention joined in support of an independent ticket for La Follette. Farmer-Labor organizations throughout the Northwest withdrew their support of the convention. The American Federation of Labor warned all trade unions to have nothing to do with the meeting. There was a question for a time as to whether the convention would be held at all. It did meet, but with scarcely more than a third of the more than a thousand delegates originally certified.

Congress adjourned June 7. Before adjournment, however,

Senator La Follette introduced a joint resolution calling for a reconvening of Congress on July 7 after the two national party conventions. In the resolution attention was called to the serious financial condition of farmers in the wheat and corn belt and cited Department of Agriculture figures showing that in the fifteen wheat states alone 26 per cent of the farmers were bankrupt. La Follette cited figures on bank failures and declared that "the alarming conditions are not only increasing but threaten the financial and commercial stability of the entire nation." The resolution also provided that when Congress reconvened, it should consider emergency legislation for the relief of agriculture, the Howell-Barkley bill for settlement of disputes between carriers and their employees, amendment of the rate-making sections of the transportation act, and reclamation relief legislation.

The resolution was defeated and La Follette commented that "the administration has literally turned its back on the farmer." In his argument supporting the resolution, the senator from Wisconsin declared:

"The truth is that the farmer is suffering from artificial disadvantages which have been saddled upon his back by act of Congress or by the policies of the executive branch of the government.

"The Esch-Cummins railroad law of 1920 brought a gigantic freight rate increase . . . which has made it impossible for farmers in many sections to move their products to market at a profit.

"The ruinous 'deflation' policy of the same year . . . plunged thousands of farmers into bankruptcy and has made credit unavailable on fair terms to agriculture . . .

"To them has been added a robber tariff which imposes enormously increased taxes on everything he buys."

The Wisconsin delegates to the Republican convention in Cleveland were pledged to La Follette. He wrote the chairman of the convention, Governor John J. Blaine, that he did not want his name to be placed in nomination and urged the delegates to concentrate on obtaining adoption of the Wisconsin platform. In brief, that instrument provided:

1. A complete housecleaning in the Departments of Justice, Interior, and other executive departments.

2. Recovery of naval oil reserves, public ownership of water power.

3. Repeal of the Esch-Cummins railroad law, eventual public ownership of railroads.

4. Reduction of income taxes on moderate incomes, increase of inheritance taxes on large estates, taxes on excess profits, publicity on income tax returns, curtailment of naval expenditures, and prosecution of war profiteers.

5. A constitutional amendment permitting Congress to override, by re-enacting a law, Supreme Court decisions finding it unconstitutional, election of federal judges for terms not exceeding ten years.

6. Reduction of Fordney-McCumber tariff rates, revision of Federal Reserve and Farm Loan systems.

7. Abolition of use of injunctions in labor disputes.

8. Adjusted compensation for veterans to be paid by taxes on wealth in accordance with ability to pay.

9. A Great Lakes to the sea deep waterway.

10. Constitutional amendments to provide for direct nomination and election of president, extension of initiative and referendum to federal government, and popular referendum on war except in case of invasion.

11. Revision of Treaty of Versailles in accordance with Armistice terms, outlawry of war, reduction of armaments, and abolition of conscription.

When the report of the resolutions committee was presented for adoption, Henry A. Cooper of Racine, a veteran member of the House of Representatives, presented the minority report, which incorporated the Wisconsin platform. He was greeted with hisses and boos and the convention threatened to become unruly. Cooper paused a moment while the chairman gaveled for order. He then quietly reminded the audience that he had had the privilege of offering the minority report at every convention beginning with 1908. The audience was sobered into attention with his sharp reminder that of the thirty-one planks offered by the

Wisconsin delegation since 1908, all of which had been rejected as being too "radical" by Republican conventions, twenty-six had been written into law. The speaker was given an ovation when he finished but the report was not adopted.

The convention moved without a hitch to the nomination of President Coolidge, with Charles G. Dawes as vice-presidential candidate. La Follette's challenge to the Republican party went unheeded.

Democrats meeting in New York were deadlocked when delegates to the Conference for Progressive Political Action met in Cleveland in the same hall recently occupied by the Republican convention. This time there was no booing or jeering of the name La Follette. Instead, a huge photographic portrait of the Badger senator dominated the platform decorations. The conference included all shades of liberal thought in the United States. A few farmers were there. Senator Lynn Frazier apologized for the small number and explained that they just couldn't afford to come. Representatives of the Railway Brotherhoods were there in force. Morris Hillquit and Victor Berger were there representing the Socialists. Congressman Fiorella La Guardia was present. William H. Johnston of the International Machinists Union served as temporary chairman.

There was a grim seriousness in the voice of every speaker. They were met for one purpose—to nominate an independent candidate for the presidency of the United States. They were unanimous in their denunciation of the candidates already chosen or being chosen by the two major parties. They sought simple justice and they knew who their leader was. The mere mention of his name brought the delegates to their feet cheering. But Robert M. La Follette had not indicated what he would do.

It was getting toward five o'clock in the afternoon of the first day when a sudden expectancy permeated the convention hall. Robert M. La Follette, Jr., was seen going to the platform. The report of the chairman of the credentials committee was interrupted and the jaunty, smiling young man was introduced. He was given an ovation, for he bore the message from his father that was so eagerly expected. Seriously and proudly he began to read the senator's message.

"In the most momentous crisis which has confronted the nation in our time, you have called upon me to accept the leadership in a national political campaign to wrest the American government from the predatory interests which now control it, and to restore it to the people. . . .

"I am convinced that the time has come for a militant political movement, independent of the two old party organizations, and responsive to the needs and sentiments of the common people.

"I should be unwilling to participate in any political campaign at this time which would imperil the steady advance of the Progressive movement or diminish the number of true Progressives, nominally elected as Republicans and Democrats, who are now serving the public in the House, the Senate, and in many of the state governments. The ground already won must not be abandoned. We must consolidate our present gains and press forward, without compromise or surrender."

There followed a blistering condemnation of both Republican and Democratic parties. They had betrayed the people's trust. Senator La Follette, through his son, told the convention that he would not accept a nomination or an election if "doing so meant for Progressive senators and representatives and Progressive state governments, the defeat that would inevitably result from the placing of complete third party tickets in the field at the present time.

"Permanent political parties," the senator went on, "have been born in this country after, and not before national political campaigns, and they have come from the people, not from the proclamations of individual leaders. . . .

"If the hour is at hand for the birth of a new political party, the American people next November will register their will and their united purpose by a vote of such magnitude that a new political party will be inevitable."

With that admonition, Senator La Follette announced that he would submit his name as an independent candidate in every state.

"I am a candidate upon the basis of my public record. . . . I shall stand on that record exactly as it is written, and shall give

my support only to such progressive principles and policies as
are in harmony with it." La Follette closed his message to the
Conference for Progressive Political Action with the warning that
the only platform he would run on was the platform that had
but recently been rejected by the Republican national convention. With that announcement the convention adjourned for
the day.

Next morning La Follette was nominated by acclamation and
his platform adopted without change. Choice of a vice-presidential candidate was left to a campaign committee representing
both the Conference for Progressive Political Action and the La
Follette-for-President committee. The unanimous choice of the
group was a comparatively new man in Progressive circles. He
had, however, fought strenuously at the Democratic national
convention in New York to secure acceptance of progressive
principles and was almost bitter in his denunciation of the ultimate choice of the convention, John W. Davis of West Virginia.
When Burton K. Wheeler, senator from Montana, returned to
Washington from the Democratic convention he gave out a public statement that "when the Democratic party goes to Wall
Street for its candidate, it cannot take me with it."

In accepting the Progressives' bid on July 19, Senator Wheeler
wrote:

"I have no desire, as you know, to become a candidate for
any office in the approaching election, but have decided it is my
duty to accept your call because it appears to me that by doing
so I can best serve the highest interest of the American people."
He condemned the reactionism of the Democratic party and
concluded:

"In accepting this call, I do not abandon my faith in the
democracy of Thomas Jefferson. I am a Democrat but not a Wall
Street Democrat. I shall give my support and whatever influence
I may possess to those candidates for office who have proved
their fidelity to the interests of the people wherever they may be
found, but I shall oppose every man on whatever ticket he may
appear who bears the brand of the dollar sign."

In its candidates for the highest offices in the United States,
the Conference for Progressive Political Action symbolized the

fact that progressivism knew no party lines but had to work within the framework of the major parties to secure progressive legislation.

Senator La Follette summed up Progressive philosophy and at the same time sounded the keynote of the Independents' campaign in a special article for the New York *Times*. He wrote:

"The Progressive movement in the United States, as I see it, has for its fundamental objective the economic and political freedom of the American people and the restoration of the Government to the services of the great mass of our citizens.

"We are fighting for the basic principle of Republican government. We are opposed to any form of class dictatorship either of the plutocracy or of the proletariat.

"We are organizing to meet the equally sinister and destructive influence of unprecedented wealth in the hands of a few men, which largely controls the Government and threatens the mass of the people with economic servitude.

"The issues are plain and clearly defined. The specific proposals of the Progressives are constructive measures advanced to meet the supreme issue of the 1924 campaign—to break the power of private monopoly and restore government to the people."

The Independent ticket, of course, ran into difficulties. Organizationally, matters were not so bad as they might appear to have been. The Conference for Progressive Political Action had branches in thirty-two states, the Farmer-Labor party helped in the Northwest, and the La Follette-for-President committee had the beginnings of an organization that it put into the battle. Financially, the candidates were dependent on small contributions. At every meeting the hat was passed. The precedent was set at the Cleveland meeting, where nearly $2,500 was collected by passing the hat. Herman Ekern, Wisconsin attorney general, had been named chairman of the finance committee of the national organization. His first announcement was that "this is a cash-and-carry campaign." Wherever the two candidates spoke, blocks of seats were sold at a dollar each to help defray campaign expenses.

At the close of the campaign, when Senator La Follette went

to his home in Madison to vote and listen to the election returns, he was greeted at the railroad station by a large and enthusiastic group of supporters. To Eric Onsted, Wisconsin campaign manager for the La Follette-Wheeler presidential ticket, this was too good an opportunity to pass by. He grabbed a couple of water pails on the station platform and circulated through the crowd soliciting their small change. He got nearly $200.

La Follette was attacked for his war record. Wheeler was attacked as subversive because of his senatorial investigation of the Department of Justice, one of the aftermaths of the oil scandals. During that investigation, Senator Wheeler had forced from Gaston Means testimony concerning the looting of Senator La Follette's office on orders from Jesse Smith. The "investigation" of La Follette's files, Means testified, was ordered immediately after the senator had introduced his resolution calling for the investigation into the leasing of Teapot Dome and the Elk Hills naval oil reserves.

Wheeler's enemies went so far as to get a criminal indictment charging him with accepting, as a senator, a retainer for services rendered in handling a case before a federal bureau. Both major parties made use of the point that if the Independent ticket succeeded in gaining the electoral votes of even five or six states, the election might be thrown into Congress with resulting chaos. Republicans, however, as the final vote showed, were the more successful with their "Coolidge or Chaos" slogan. The constitutional amendments suggested by the Independent platform were bitterly attacked, especially the proposals concerning election of federal judges and Congressional review of Supreme Court decisions. In a speech in Milwaukee on September 11, the Republican vice-presidential candidate, Charles G. Dawes, declared:

"La Folletteism in this campaign represents the quintessence of demagogism, animated by the vicious purpose of undermining the constitutional foundations of this republic." The Republican party, he held, was the only watchman worthy of entrusting with the job of guarding those constitutional foundations which were in danger of being shattered by the radicals.

Newspapers announced the results of the 1924 presidential election as a "Coolidge landslide." In terms of the number of electoral college votes it was true. Wisconsin was the only state the La Follette-Wheeler ticket carried. Wisconsin voters gave La Follette 435,000 votes, Coolidge received 311,000, and Davis got 68,000 votes. Cleveland was the only large city that gave the Independents a plurality. But nearly five million voters in the United States were willing to go into the Independent column to cast their votes for the Progressive candidates. It was the largest "third-party" vote ever recorded in the United States. In a postelection statement Senator La Follette said:

"I am wholly unable to believe that the election of Mr. Coolidge can be accepted as an endorsement of the Harding-Coolidge record by the American people. I have too much faith in the integrity of the plain people of our country. I believe that the Republican landslide resulted wholly from other causes . . .

"During August and September the reports brought to the managers of the Republican and Democratic parties showed an amazing swing to the Progressives which unless checked indicated the defeat of the old parties.

"The Private Monopoly System sounded the alarm. The industrial, financial, and commercial strength of the nation was mobilized for action. . . . The economic thumbscrews were twisted down upon the farmer, the wage earner and the independent business man. 'Elect Coolidge or starve' was the slogan. . . . The fear of hunger and ruin was made to stalk in the homes of the poor. . . . Notices were posted in the shops that only the foremen need report for work on the Wednesday after election unless Coolidge was elected. The farmers were quietly informed . . . that there would be no extension of mortgages unless Coolidge was elected . . . merchants whispered to housewives that prices would advance and no credit could be had unless Coolidge was elected. Business men were given fat orders subject to cancellation if Coolidge was not elected. The Private Monopoly System had demonstrated its ability to create a financial panic as far back as 1907. It now demonstrated its ability to create a political panic, the like of which had not been witnessed before in this country . . .

"The priceless heritage of our free institutions is not to be yielded up because one battle with the enemy of progressive democracy has been lost. Our ancestors did not surrender in the face of hardship and suffering . . .

"The Progressives will close ranks for the next battle. We are enlisted for life in the struggle to bring government back to the people. We will not quit and we will not compromise. . . . Without money and little organization we have shaken the mighty in their seats . . .

"Our task is great, but our cause is greater."

Even as he had lost in his bid for the presidency, Senator Robert M. La Follette could find welcome news in the election returns. The younger of his two sons, 27-year-old Philip, had been elected district attorney of Dane County. Forty-six years earlier, in 1881, the senator had embarked on his public career by being elected to the same office by the narrow margin of 93 votes over his opponent. In the 1924 election his son Phil received 25,000 votes to his opponent's 6,400. As presidential candidate, the father had carried all but six precincts in the county and tied with Coolidge in one. Son Phil carried every precinct but one, in which the vote was tied.

It was during the 1924 presidential campaign that radio was first extensively used by the candidates. To a public speaker of the old school like Senator La Follette the new medium of communication was a snare and a delusion. George F. Authier, a New York *World* correspondent who traveled with the La Follette entourage during the campaign, recalled the senator's reaction to radio speaking in a letter to Fred L. Holmes of Madison in these words:

"I have always regarded Senator La Follette as one of the last representatives of a vanishing race—namely, the race of public orators, who spoke without benefit of radio, loudspeaker or any other gadget that would amplify the human voice. As you well know, the Senator was very active on his feet when he made a speech. He entered into the spirit of it with his complete physical person. I heard him make his first radio speech. He was seated before the microphone and had great difficulty in keeping his hands and feet still. At times he would forget and I was fearful that he was going to jump into the 'mike' itself. During the campaign he would complain bitterly when before the radio or loudspeaker because, as he explained it, he felt that he 'was tied to the floor.'"

Almost before final election returns were in, Washington political circles buzzed with gossip about how the new Republican majority in the Senate would discipline Senator La Follette for daring to run as an independent candidate for the presidency against the man chosen by the party convention. According to the gossip, the other insurgent Republican senators, Ladd, Brookhart and Frazier, also were to be made to feel the lash of party displeasure. At the caucus of Republican senators on November 28 a resolution was adopted that "Senators La Follette, Ladd, Brookhart and Frazier be not invited to further Republican conferences and be not named to fill any Republican vacancies on Senate committees."

Democratic Congressional leaders refused to take any action against Senator Wheeler.

CHAPTER XI

Death and Succession

DURING MUCH of the time in his later years Senator La Follette fought a battle against ill-health. Several times he had been put to bed with pneumonia, and his failure to ease up on the strenuousness that characterized everything he did had finally brought about a weakened heart. Just before the 1924 presidential campaign he was recuperating from pneumonia. He had not attended the Republican national convention in Cleveland because his physicians thought it better that he relax at Atlantic City.

La Follette was still far from well when the Conference for Progressive Political Action met in Cleveland. The speaking tour arranged for the independent presidential candidate during that campaign was postponed until mid-October. A schedule of speeches on the Pacific coast was canceled because physicians forbade La Follette's crossing through the high altitudes of the Rocky Mountains. On more than any other member of his personal entourage, Senator La Follette depended on his eldest son, Robert Jr., to handle the details of the campaign.

Early in 1925 Senator La Follette again fell victim to pneumonia and during the winter months went to Fort Lauderdale, Florida, to recuperate.

Despite his illness, La Follette continued to write the editorial comment for *La Follette's Magazine* and kept abreast of legislative developments on Capitol Hill. He lost little sleep over the outcome of the 1924 campaign. One subject about which he wrote with vigor was education—especially the educational services rendered by the state universities and their extension divisions. He was skeptical of the real value of huge gifts made by industrialists to institutions of higher learning.

In the January, 1925, issue of his magazine La Follette called attention to a report of the United States Bureau of Education tracing the growth of such benevolences to colleges and universities since the Civil War. He warned his readers that there had developed a "degree of control over the teaching of professors in our colleges and universities which constitutes a most serious menace."

A month later he wrote that "if our colleges and universities are to pass under the domination of those who make their enormous profits in exploiting the people, it will be hard to justify general tax levies upon the people for the support of state institutions of higher learning."

In one of his last editorials Senator Robert M. La Follette reverted to an issue that to him was of utmost importance—the power of the Supreme Court to declare legislation unconstitutional. The immediate reason for the comment was a Congressional investigation into the activities of Federal Judge George W. English of Illinois. Judge English had been accused of using funds held in trust by the court for his own enrichment.

Another federal judge, John C. Pollock of Kansas, had stated publicly that the 17th and 19th Amendments to the Constitution were "crimes." Judge Pollock complained that the popular election of senators had degraded the essentially aristocratic tone of the Senate. He declared that the right granted to women to vote was "backed by organizations of radical leaders."

La Follette also reminded his readers that a justice of the District of Columbia Court of Appeals, in holding unconstitutional the minimum-wage law, had said: "It should be remembered that of the three fundamental principles which underlie government, and for which government exists—the protection of life, liberty, and property—the greatest of these is property." But, La Follette wrote:

"The federal judiciary was hailed in the last campaign as 'the guardian of the lives, liberties and property of the American people.'

"The common people of the country should reflect upon the wisdom of the reposing the enormous power this characterization implies in men like Judge Pollock and Judge English and Judge Van Orsdel."

Regular Republicans were still bitter about La Follette's effrontery in running as an Independent for the presidency in 1924. That bitterness permeated even the executive departments. The Department of State, headed by Frank Kellogg, refused to issue letters of identification requested by the senator for Robert M. La Follette, Jr., who was planning an extended trip through Europe. It was reported from Washington:

"Refusal is said to have been made on the ground that since Senator La Follette has been 'demoted' by the Republican Senate caucus, he is no longer chairman of any Senate committee and therefore is a 'mere senator' and not entitled to special consideration."

Robert M. La Follette, Jr., went to Europe without the credentials requested by his father. On his return he found the senator critically ill with a bronchial asthma and heart condition that had resulted from the earlier attack of pneumonia. Senator La Follette knew he would never survive that illness and shortly before he sank into the final coma he told his son, Robert Jr.:

"I am at peace with all the world, but there is still a lot of work I could do. I don't know how the people will feel toward me, but I shall take to the grave my love for them which has sustained me through life."

Robert M. La Follette died June 18, 1925, four days after his seventieth birthday.

Contemporary appraisals of the life and work of any man who impresses himself upon his fellow men are not usually the verdict of history. They do, however, provide some measure of reaction to what that man accomplished or tried to do. Editorial writers throughout the nation cast up their accounts on Robert M. La Follette at his death and the verdict was mixed.

William Allen White wrote in his Emporia *Gazette:*

"For thirty years Robert M. La Follette has been a dominant

force in American politics. He has led the ultra progressives. And the causes he has espoused in his generation have made over our country. He has stood courageously and without compromise for practically every one of the great political and economic changes that have remade America. . . .

"He used his talents well. No other man of his time has more constructive legislation to his credit than Robert M. La Follette. He has been a good and faithful servant to the forces of righteousness which are rebuilding Christian civilization somewhat along Christian lines."

The New York *Times,* however, took the dim view that "For a man who for so long filled so large a space in our political annals, Senator La Follette left behind him a meager record of attainment. Perhaps he preferred to live a life of contest rather than achievement."

The New York *World* suggested that "La Follette wrote his own record on the statute books." But the Kansas City *Star* saw in Senator La Follette only "a successful governor whose growing egotism, intolerance, and ambition made the rest of his career a disappointment and an anticlimax."

It remained for the American correspondent of the London *Morning Post* to describe the mixed feelings regarding Senator La Follette. The correspondent wrote his paper:

"There is no midway public opinion about Senator La Follette. He was very great or utterly base . . .

"Go out into the street of any large American city, pick at random a dozen men and women, and ask them to tell you in a word or two what Senator La Follette is, and you shall have as many answers as there are persons. You will be told that he is a demagogue, a man with no convictions, consumed by his vanity, a patriot, a defeatist, a pacifist, the one honest man in politics, a Socialist, a second Lincoln, the friend of the people, the enemy of monopoly and greed.

"He sustained, however, in the highest measure the American political tradition. He was born in a log cabin . . . he had to go to work at a tender age. . . . Without money he went to college, where he supported himself.

"At the outset of his political career he fell under the displeasure of the local boss who, with the prescience of a boss, saw that he was dangerous because he was honest and independent. That is the tradition to delight Americans and La Follette fulfilled it.

"They proudly say, 'The Republic is opportunity,' and they like to think of the self-made man, overcoming all obstacles, proof against temptation, scorning the easy road to wealth and success, and enduring hardships because he has a mission."

One newspaper editor who might have been expected to voice an appraisal echoing that of the New York *Times* and who for personal reasons might have written a bitter, cynical, derogatory appraisal, wrote a remarkable tribute to Senator La Follette. Aaron M. Brayton, editor of the *Wisconsin State Journal* of Madison, reminded his readers that he had always opposed the senator's political doctrines and wryly called attention to the fact that La Follette had once sued him and his paper for libel! But Mr. Brayton came to the conclusion that

". . . the record will attest that he possessed a clear vision and a practical application of which has been that in almost every case the tested products of his labors have proven surprisingly sound, considering that in almost every instance he was breaking new ground. This is one of the good fortunes of Senator La Follette: the world is progressing.

"The man who sees farther ahead than his contemporaries will be out of step with the average mind, which too often is more critical than informed. But the years go on, testing and sifting, and soon the average mind comes to the spot where that of the pioneer stopped at the Imperial Summons. And so tomorrow's historian will judge the work of Senator La Follette in the enlightenment of his later day. The progressive always grows in history, the reactionary shrinks."

Nearly four years later the eminent historian Claude G. Bowers declared, at the unveiling of Wisconsin's statute of Senator La Follette in Statuary Hall:

"The meaning of this man to posterity can be expressed briefly. In a century and a half of history he was one of the keenest and most constructive champions of democracy in the never-ending war against reaction; one of the most persistent and devastating enemies of privilege; one of the most uncompromising foes of corruption; one of the greatest commoners of all time, standing always for social justice and the humanizing processes of government."

This, then, was the heritage to be passed on to the successor of Robert M. La Follette as senator from Wisconsin. Often, in the heat of argument over specific issues, the real, solid achievements of the man were lost sight of. Because of his intensity of purpose, he was more often considered an obstructionist than an innovator. Yet it is impossible to overlook or to dismiss the many contributions Senator Robert M. La Follette made in behalf of a more democratic government.

Perhaps the major reason he was so often characterized as a mere agitator or obstructionist was psychological. Whenever he objected La Follette always provided something in place of the proposal to which he objected. His objections and opposition were never halfhearted. For that reason, possibly, the proposals he made were often overlooked. He is remembered for his opposition to the Payne-Aldrich tariff measure. Actually, his opposition was a fight to provide a sound economic tariff measure that would not throttle the purchasing power of the average citizen and would provide the widest opportunity for a truly free competitive economy.

Senator La Follette was opposed to war. His opposition was dramatic and in the heat of superpatriotism he was reviled as a traitor. Forgotten were his efforts to set up the machinery of international arbitration before war actually came. His proposals for popular referendums and public opinion sampling also were forgotten. That those proposals were motivated by a deep-rooted and almost fearful love of humanity and were put forward to protect human beings against the ravages of war was a point completely missed in the heat of the times. He was opposed to war and voted against the war resolution. That was sufficient for the mob spirit of the time.

When he became governor of Wisconsin, Robert M. La Follette discovered a state in the tight grip of a small group of politicians whose sole interest was exploitation at the expense of others. He broke that grip. He established the direct primary.

As a senator he helped break the grip of special interests on the
Senate of the United States and assisted in establishing the direct
election of senators.

As governor of Wisconsin, he fought to make the lot of the
laboring man and woman happier in Wisconsin. Shorter hours
of labor were established by law. A workman's compensation act
was put on the statute books. As a senator, La Follette fought
for and secured laws limiting continuous hours of labor for railway employees. He fathered the federal employers' liability law.

Governor La Follette established civil service in the government of the state. Senator La Follette was responsible for many
improvements in the federal civil service.

One of the major subjects with which La Follette wrestled as
governor was the manner by which the railroad interests were
exploiting the citizens of his state. He got a railroad commission
with power to regulate the common carriers. He fought for the
same principle in the Senate. His record as senator was foreshadowed by his achievements as governor. As senator, he helped
to translate the problems and solutions to those problems of a
progressive state into national terms and situations. If, at times,
the translation was unclear to some, it was simply because certain citizens could not recognize the cardinal principle for which
Robert M. La Follette always stood—fair dealing and exact justice between man and man.

La Follette's death, scarcely three years after he had been
re-elected for a fourth term in the Senate, naturally raised the
question of succession. Stalwart Republicans of the state, organized as "The Republican Party of Wisconsin," believed they
could defeat any candidate the Progressive Republicans might
put up. A great deal of pressure was put on the senator's widow,
Belle Case La Follette, to run for the unexpired term. On July
28 Mrs. La Follette announced she would not be a candidate. On
July 30 Robert M. La Follette, Jr., announced simply, "I am a
candidate for United States senator."

Senator George W. Norris had written a friend in California
that Mrs. La Follette "had the senatorship practically laid at her
feet" but that she had no ambitions and unhesitatingly declined.
Norris wrote that he had originally thought the best solution of

the question of a successor would be Philip La Follette. He discovered, however, that Philip could not qualify under the Constitution because of his age. He was twenty-eight. "It is quite likely that Robert Jr. will become a candidate. I think that is practically settled but he will not have it without opposition." Norris was writing his California friend under a June 26, 1925, date. The letter, subsequently published in *Labor News* of Long Beach, California, carried this personal estimate of Senator La Follette's elder son:

"I consider Bob Jr. very well qualified for the place. He has been his father's confidential man for several years, and for more than a year has done a great deal of the work that has come to the office. He is very well acquainted with the various public questions, and I think is fundamentally right in his belief on the fundamental principles of government."

La Follette's death had hit Senator Norris hard and he was concerned about the possibility that the Stalwart Republicans might be able to get their candidate elected if Progressives fell out over the question of succession. He even issued a public statement calling on Progressives of Wisconsin "to make no mistake at this critical hour. . . . Petty jealousies and personal ambitions must be forgotten . . ."

Apparently Senator Norris had become alarmed by rumors of a possible split in the Progressive group. Robert M. La Follette, Jr.'s announcement on July 30 put to rest any rumors or dope stories that Stalwarts had been busily trying to spread in order to force a split.

In the meantime Stalwart Republicans made a disconcerting discovery. There were several in their own ranks who wanted to run and who refused, even on the plea of harmony, to withdraw from the race. Among them was a former Progressive, Governor Francis McGovern.

On August 17, immediately after Governor John J. Blaine had announced the special election—the primary to be held September 15 and the general election September 29—Robert M. La Follette, Jr., elaborated on his previous statement that "I am a candidate for United States senator." He said, in part:

"I am a candidate for the nomination of United States senator to fill the unexpired term at the Republican primary. The Republican party of Wisconsin is a progressive party. . . . It is to the progressive voters of Wisconsin that the state ówes its position of leadership in the nation.

"I am a progressive candidate and seek the support of the progressive men and women of the state.

"I am a candidate on the platform endorsed by the voters of Wisconsin three years ago when Robert M. La Follette was elected to his fourth term in the United States Senate. If I am chosen to fill out the unexpired term, I shall do all in my power to fulfill the pledges and carry out the program outlined in that platform . . .

"I do not ask the support of the people of Wisconsin because I am Robert M. La Follette's son. I am well aware that this relationship in itself does not entitle my candidacy to consideration. At the same time that relationship does not disqualify me.

"I believe long association with my father in his public service, intimate knowledge of his work in the past and his plans for the future—the policies involved, the issues at stake, together with years of contact with progressive leaders in and out of public life, will, if I am elected to the Senate, enable me to keep the record straight and to render good service to the state of Wisconsin and the nation for the next three years."

The candidate's platform pledged government operation of the Muscle Shoals power plant, repeal of the Esch-Cummins railroad law, maintenance of the right of labor to bargain collectively, and prevention of the unjust use of the injunction in labor disputes. He pledged continuance of the fight to pass the resolution introduced by his father instructing the Interstate Commerce Commission to reduce freight rates on agricultural products. He favored reduction of the armed services of the United States to a strictly defense basis and insisted on full payment of the Allied war debts owing to this country.

Robert M. La Follette, Jr., pledged his abilities in the fight to secure a federal tax program based on ability to pay and repeal of the special war "nuisance taxes." In the field of foreign relations the senatorial candidate favored the promotion of friendly relations with Mexico and the Central and South Ameri-

can republics, treaty agreements to outlaw war, abolish conscription, and provide for referendums on questions of war and
peace. He opposed entry of the United States into the proposed
World Court.

With that platform Senator La Follette's elder son plunged
into the campaign for nomination with all the vigor his father
used to display. Wherever the young La Follette went during his
campaign he was greeted by crowds which observers declared to
be as great as those which had gathered to listen to the elder
La Follette. Those who flocked to the young candidate's meetings at first went probably more out of curiosity than from any
other motive.

Citizens who had supported "Old Bob," as he was affection-
ately called, wanted to see for themselves whether "Young Bob"
would measure up to his illustrious father. It was a grueling
assignment for the 30-year-old campaigner but he was not
unknown to the voters even though his younger brother Philip,
who had just been elected district attorney of Dane County, was
acclaimed his father's successor as an orator. Robert M. La
Follette, Jr., had served as chairman of the State Republican
Committee since 1922 and had managed his father's senatorial
campaign that year.

In preparing for the campaign, Robert M. La Follette, Jr.,
knew he would be measured against the oratorical abilities of
his father. He realized that he would also be measured against
the solid basis of his father's wide and intimate knowledge of
affairs. He began his preparation by writing a speech that ampli-
fied his announced platform plank for tax reduction. He mem-
orized that speech and, with a close friend for critic, went out
into the hayloft on the La Follette farm at the outskirts of Madison and practiced delivery.

That maiden campaign speech was delivered on August 24 at
Stoughton, a few miles southeast of Madison. Old-timers were
not too impressed with the rather stiff formality of the speaker,
who seemed to be tied down to his notes. Within a couple of
days, however, Stalwart Republican headquarters was worried
over reports that Robert Jr.'s speeches were being enthusiastically
received. At Sheboygan, for instance, the crowd was so en-

thusiastic that following his speech so many people rushed up to shake his hand and congratulate him that the meeting was turned into a triumphal reception.

Somewhere between Stoughton and Sheboygan the briefcase containing all his notes and prepared speeches had been lost. The candidate was forced to speak without the benefit of notes, and Robert M. La Follette, Jr., discovered an unsuspected effectiveness in public speaking.

In the following three weeks three, four, and even five meetings a day with long night drives to get a running start the next day were not uncommon. A growing enthusiasm for the young man went before him. Despite the fact that meeting halls were often impossible to get because Stalwart Republicans saw to it that available halls were "engaged," the outdoor meetings were largely attended.

Robert M. La Follette, Jr., was nominated as the Republican candidate for the unexpired term of his father at the September 15 primary. Out of a total of 352,000 votes cast in the September 29 general election, young Bob received 238,000. He carried all but eight of the seventy-one counties in the state.

Just six months older than the constitutional minimum age for senators, Robert M. La Follette, Jr., was the youngest man up to that time to be elected to the United States Senate by direct vote. Henry Clay was twenty-nine when he was elected to the Senate by the Kentucky legislature and, more recently, Rush Holt of West Virginia barely met the minimum age requirement.

Young Bob La Follette took his oath of office in December, 1925, became Wisconsin's senior senator in 1926, when former Governor John J. Blaine defeated Irvine L. Lenroot for the senatorship, and continued as Wisconsin's senior senator until December, 1946.

CHAPTER XII

Robert M. La Follette, Jr.

ONE OF THE MOST illuminating and descriptive things ever written about Robert M. La Follette, Jr., is the five and a half lines of type in the 1946 *Congressional Directory* devoted to his biography. It follows:

"ROBERT M. LA FOLLETTE, Jr., Progressive, Madison, Wis.; born February 6, 1895; married Rachel Wilson Young September 17, 1930, has two sons, Joseph Oden and Bronson Cutting; elected to the United States Senate on September 29, 1925, to fill the unexpired term of his father, Robert M. La Follette; reelected November 6, 1928; reelected November 6, 1934, and November 5, 1940; his term expires 1946."

That official biography is the shortest of the entire Wisconsin delegation. It is a modest and almost shy statement of certain aspects of the man's life. It hides a lifetime devoted to the public service and is of interest more for what it does not say than for the meager facts it discloses. It says nothing, for instance, about the fact, found thirty pages farther on in the *Directory*, that Robert M. La Follette, Jr., after twenty-one years of service in the Senate ranked fifth among the members of the United States Senate in length of continuous service. It reflects, with almost stark simplicity, a man's pride in two things—his family and his job.

Robert M. La Follette, Jr., is short of stature—less than the average in height. Self-possessed and quiet, his face has a

143

studious expression. He listens well and when he speaks he
wastes no words. He never fumbles or reaches out for words.
He talks with conviction. One is struck by the air of innate
modesty about the man. "Surely," you say to yourself on meeting
him the first time, "this can't be the man who almost singlehand-
edly got Congress to reorganize itself. This isn't the man who
conducted the famous Civil Liberties investigations."

As you visit with him in his office you can't escape an impression of relaxation on his part. His face is grave, yet there is a
certain contagious serenity in his manner even though he
punctuates what he may be saying with short, almost nervous
gestures. His scholarly manner carries no suggestion that he
is a rabid baseball and football fan. He bemoans the fact that
pressure of senatorial duties too often keeps him away from
Griffith Park when the Washington Senators are at home. No
other "old alumnus" is a more enthusiastic supporter of the University of Wisconsin football team than he.

This is the man who on occasion has played merry hob with
the well-laid plans of the conservative Senate. One is never long
in doubt about La Follette's stand on a particular issue. His independence of thought and action have often been an embarrassment to the Senate Republican leadership. To a regular, Old
Guard Republican like the late Senator George H. Moses of
New Hampshire, Robert M. La Follette, Jr., was one of the
"Sons of the Wild Jackass," an appellation the New Hampshire
senator created as a pleasant wisecrack to add to the gaiety
of a New England manufacturers' meeting in the fall of
1927.

But Robert M. La Follette, Jr., was not disturbed by such
barbs. He had been raised in an atmosphere of politics. When
his father was given the unanimous endorsement of the Republican convention for the governorship in 1900, the nearly six-year-
old Robert, Jr., was busy collecting convention badges from delegates. He heard, at the Governor's Mansion in Madison, the
planning between his father and his associates for all the measures initiated by the progressive Republicans of Wisconsin that
gave it the lead in the movement to make government responsive
to the needs of all the citizens. Politics and the economic and

social problems of the day were familiar to Young Bob "almost before he learned the multiplication tables."

His political education broadened to include the national scene when the elder La Follette moved to Washington as senator. Young Bob watched and listened to the debates in which his father fought for effective railroad legislation. The youngster's understanding of economic forces and their interrelation with political institutions was sharpened by his father's bitter fight against the Payne-Aldrich tariff measure.

He was an observant and intensely interested lad of seventeen when the elder La Follette led the campaign to liberalize the Republican party in the 1912 campaign.

Having graduated from the Washington, D.C., high school system, Robert Jr. entered the University of Wisconsin, which he attended with indifferent success. Academic work was pallid stuff to the young man who had vivid impressions of the long, serious discussions in his own home where such men as Jonathan Dolliver, Albert Beveridge, the Pinchot brothers, and others often gathered. He was dogged, also, by sporadic illness that often kept him from classes for considerable periods of time.

It was at the height of the war hysteria early in 1917 that Young Bob became desperately ill with a streptococcic infection. That was the period when Senator Robert M. La Follette dropped out of public life to devote himself to the task of nursing his son back to health. A year later, following his convalescence in California, Robert Jr. was back in Washington. He was made a clerk of the Committee on Manufactures of which his father was chairman and took over many of the small but burdensome details of the senator's office. In 1919, Young Bob became his father's private secretary.

With his father as teacher, Robert M. La Follette, Jr., learned about all the complicated postwar problems that were troubling the nation and the world. He was at his father's side when the plans were made for the Senate resolution that blew open the Teapot Dome oil scandals. He watched and studied the operation of the Senate. With his father explaining the nice details, Young Bob early became well grounded in the parliamentary procedure that in later years served him so well.

Young Bob developed politically. In 1922 he was named chairman of the Republican State Central Committee and managed his father's campaign for re-election. He played an important part as the elder La Follette's personal representative and as a member of the Wisconsin delegation at the 1924 Republican national convention in Cleveland. He was also his father's representative at the Conference of Progressive Political Action that named the elder La Follette as Independent candidate for the presidency. During that 1924 campaign, John W. Owen of the Baltimore *Sun* staff wrote of Young Bob's political sagacity:

"Those who have to do with him in Washington have come to realize that he usually has Congress, what it might do and what it will do, sized up in an extremely realistic way; that he is fully cognizant of all the moves under way out in the country; that he moves quickly when the chance to take a trick presents itself; and that whether the breaks are good or bad he is as cool as a cucumber . . .

"He knows his cards and he is not afraid to play them. He could be set down in a political poker game with William M. Butler, C. Bascom Slemp, Will H. Hayes, and Senator Charles Curtis, who would certainly constitute the nucleus of a political poker game of some ferocity—'Young Bob' could be seated in that kind of a political poker game and he would be so collected that not even his little toe would twitch. Even 'Charley' Curtis would hesitate to try to 'steal' a hand."

Had any young man deliberately set out to secure an education fitting him for a political career he could not have chosen better than the almost fortuitous twist of circumstances presented to Robert M. La Follette, Jr. As a matter of fact, the mantle of the elder La Follette was to have fallen upon the shoulders of Robert's brother Philip who had his father's flair for public speech. During the 1924 campaign he took the stump in his father's behalf and favorably impressed those who heard him. Robert worked behind the scenes, so to speak. He was not much in the public eye, for he was not much of a speaker. Senator Robert M. La Follette's death in 1925 altered matters. Philip could not qualify because of age. The boys' mother refused the opportunity to succeed her husband—even the Stalwart Republi-

can organization had announced it would offer no candidate at
the special election if Mrs. La Follette wanted to run. It was
considered essential that a La Follette make the run for the unexpired term, and Robert Jr. was the only one available.

On December 7, 1925, the "youngest Senator since Henry
Clay" took his oath of office as senator from Wisconsin. Exactly
forty years earlier, on December 7, 1885, the "youngest member"
to be elected to that Congress, 29-year-old Robert M. La Follette,
took the oath of office as a member of the House of Representatives.

The election of Robert M. La Follette, Jr., put the Old Guard
Republican leadership in a quandary. A year earlier they had
read out of the party the new member's father for his insurgency
during the presidential campaign and had deprived him of all
committee assignments. They quickly learned that the passing
of the elder La Follette did not mean the passing of the political
independence for which he was noted.

The new member from Wisconsin received an invitation to
attend the Republican Senate conference. Newspapers reported
"indications that the men who were most bitter against Senator
La Follette's father last spring are not so antagonistic." Senator
Walter Edge of New Jersey was quoted as saying that "if Mr.
La Follette wants to return to the Republican party and function with it, by all means let's give him a chance." Press accounts
went on to report that, should he attend the conference, La
Follette's "brand of Republicanism" would not be questioned.
The new senator did not attend the party conference. But when
the Committee on Committees settled down to work to make
appointments, the fun began.

The committee discovered itself deadlocked over the question of whether Robert M. La Follette, Jr., should be classified
as a Republican! The question was referred to the Senate Republican caucus. In the meantime the committee sent messengers
to the White House to find out if President Coolidge favored
treating the young man as a Republican. That action was of little
help in solving the committee's dilemma for the two messengers
reported substantially different notions of their understanding
of Coolidge's position!

The committee was further embarrassed when it was discovered that through a clerical error Senator James Wadsworth
of New York, a member of the committee in the preceding Congress but who had retired in favor of Senator Rice Means of
Colorado, had met with the committee and had voted with
Senators Moses, Reed, and McNary to recognize La Follette as a
Republican. The four who had voted against the recognition were
Senators Watson, Smoot, Ernst, and Cameron. Everyone had
forgotten, including the senator himself, that Wadsworth was no
longer a member.

On December 15 the committee finally accepted Robert M.
La Follette, Jr., as a Republican and announced his appointment
to the Committees on Manufactures, Indian Affairs, and Mines
and Mining. On the same day, however, La Follette made public
a letter he had just written to the committee chairman, Senator
"Jim" Watson. He wrote:

"I am informed through the newspapers of this morning that
the Committee on Committees has voted to report my committee
assignments to the Senate. Before this formal action is taken by
the committee, it seems important that there should be no misunderstanding as to my position.

"At the recent special election held to fill the vacancy created
by the death of Robert M. La Follette I was designated as the
regular Republican nominee by the voters of Wisconsin at the
primary, and duly elected under such designation.

"In announcing my candidacy, and throughout my campaign,
I declared my allegiance to the progressive principles and policies
of government as interpreted and applied by the late Robert M.
La Follette throughout his entire public career. The platform
upon which I was nominated and elected was that upon which
he announced his successful candidacy for the Senate in the
Republican party of 1922, and upon which the Republican
members of the House of Representatives from Wisconsin were
elected at the same time.

"I shall, during my service in the Senate, adhere to the
letter and the spirit of the platform upon which I was elected,
and shall follow the independent course which I have marked
out for myself.

"With these facts before the committee, should they assign me to committees as indicated by the press, I shall accept such formal assignments."

Such independence on the part of a new member was unheard of, but the Old Guard let the matter stand as decided. Despite occasional protests and skirmishes, La Follette received his committee assignments as a Republican throughout his twenty-one years of service in the Senate.

Senator La Follette served continuously on two regular Senate committees during his entire service in that body: the Committees on Indian Affairs and Manufactures. In 1928 he was appointed to two additional committees. In 1929 he was appointed to the Foreign Affairs Committee relinquishing his post on the Post Office and Post Roads group. In 1930 La Follette was made a member of the Finance Committee and dropped from the Commerce Committee. In 1932 he became a member of the Education and Labor Committee, giving up the Mines and Mining post.

From 1932 through 1941, Senator La Follette held membership on six regular committees: Education and Labor, Finance, Foreign Relations, Post Office and Post Roads, Manufactures, and Indian Affairs. Beginning with 1942 he held membership on five regular committees, giving up the Committee on Post Office and Post Roads.

Besides these regular committee assignments, Senator La Follette served on the following joint committees of Congress: On the Economic Report (1946); On Internal Revenue Taxation (1937); On the Organization of the Government (1937); On the Reduction of Nonessential Federal Expenses, and for a short time on the Interparliamentary Union Committee.

Senator La Follette was chairman of the Joint Committee on the Organization of Congress whose work resulted in the passage of legislation to reorganize Congress beginning with the 80th Congress, meeting in January, 1947.

One looks in vain through the files of the *Congressional Directory* for mention of one committee that brought to the Wisconsin senator much national attention and acclaim—the so-called Civil Liberties Committee. That committee was established by a Senate resolution introduced by La Follette on April 10, 1936. He was named chairman of a subcommittee of the Education and Labor Committee to carry out the provisions of the resolution "to make an investigation of violations of the rights of free speech and assembly and undue interference with the right of labor to organize and bargain collectively." Other members of the subcommittee included Senators Louis Murphy of Iowa and Elbert D. Thomas of Utah.

Thus was established the Civil Liberties Committee, which revealed labor policies and practices that made industrialists throughout the nation squirm in shame. It also laid the basis for legislation establishing the Farm Security Administration.

The January, 1930, issue of the *Congressional Directory* listed La Follette for the first time as a member of the Senate Finance Committee. In December, 1929, Senator Walter Edge had resigned from the Finance Committee and La Follette threw the Republican Old Guard into a frenzy when he declared that he expected, because of his seniority rank, to be named to the vacancy.

The situation even attracted the attention of the White House. President Hoover let it be known that he looked with complete disfavor on the recognition of the progressive bloc in the Senate by having La Follette named to the Finance Committee. Various plans were considered to head off his claim to the post. It was even suggested that Senator Guy D. Goff, of West Virginia, whose seniority rights were superior, resign from the Interstate Commerce Committee and thus be in line for the vacancy on the Finance body. Old Guard leaders and President Hoover agreed that recognition of one of the progressive senators would make the 1930 campaign tough. They wanted a "Hoover Senate" and were supporting conservatives against the progressive senators up for re-election. Senator Reed Smoot of Utah, chairman of the Finance Committee, strenuously opposed any recognition of progressive senators in important committee assignments.

La Follette was assured of his place on the committee, however, when the Senate Republican caucus, voting on the question, cast a tie vote. In the meantime it was announced at the White

House that President Hoover would take no part in the argument. The struggle had reached such proportions that the *Christian Science Monitor* was finally moved, late in January, 1930, to comment:

"Insurgent victories in the reapportionment of United States Senate committees should be recognized as something more than mere personal triumphs for a few colorful and untamed senators. Readjustments in the Senate can be more adequately understood if regarded as belated expressions of profound political realignments in the nation. The most spectacular of the changes—admission of Robert M. La Follette to the Finance Committee, that final stronghold of the Old Guard—means . . . that in the North and West millions of Republican voters with Progressive leanings will have a spokesman on that powerful committee, so long considered a 'standpatters' club.'

"It has been too easy to look upon the insurgents in the Senate as political accidents, representing merely their own unorthodox views . . . Gradually the impression has percolated that they do speak for a great mass of opinion. Apparently they are in the Senate because a good many Americans want them there . . . The Borahs, La Follettes and Norrises cannot be dismissed as evidences of a temporary revolt; persistent constituencies have so repeatedly re-elected them that many of them have come to key positions on committees through seniority."

During his first session as a freshman member of the Senate, albeit a freshman with an enormous store of knowledge about that body and its operations, Senator Robert M. La Follette, Jr., preferred to listen. As in the campaign when he ran for election to the unexpired term of his father, he was under the handicap of constantly being compared to his illustrious sire.

When he entered the Senate that body had under discussion American membership in the World Court. La Follette listened for weeks to the debate on the Court issue. On January 22, 1926, Young Bob made his bow as a speaker in the Senate. He boldly took his stand as an "irreconcilable" and for three hours discussed the issue as he saw it. His speech, delivered without the traditional La Follette oratorical frills, commanded respect and attention from both his colleagues and the Senate galleries. At the

close of his address, Senator Reed of Missouri rose and complimented La Follette.

"I don't know how it impressed other senators," Reed commented to his fellow members, "but in my opinion we have just
listened to a great speech from the senator from Wisconsin."

As a Progressive Republican La Follette was named to two
important investigating committees during his first session. One
was an investigation of the Tariff Commission and the other was
the investigation into use of "slush funds" by William S. Vare,
a senator-elect from Pennsylvania, and Frank Smith, senator-elect
from Illinois. On both committees La Follette displayed an ability
to get at the facts of the situation through careful, patient questioning and digging. The tariff investigation, in which the young
Wisconsin senator took a leading part, was characterized as a
model of its kind and demonstrated to a startled nation that instead of being a "fishing expedition" it could, and did, produce
solid facts and fully supported evidence for the information of
Congress and the public. As a result of the slush fund investigation, both Vare and Smith were denied their seats in the Senate.

Beginning early in 1927 there was much discussion about the
presidential elections of the next year and some talk about
another term for President Coolidge. In the spring Senator La
Follette caused acute pain, both to the Old Guard Republicans
in the Senate and to the occupant of the White House, by introducing a resolution that would, if passed, have put the Republican-dominated Senate on record as opposing a third term for
the President. A "draft Coolidge" movement seemed to be gaining
some headway at the time and after hurried conferences between
the White House and Republican Senate leaders steps were taken
to block consideration of the resolution.

During the summer President Coolidge issued his famous "I do
not choose to run" statement. It helped to crystallize sentiment
in favor of the resolution against the third term. La Follette bided
his time and pitted his knowledge of parliamentary procedure
against the opposition of the Old Guard.

In December, 1927, La Follette introduced an amended
form of his original resolution that caught his opponents flat-
footed. The Wisconsin senator took the President at his word

and complimented him for adhering to American tradition with respect to the presidency. The resolution still called for a vote opposing the third term. Conservative Republicans were nonplused. If they opposed the resolution they were in the embarrassing position of withholding praise from their President! The usual parliamentary tricks were set in motion to delay consideration. La Follette, however, was not asleep. A sudden opportunity developed early in 1928 for him to drag out his resolution and make it the order of business. Catching the Republican leadership off guard, he requested and gained unanimous consent to place the resolution before the Senate.

Angry and confused by their own ineptness, the conservative Republican leadership made every effort to head off the vote but La Follette's superior knowledge of parliamentary tactics won out and the resolution putting the Republican Senate on record as opposed to a third term for their Republican President passed almost a year after it had been introduced.

Such feats might have been considered primarily as a sort of free-lance insurgency the background of which could easily be traced to the record of the elder La Follette. He, like other titans of progressive insurgency at the turn of the century, got his liberal inspiration from the agrarian revolt. Those liberals battled with all their might to lop off abuses and to assuage the popular suspicion of big business by pressing for regulation. Many of their reforms seem unexciting enough today yet when they were first proposed and fought for they were milestones in the progress of democracy.

In their headlong plunge toward reform, those turn-of-the-century liberals did not fully understand the economic implications involved in the development of the emerging industrial society; nor, for that matter, did the new industrial and financial giants who were interested solely in using the newer developments for their own personal gain. Important issues were raised by the insurgent progressives and they labored to ameliorate the worst evils but they did not fully appreciate the interrelation of the social and economic and political forces at work. It remained for a newer group of progressives, grounded in the "dismal science" of economics and possessing the fire of conviction in the rightness of their programs, to bring new meaning and direction to the liberal movement. It was, in the final analysis, the difference between a regional and a national point of view .

In October, 1940, Senator Robert M. La Follette, Jr., confessed that as a Progressive he had had to choose between the New Deal proposals and the do-nothing policies of reactionary Republicans and Democrats. Confronted with that alternative, "I have unhesitatingly supported measures which, although inadequate and often piecemeal, broke new ground in attempting to cope with the basic problems of our day and generation."

That statement was part of his formal announcement that he would support President Roosevelt for re-election. La Follette faced a bitter and well-financed opposition in his bid for re-election to the Senate. The political situation in Wisconsin was none too reassuring. His brother Philip had been defeated in the governorship race in 1938 by a coalition of Democrats and Republicans. Announcement of Senator La Follette's position had been awaited with interest, for a number of Washington correspondents had recalled his anti-third term resolution of 1927. In his statement La Follette said:

"Since 1933 I have fought to the best of my ability for a sound, comprehensive, and fundamental Progressive program. My record shows that on the vital issues presented during this economic crisis my first fight has always been for the passage of legislation embodying the Progressive solution of specific problems at stake . . .

"I am heartily in favor of the program to re-arm America to make it invulnerable against attack by any nation or group of nations. But the tragic lesson of the war is that a nation which fails to put its social, economic, and spiritual house in order can be overwhelmed by a nation with dynamic, expanding economy. We must learn that our domestic front is as vital as our military front . . .

"As a Progressive I refuse to join those pessimists who see disaster lurking around every corner. I believe with every fiber of my being that we can put our manpower, capital, and resources to work. I am convinced that we can give youth its chance in life, assure the farmer a decent return for his productive efforts, provide the opportunity for real jobs to our able-bodied men and women at a living wage and under humane working conditions, and establish a national pension plan which will provide security, comfort, and respect for our senior citizens . . .

"We must put our social, economic, and spiritual house in order if democracy is to survive in the New World. Time and events press. We must not fail to seize our opportunity to prove to ourselves and the world that the democratic way of life is man's only hope on earth of working toward the teachings of the Master.

"I have searched my mind and heart. I have not been unmindful of the fact that I sponsored an anti-third term resolution in the days of the false prosperity of President Coolidge. But, for myself, choosing between the two present candidates in this critical period, I can come to only one conclusion:

"On the record as made by the candidates for President, the American way of life has the better opportunity of working out its destiny in the next four years under the administration of Franklin D. Roosevelt. I shall vote for him on November 5."

That concern on the part of Senator La Follette for the national welfare had begun to emerge with the inauguration of the Hoover administration in 1928. Despite the apparent prosperity of the country, La Follette was at loggerheads with the Administration over its do-nothing policies. As he read the trends and events of the time, the Wisconsin senator saw trouble ahead and raised storm warnings that were ignored. He began his unrelenting battle to build a national tax system based on the principle of ability to pay and criticized sharply administrative efforts to "untax wealth," as he once expressed it.

La Follette declared in a nation-wide radio talk in April, 1934, that when taxes were collected on the principle of ability to pay the nation would have an important weapon against the concentration of wealth that threatened democratic institutions. That weapon would help provide purchasing power for the masses and would aid in establishing economic stability.

Senator La Follette was scorned in 1928 when he undertook to call attention to the mounting unemployment situation. At the same time he uttered what was considered almost treasonable

economic heresy when he urged the Senate to pass a resolution
to instruct the Federal Reserve Board to tighten up on credits
in order to stop a possible financial crash. As he saw the situation,
there was close correlation between the unemployment of the
time and the growing frenzy for stock market speculation.

He wasted no time chortling "I told you so" when the economic collapse of 1929-1930 proved his warnings to have been
sound. He set to work collecting data on unemployment from
the mayors of American cities and from labor organizations. He
could not get Administration spokesmen to admit, even in the
face of the evidence, that there was anything seriously wrong or
that the federal government had any responsibility in the matter.

In December, 1931, defying both the White House and the
Senate Republican leadership, La Follette introduced a measure
for federal unemployment relief. Senator Edward Costigan introduced a similar bill. The two were referred to the Committee
on Manufactures of which La Follette was chairman. After full
consideration and public hearings, the two bills were merged
and reported for passage. The La Follette-Costigan relief bill
raised bitter debate and was finally defeated by a 48-to-35 vote.
But the realities of the unemployment situation had been revealed.

It remained for the Roosevelt administration two years later
to adopt the proposals of the relief measure sponsored by La
Follette and the emerging group of Progressives who had embraced the national viewpoint. La Follette's efforts to persuade
the Hoover administration to set up a public works program
to help solve the unemployment problem was brushed aside as
being unworthy of consideration.

With the advent of the New Deal, Senator La Follette received a more respectful hearing for his economic and social
program. He was often critical, however, of the failure of the
Roosevelt administration to take all the steps he considered necessary for the solution of the many problems that confronted it.
He did not approve of the political expediency to which the Administration sometimes bowed when important economic or social
legislation was under consideration.

La Follette took sharp issue with President Roosevelt on much
of his international policy but did support wholeheartedly the

Latin-American Good Neighbor policy. The reciprocal trade agreement policy had his full support. He differed with the Roosevelt administration over tax policies and criticized New Deal borrowing to finance relief and rehabilitation programs.

While his role in the development of the new social and economic policies of government as inaugurated by the Roosevelt administration was inevitably a subordinate one, yet it was Senator La Follette who laid the basis for much relief legislation and played a major part in the shaping of legislation in behalf of labor. An efficient worker, La Follette contributed much of a constructive nature to American democratic government.

When the nation went to war in 1941, Senator La Follette kept reminding the Administration that it must not lose sight of the importance of meeting and solving the domestic issues. As had his father at the beginning of American participation in World War I, Senator La Follette argued and pleaded with the Administration to adopt a fiscal policy that would provide more adequately for war costs to be paid out of current revenues. He did not want to see a re-enactment of the situation that had made possible the "war millionaires" of the earlier war.

La Follette warned against cutting of appropriations for WPA, contending that the defense and war program would not absorb all the unemployed. When, in the summer of 1941, the Senate cut out WPA appropriations, La Follette observed:

"There is tragic irony in the Senate's action. A Congress that can afford to give away $7,000,000,000 to friends across the sea says it cannot afford to spend $1,250,000,000—less than one-fifth as much—to provide jobs, food and clothing for our own needy unemployed!

"A Congress that says our national defense must be extended 3,000 miles beyond our shores overlooks our first line of defense: the morale of the rank and file!

"A Congress that is willing to appropriate more than $40,000,-000,000 for an outward covering for defense is unconcerned about letting part of the core rot . . ."

One of the most articulate opponents of the conscription act passed by Congress in 1941 was Senator La Follette. The older members of the Senate could hear the echo of the voice of the

elder La Follette who had spoken so forcefully against conscription in the first World War. In 1941 La Follette, Jr., was
aroused at the niggardly attitude of Congress with respect to
base pay provided for inductees. He helped crystallize the public
criticism over this policy which finally forced the Administration
to authorize establishment of an Interdepartmental Committee
to make recommendations for revisions in Army and Navy pay.

The committee finally offered to Congress a report recom-
mending increases for high-ranking officers and only moderate
increases for enlisted personnel. A bill modifying the increases
for high-ranking officers and incorporating some of the suggested
increases for enlisted men was presented for action. It had been
languishing in committee but La Follette forced it out for consideration. To those senators who asked for more time for committee consideration, La Follette retorted:

"The enlisted men have already lost several months' increase
in pay because of the delay . . . the only object there can possibly
be for holding this bill in conference is to chisel a few dollars
out of the enlisted pay of the men in the service of the United
States.

"I know it is whispered around here that the men in the armed
services cannot be trusted with all this money. That kind of
argument makes my blood boil. We are willing to trust them with
the future and fate of this nation, baring their breasts to the
bullets of the enemy—but it is stated and whispered that these
men are not to be trusted with an extra $10 a month to spend!"

With that stinging rebuke ringing in its ears, the Senate approved the increase in base pay of enlisted personnel in the
armed forces to $50 a month.

Senator Robert M. La Follette, Jr., supported and voted for
American participation in the United Nations. He supported the
Bretton Woods international monetary agreement and voted for
funds for the Export-Import Bank. Recalling his father's opposition to the Versailles Treaty and the League of Nations after the
first World War, many individuals professed to see a vital difference in point of view between father and son on international affairs. But the father would have fully approved and supported
the son's position as he stated it in May, 1946:

"In the field of foreign policy, the genuine progressive way calls for American participation in every practical instrument of international cooperation. I am deeply convinced that, more than merely joining the various international organizations, we of the United States must play a positive role in shaping a just and democratic peace settlement that will strike at the very causes of war, which are imperialism, power politics, spheres of influence, suppression of minorities, social and economic dislocations, armament competition, racial and religious intolerance, and treaties based on malice and vengeance rather than justice and charity."

To the discomfiture of the Administration leaders and the ardent internationalists who were whooping through the Congress approval for a four billion dollar loan to Great Britain in the late spring of 1946, La Follette analyzed, in a three-hour speech in the Senate, the long-range economic effects of the loan. It was such an effective declaration of opposition that there was much backstage scurrying around to counteract it. He cautioned the Senate against blind acceptance of the argument that the proposed loan would be helpful to both nations. He cited the testimony of top-flight economists of both the United States and Great Britain who held the opposite view, and concluded:

"It would be a great calamity to world peace if our country, as one of the major pillars in the United Nations, crumbled financially under the weight of excessive commitments. These extremists who blindly support any project that is labelled international are doing this country a great disservice. They are building up a pressure of disillusion and reaction that will swing the pendulum far back in the opposite direction to a sure-footed and sane international cooperation."

Senator La Follette fought against the uneven distribution of defense and war contracts and urged that the smaller businessmen of the nation be given an opportunity to bid on contracts. He believed it bad policy to concentrate orders for war material in the hands of a comparatively few large industries. He warned of the troubles sure to come if the federal government failed to take positive action on the problem of housing. He foresaw the dislocations resulting from concentrations of people in a few large cities that were the industrial centers of the nation.

In all this, Senator La Follette was motivated by the philosophy he had expressed in a public statement in October, 1940:

"I believe with every fiber of my being that we can put our manpower, capital, and resources to work. I am convinced that we can give youth its chance in life, assure the farmer a decent return for his productive efforts, provide the opportunity for real jobs to our able-bodied men and women at a living wage and under humane working conditions, and a national pension plan which will provide security, comfort, and respect for our senior citizens.

"The achievement of these objectives will remove once and for all the menace of fifth column activities whether they work from the left or right—whether they spring from communist, fascist, or nazi ideology. It will maintain the precious right to worship God according to the dictates of each person's conscience. It will guarantee for the future the right to enjoy our priceless liberties.

"We must put our social, economic and spiritual house in order if democracy is to survive in the New World. Time and events press. We must not fail to seize our opportunity to prove to ourselves and the world that the democratic way of life is man's only hope on earth of those working toward the teachings of the Master."

This statement reiterated the progressive doctrine for which Senator Robert M. La Follette, Jr., stood and which was the basis for all the measures he endorsed throughout his service in the Senate. It was the transplanting of the Wisconsin Idea, developed by the elder La Follette, to the national scene. The Wisconsin Idea, which an editorial comment in *Life* credited the younger La Follette with keeping alive, "is a far purer and more consistent body of radical doctrine than was the New Deal, being built not only on social welfare, but on a deep faith in small business, equal opportunity and individual freedom. It is a peculiarly American kind of radicalism, free from all taint of 'foreign ideologies' . . ."

On the basis of his long record in the Senate, Robert M. La Follette, Jr., ran as a Republican for nomination and re-election in the 1946 campaign. He had been elected as a Progressive in

1934 and 1940. When the votes were counted, he had lost to the Stalwart Republican candidate, Joseph R. McCarthy. Perhaps the least surprised person in Wisconsin was Senator La Follette himself. With that sixth sense developed by men long in public office, he sensed that the primary vote would be light. He also realized more clearly than many of his supporters that people were not excited enough or concerned enough in the election to go to the polls. His opponent had the support of a Stalwart Republican machine determined to "retire La Follette." Because he had stayed on the job in Washington to get the Congressional reorganization bill through Congress, La Follette actually had only ten days to conduct a personal campaign. He lost the nomination by a scant 5,000 votes.

Many citizens were so sure that La Follette would be nominated that they did not go to the polls for the primary election. Some of them, writing to the senator of their sorrow at his defeat, admitted that they had not gone to the polls because they knew he would be nominated but that they had planned to vote for him in the November election!

On the morning after the primary, Senator La Follette issued a statement in which he said:

"I want the people of Wisconsin to know that I deeply appreciate the opportunity they have given me to serve them during the last 21 years in the United States Senate.

"I have served to the best of my ability during these years and I always have realized that an elective office is not a vested right, but rather a temporary honor and privilege accorded by the citizens of a democracy.

"I sincerely thank all who gave me their support in this and past elections."

CHAPTER XIII

The Fight Against Depression

Senator Robert M. La Follette, Jr., carried to the Senate a firm conviction that the civil and political freedoms guaranteed to American citizens were meaningless unless the government established to maintain those freedoms also guaranteed equal economic opportunity. It was inevitable that he should clash head on with the conservative economic doctrine held by the Hoover administration that all would be well if the well-being of the business interests of the nation were maintained.

As Senator La Follette analyzed the situation, protection of big business against the sharp agonies of depression in the form of high protective tariffs, of loans to big industrial and financial institutions, and the policy of lowering taxes on the wealthy in the face of lowered national revenues were complete distortions of both the spirit and the letter of the principles of government stated by the Founding Fathers. He rejected in short, blunt words the Administration's view that the federal government had no responsibility to the small businessman, the farmer, or the wage earner who through no fault of his own was a victim of the economic debacle that came in 1929.

Senator La Follette's deep concern at getting at the root of the trouble was foreshadowed by his appeal to Congress several months before the stock market crash in the fall of 1929, to instruct the Federal Reserve banking system to take action that would put a stop to unregulated speculation. At the December session of Congress in 1929, La Follette began his militant opposition to the Administration's policies. He insisted that the federal government could not shirk its share of the responsibility for the victims of a depression resulting primarily from mistaken policies of past administrations. He shocked the conservatives by demanding that the government launch a nation-wide program of useful public works to provide jobs for the unemployed, stimulate business, and check deflation.

Within sixty days after the stock market crash President Hoover asked Congress to enact as quickly as possible a bill to reduce federal taxes by $160,000,000 on incomes for 1929, the taxes on which were already payable. Administration spokesmen defended the bill as a means of "pegging" the falling stock market by reducing tax payments on big incomes and corporations. La Follette opposed the bill as "sleight of hand" and warned that the depression was too serious to be checked by such methods. He demanded that the taxes already payable under existing law should be collected to meet the need for genuine relief which he predicted would soon become necessary.

The Wisconsin senator smiled grimly to himself when President Hoover announced on March 8, 1930, that the crisis was past and predicted that unemployment would cease to be a problem "within sixty days." During the recess before Congress convened in December, 1930, La Follette sent out questionnaires to the mayors of all cities of 5,000 population and over to get firsthand information on unemployment in every part of the country. The replies to his inquiries belied the Administration's claim that prosperity was "just around the corner." In the face of La Follette's carefully prepared documentation of his argument that unemployment was real and getting worse, Congress refused to take action. The senator took the floor on February 10, 1931, to protest against adjournment on March 4 without any action on the part of Congress to enact federal relief legislation. He said:

"The evidence is overwhelming that the urban centers are now suffering from a more serious economic crisis than has ever confronted the country . . . With at least 6,000,000 unemployed,

with another 5,000,000 on part time, it is a very conservative
estimate to say that, with their dependents, at least 22,000,000
people are affected.

"To fail to provide any relief for this great group is a breach
of faith with the American people. . . .

"It has been argued in this controversy by those supporting
the administration that the local communities should be called
upon to take care of the unemployed.

"I for one cannot see the logic of that argument. If any governmental entity is responsible, or has any share of responsibility
in producing this economic crisis, then surely it is the federal
government. The governments of the cities and the governments
of the various states cannot be said to have enacted legislation
which has contributed to the present business depression. It is
only the federal government, in enacting legislation affecting economic conditions in the country, which has any responsibility in
this matter; and yet it is argued that Congress is the one governmental agency which should not afford any assistance in the existing crisis."

A few days later Senator La Follette revealed another aspect
of his fight against depression by introducing a bill providing
for establishment of a national economic council. The bill, however, received the same treatment his other proposals had. Nothing was done at that session. La Follette reintroduced the bill the
following December. In the meantime the proposal created much
discussion. From Gerard Swope and the United States Chamber
of Commerce came counterproposals. Senator La Follette's original bill would have established a council of fifteen members representing the various segments of economic life and appointed
by the President to keep an eye on the general economic conditions, to formulate proposals looking to the solution of possible
trouble, and to submit those proposals to the President and Congress for appropriate action.

It was La Follette's belief that depressions could be avoided
in large degree by study and planning.

"This piece of legislation is a challenge to the fixed belief
that hard times and good times alternate in cycles," La Follette
told Washington news reporters. "I do not believe hard times

are necessary provided it is possible to look ahead and plan to meet the emergencies that may arise.

"It is quite evident in considering the factors that are responsible for the present depression that the only sound approach to the problem of unemployment and industrial instability is the creation of the necessary public machinery of planning and control."

Convinced that the 1930-1931 session of Congress would do nothing to alleviate the plight of the people of the nation, Senator La Follette joined with four other progressive senators in issuing a call for a conference of Progressives in Washington to outline a program of legislation dealing with the economic situation for presentation to the new Congress. Besides La Follette, Senators George W. Norris of Nebraska, Edward Costigan of Colorado, Bronson M. Cutting of New Mexico, and Burton K. Wheeler of Montana signed the call. In announcing the conference for March 11 and 12, 1931, the committee noted the failure of Congress to approve measures for the "solution of one of the greatest economic crises ever confronting the nation."

"We believe," the committee declared, "that a constructive solution for these problems can be found by men and women who are aligned with different political parties. We hold that the magnitude of these problems demands an intelligent effort to solve them without regard to partisan or political advantage.

"We assure you that this conference is not called to form the basis for a new party. To this end, it is our purpose that the conference shall be nonpartisan in character, and shall be devoted to the exchange of ideas looking solely to the formulation of a sound legislative program to be advanced at the next session of Congress."

The conference created uneasiness among Congressional Administration leaders. Senator James E. Watson of Indiana, apparently in an effort to draw the attention of the conference from the avowed subjects announced for discussion and also to cast doubt on the political purpose of the meeting, wrote a letter to Senator George W. Norris as chairman propounding a series of questions for the conference to answer. In a humorous reference to the letter in his opening address, Senator Norris suggested that it was apparent from the questions asked that Senator

Watson was not aware of the fact that the conference was non-partisan.

The two-day conference sparkled with the ideas presented by such speakers as Edward J. Jeffries, Harold L. Ickes, Milo Reno, Charles Beard, Sidney Hillman, William Green, Frank Murphy, Robert P. Scripps, Donald Richberg. The senators who called the conference added their observations, which in no case were given to denunciation of the Administration for its failure to act. Rather, the discussions were exploratory with the aim of demonstrating that seemingly unrelated topics such as the tariff, representative government, unemployment, agriculture, and public utilities were fundamental parts of the over-all problem of the economic distress of the nation.

The committees on unemployment and agriculture presented reports that acknowledged the lack of enough pertinent factual material on which to base programs for specific action but pledged that they would continue investigations to get the facts. The committee on the tariff excoriated the recently passed Smoot-Hawley tariff law and reported:

"Since certain provisions of the Smoot-Hawley Tariff Law are inimical to the interests of American agriculture, to labor, average business and consumers generally, a scientific revision of various important tariff rates and administrative clauses should be made, with a view to the maintenance of fair and wholesome competition, more liberal commerce with other nations, restored confidence and reawakened prosperity."

The committee on representative government, headed by Senator Bronson Cutting, presented a report prophetic of the reorganization of Congress law passed fifteen years later. The report called for the more adequate control by Congress of policy and lawmaking, for provisions to eliminate from the floor of Congress the great mass of private, local, and sectional bills, "leaving Congress free to give more adequate consideration to measures of major importance," and for scrutiny and revision of House rules of procedure affecting control over legislation.

Meanwhile, three months before, in January, 1931, Senator Robert La Follette's brother Philip had taken the oath of office as governor of Wisconsin. Philip La Follette had amazed all the political dopesters by entering the primary contest the summer before as a candidate against Governor Walter Kohler. Kohler had given the state a good administration and his re-election was practically conceded—even by Progressive Republicans. The governor was well liked and had heavy financial support for his bid for re-election. Phil La Follette entered the contest with little hope of winning but felt that his candidacy was in the nature of a challenge to the Stalwarts and the beginning of a campaign by Progressives ultimately to win.

Rallying behind Philip La Follette's leadership, Progressive Republicans elected not only a governor but a majority of the state assembly. Fifteen of the thirty-three members of the State senate were Progressive Republican and with the occasional aid of two independent members were able to control the upper house of the legislature.

During his first year as governor, Philip La Follette found, as had his brother Robert, that local resources were not enough with which to fight the depression. Warned by the conservatives that he would "bankrupt the state treasury," Governor La Follette requested and finally secured six million dollars for direct relief and state aids for local public works programs. A road-building and grade-crossing separation program was provided to help take up some of the unemployment slack. The governor also suggested and put through legislation to provide employment for younger unmarried men who he declared had been overlooked by everyone even though their plight was as desperate as that of others. Out of this suggestion came a reforestation program and a fire-protection project for northern Wisconsin. With some modifications that plan was later adopted by the federal government and became the Civilian Conservation Corps.

Encouraged by the response to the Progressive Conference, Senator La Follette spent the recess of the summer of 1931 in continuing his investigation of unemployment and sent out a second questionnaire to mayors of cities. On December 9, 1931, just a few days after the new Congress assembled, Senators La Follette and Costigan introduced separate bills for federal relief. La Follette's bill was referred to his Committee on Manufactures while the Costigan bill was referred to the Commerce Com-

mittee. Senator Costigan immediately got in touch with Hiram
Johnson, chairman of the Commerce Committee, and with his
co-operation had the bill rereferred to the Manufactures Committee.

Senator Costigan explained to the Senate that his bill had
been the result of independent investigation and work. On his
own initiative he had, as had Senator La Follette, called social
workers and labor leaders from various parts of the country into
conference before he drafted his bill. Although La Follette had
been called in to meet with the people Senator Costigan was
conferring with, neither man realized that both were actually
working on the same thing! Working together, La Follette and
Costigan merged the details of the two bills into the one that
was reported to the Senate on February 2, 1932.

The bill provided for an outright grant of $500,000,000 to the
states to be administered by a federal emergency relief board.
Opening the debate on the bill, La Follette called attention to
the failure of the government, after two winters of unprecedented
economic depression, to do anything for those who felt the effects
most severely—the wage earners. His voice tinged with sarcasm,
he reminded the Senate that the major portion of the President's
reconstruction program called for the creation of the Reconstruction Finance Corporation which he had previously characterized
as "a measure to afford hospitalization to the casualties of this
depression."

"The objective of that measure," La Follette said scornfully,
"was to provide up to $2,000,000,000 credit, furnished by the
people of the United States, to stem the tide of bankruptcy, of
railroad receiverships, of bank failures. In other words, the Congress of the United States and the administration, passed through
and enacted the Reconstruction Finance Corporation measure for
the relief of those who are interested in these corporations, insurance companies, and banks.

"Two billion one hundred and sixty million dollars has already
been provided by the Congress and the administration during
this depression for the relief of those who own property and
securities in the United States. Now, when it is proposed that
the Congress shall give consideration to a measure providing for

the relief of those in the United States who, through no fault
of their own, find themselves destitute, cold, hungry, and home-
less, the contention is raised that there is not sufficient evidence
to demonstrate the necessity for Federal action in this crisis."

For five hours Senator La Follette reviewed past actions of
the Congress in meeting demands for relief of various crises
throughout the world. He read into the record the considered
judgments of nationally known social workers and economists
concerning the national effects of the depression. He presented
the testimony of hundreds of mayors of cities throughout the
nation to refute the Administration's claim that there was no
demonstrable need for relief. He called attention to the fact that
he was sponsor of a $500,000,000 public works program which
was before Congress for consideration but said:

"Mr. President, I hope Congress will consider the proposal
for a stupendous public works program as a means of stemming
the tide of deflation in the United States, but to advocate it
now in this critical emergency as a substitute for relief is to
befog the issue. We could not get a public works program in
operation in time to meet this critical situation."

La Follette presented evidence showing that local governmental units in trying to meet the needs for relief had practically
exhausted their credit and that the problem of municipal revenues had been aggravated by mounting tax delinquencies due to
the inability of property owners to pay taxes. He closed his plea
for prompt and affirmative action on the La Follette-Costigan
relief bill with the warning:

"Proceed, if you will; make the record that you will extend
relief to organized wealth in this situation to the tune of
$2,160,000,000 and that you will turn your backs upon millions
of upstanding Americans who are suffering want, privation, and
misery. But I say that if you fail to meet this issue now, you will
meet it later. You cannot duck it; you cannot dodge it; you cannot meet it by offering substitutes that fail to meet the emergency
character of the situation.

"Senators say that this is a problem for local government;
that it is no concern of the Federal Government.

"Mr. President, the Federal Government is just as much concerned in the future citizenship of this Republic as the local communities, if not more so. If we permit this situation to go on, millions of children will be maimed in body, if not warped in mind, by the effects of malnutrition. They will form the citizenship upon which the future of this country must depend. They are the hope of America."

Scholarly, shy Senator Edward Costigan immediately took the floor in behalf of the pending relief bill. In a deceptively mild voice he said:

"More than a hundred years ago America rang with Pinckney's flaming sentence, 'Millions for defense, but not one cent for tribute.' If, following the legislative record already made at this session, this body refuses to admit the justice of the pending measure . . . a new slogan of sinister significance and far-reaching consequence will be heard in America. That slogan, I fear, may be, 'Billions for big business, but no mercy for mankind; billions for doles from the people's taxes for bankers, railroad executives, and financial institutions through government in business and financial corporations, but not one Federal cent for humanity.'"

Senator Costigan added to the already impressive mass of evidence testifying to the critical need for action. Between them, Senators La Follette and Costigan read into the record evidence which took 408 pages of the *Congressional Record* to present! The La Follette-Costigan relief bill, brought to a vote on February 16, 1932, was defeated by a 48-to-35 vote.

Following this defeat, Senator La Follette supported a proposal by Senator Wagner of New York which provided for reimbursable loans to the states rather than outright grants. Senate Republican leaders would not permit action even on that bill until it had been incorporated in the Administration's emergency relief and construction bill which gave administration of relief loans to the Reconstruction Finance Corporation.

Senator La Follette was not yet willing to give up to the theory that the depression must run its course. Subscribing as he did to the theory that government should undertake action to check the process of deflation and endeavor to stimulate recovery, he introduced, in the closing days of 1931, a bill proposing a five and a half billion dollar bond issue to raise funds for public works and relief. Terming it a "prosperity bond plan," La Follette proposed that the federal government issue the bonds to supply the funds to be used by the federal, state, and municipal governments to expand their public works programs.

Shortly after the bill had been introduced, Senator La Follette was interviewed on his proposals to soften the blows of the depression by William S. Hard for the National Broadcasting Company. In answer to a question about planned economy which La Follette advocated and the possibility of a more regularized and stable industrial and financial structure, the senator declared that such a goal must be attained:

"But I do not think of it as being regularized in a static condition. I am not interested in trying to maintain the status quo in our economic life. Devices which seek to preserve the unequal distribution of the wealth now produced will halt the progress of mankind and in the end will retard or prevent recovery.

"We have created a great industrial mechanism. It must be run so that its benefits will be more generously and widely distributed. In the last analysis, in a highly organized industrial world, the welfare of the people as a whole is, I repeat, essential to the welfare of business itself.

"My conception of a planned economy," La Follette declared, "is one which will insure an ever-rising standard of living and an ever-increasing purchasing power for all the people and which thus will press production itself to larger and larger outputs and larger and larger successes. Progressivism is not a mere protest. It is a positive program for the enlargement of consumption and production and for the lifting of all human life to higher and more satisfying levels."

In the debate on the prosperity bond bill, La Follette became angered at the lackadaisical attitude of a majority of members on both sides of the Senate. He denounced in sharp terms the failure of a coalition of Republicans and Democrats to accept the evidence of their eyes and the figures presented by able economists regarding the crisis that faced the nation. He reminded the Senate of the efforts of himself and a small group of other senators to get federal action. He castigated with devastating effect President Hoover's bland generalizations about "the essential soundness of business," the "momentarily pressing problems" that would soon be disposed of, his "committee and conference" method of ducking the problems of the depression. He called attention to the 50 per cent decrease in industrial production from June, 1929, to April, 1932, a 79 per cent decrease in building activity for the same period, a 37 per cent cut in factory employment, and a 56 per cent decline in factory payrolls.

"A further decline, La Follette warned the Senate, "will produce a cataclysmic phase in this depression which will threaten the very foundations of Government itself. I have appealed all during the crisis for action on the part of the Government to save the millions of human beings who are being ground to bits in this process . . . I wish to appeal to this body to now assert its leadership and to assume its responsibility by adopting a program commensurate with the magnitude and gravity of this crisis."

Congress adjourned without acting on the bill.

When the "lame duck" session of the 72nd Congress convened in December, 1932, Senator La Follette again got busy and directed another questionnaire to mayors of American cities to bring his data on unemployment and local relief measures up to date. The picture had blackened considerably and again the La Follette-Costigan measure was introduced. Senator Bronson Cutting also contributed to the new bill. He had introduced a separate bill to provide relief for transients. Those provisions were merged with the revised La Follette-Costigan bill.

Following to the bitter end the Administration's policy Senate Republicans seized on a substitute measure offered by Senator Wagner of New York by which to defeat the La Follette-Costigan bill. The Wagner proposal made available $300,000,000 to the Reconstruction Finance Corporation for loans to states for relief. La Follette, Costigan, Cutting, and other progressive senators considered the substitute inadequate and a mere continuation of the process of pauperization of large segments of the population. Fighting to the last for an adequate relief measure, La Follette said:

"Three million families under the existing system, which the

Wagner substitute proposes to continue, have already been ground down to this level. Millions more caught in the clutch of circumstances for which they have no responsibility and over which they have no control are rapidly being crushed and degraded.

"Mr. President, I choose my words and I weigh them carefully when I say that under existing standards of relief which the Wagner substitute proposes to perpetuate, the fiber of the nation is being weakened. The family unit upon which our civilization has been builded is crumbling and breaking under the strain. These men, these women, these little children—their fate rests in your hands. They have asked for bread. I plead with you not to give them stone."

One factor that probably helped kill the relief bill was a deep suspicion on the part of the about-to-be-replaced Republican leadership in the Senate that the Progressives supporting the La Follette-Costigan-Cutting measure had the blessing of the President-elect, Franklin D. Roosevelt. Cutting and La Follette, both Progressive Republicans, had been invited to Warm Springs in January for a conference with Mr. Roosevelt. Within a week after that conference the bill providing for $500,000,000 in outright grants to the states for relief was introduced.

Shortly after his inauguration on March 4, 1933, President Roosevelt sent to Congress a special message asking immediate action on relief measures. The message was received on March 21. On March 30, a bill abandoning the Wagner "loan" principle and providing $500,000,000 for direct grants to the states was enacted. Thus, after three years of almost lone fighting for the principle of adequate federal relief to replace the Hoover local relief policy, Senator Robert M. La Follette, Jr., saw his principles enacted into law.

Although politically subordinated throughout the Roosevelt administration, Senator La Follette was one of the major forces supporting the relief and social rehabilitation legislation of that administration. His name did not appear on any of the measures passed to give the "forgotten man" a break, but it might well have. La Follette's strength in support of such legislation was given in helping to persuade wavering senators to stay in line.

His enormous knowledge of parliamentary techniques was drawn upon time and again to break legislative log jams holding up important matters. His advice was sought by Administration leaders on strategy. His ideas were sought and incorporated in the new legislation. As a minority member of the powerful Committees on Finance and Education and Labor to which were referred much of the relief and rehabilitation legislation, Senator La Follette stood in a strategic spot to assist and offer suggestions. Withal his was the quiet, steady, sure, behind-the-scenes kind of operation that contributed much to legislative acceptance of many of the humanitarian New Deal proposals.

While the friendly climate of the New Deal gave him an opportunity to translate many of his progressive principles into law, La Follette never abandoned his independent position about which he warned the Senate Republican caucus when he first entered the Senate in 1925. He was critical of the New Deal for compromising and failing to go the whole way on many matters. He warned the Administration of the 1937 economic setback a year before it occurred. Even with the beginning of the war boom in 1940 and 1941 when the Administration showed a disposition to cut away many of the social rehabilitation projects by refusing appropriations, La Follette was critical. He fought against reductions in WPA funds in 1941 on the basis that the defense program would not absorb all eligible unemployed citizens.

There was still another aspect of the depression and the general economic situation that Senator La Follette kept before the public. He was just as much concerned over the plight of the farmers of the nation as he was over the plight of the urban workers. It was his position that measures to rehabilitate the nation fell far short of their aim if the government failed to give assistance to agriculture.

La Follette was one of the small group of western senators who practically forced on a reluctant Hoover administration the necessity of the McNary-Haugen bill. He recognized clearly the interdependence of all the groups that make up our society. In an address to the Senate on February 8, 1934, supporting an added appropriation to the Civil Works Administration, he said:

"The farmers have been fighting a losing battle against the

depression, not begun in 1929 but the depression which began, so far as their industry was concerned, in 1920. The obvious effect was a constantly diminishing purchasing power on the part of the farmer. I sometimes think that those who are not familiar with our vast agricultural section fail to realize the great economic importance of this group in our population and the absolute necessity of restoring the purchasing power of that group, if we are ever to recover from the depression and to build that recovery on a sound basis."

In that same address Senator La Follette characterized the internal crisis resulting from the depression as "more serious than any war in the nation's history and the economic, social and political consequences of losing the war against depression will be more devastating than the loss of any war, or of all wars in which this country has been engaged since its establishment." He ridiculed those who questioned the expenditure of funds for vast public works programs on the ground that it would unbalance the budget. He asked what senator would dare, in the prosecution of a war, to rise and declare that this nation could not fight the war because it would unbalance the budget!

"I think we have been trying to balance the wrong budget in this country," La Follette continued. "The budget that I should like to see set up would list upon the asset side 125,000,000 people; it would list our natural resources, our oil, our coal, our lumber, our minerals; it would list our transportation system; it would list the great industrial mechanism that has been built up in this country . . . it would list our great agricultural resources.

"On the other side of the ledger would be listed the obligation of any society and of any government worthy of the name to assure to every man, woman, and child a decent and full life. If we will discharge that obligation, if we will balance the greater budget, we will put the operating budget into balance almost at once . . ."

Drought conditions throughout the Middle West during the summer of 1934 added another burden to an already reeling agricultural economy. Reports from his own state caused Senator La Follette to hurry to Wisconsin to see for himself the extent of the damage. He knew that where farmers in other parts of the

Middle West stood to lose a crop, many of the farmers of Wisconsin were faced with irreparable losses because they might lose their valuable dairy herds. La Follette took a trip through the state to see at first hand what the conditions were. He talked with farmers and attended conferences in every part of the state. He had pictures taken of the burned and parched pastures, dried-up streams, starving and dying cattle.

When he got back to Washington La Follette had the photographs enlarged and hung them in the Senate chambers. For two days he let the pictures tell the grim story of devastation and ruin faced by the farmers of his state because of the drought. Then he told the Senate what he had personally observed and what the drought meant to the farmers and citizens of Wisconsin. It was a simple and graphic statement of fact. Supported by the evidence of the photographs, Senator La Follette secured overwhelming adoption of his amendment increasing drought relief by $75,000,000.

It was during that summer of 1934 that the Progressive party of Wisconsin was founded under the leadership of Progressive Republicans who felt that the time had come to make a clean break from the Republican party. Senator La Follette attended the conferences in Madison preliminary to formal organization and joined with his brother Philip in support of the new third party in Wisconsin.

CHAPTER XIV

The Progressive Party of Wisconsin

NATIONAL ATTENTION was focused on the Wisconsin political situation in 1934 when Progressive Republicans of the state cast off their Republican moorings and embarked as a separate party. The actual formation of the new Progressive party, however, was the culmination of a series of events that not only affected Senator La Follette personally, but which, so far as politics in the Badger State was concerned, led with some logic to a realignment of political forces. Events and personalities are still too close for a completely objective analysis. Some individuals insist that the formation of the Progressive party was the only way by which the La Follettes, Philip and Robert, could hope to be elected to office. There are those who insist that the new party was the result of a truly grass-roots demand by the people for a party that would embody in its principles those matters for which Progressives had long stood and fought. Events and circumstances that preceded the formal organization of the Progressive party of Wisconsin in May, 1934, support both views.

In the 1932 elections, Progressive Republicans in Wisconsin had given their support to Roosevelt for the presidency and to the Democrats running in opposition to former Governor Kohler and other Stalwarts in the state elections. Phil La Follette, elected governor in the 1930 campaign, had been defeated in the 1932 primary in his campaign for re-election by Stalwart Republican Walter Kohler. Their candidate defeated, Progressive

Republicans supported the Democratic state ticket. For the second time in its history Wisconsin's electoral votes were cast for a Democratic president and for the first time in fifty years a Democrat was elected governor. Democrats also controlled the legislature. Democrats of Wisconsin were not, however, fully prepared to meet the challenge. Valiant efforts on the part of the governor's friends and advisers could not hide the fact that he did not seem able to make up his mind about definite programs to meet the crisis of the time. The legislature, futhermore, proved to be without constructive leadership and in addition was thoroughly reactionary in its attitude toward the problems of the state.

To add to the difficulties of whatever administration was in office, the business depression that had begun with the stock market crash in 1929 only sharpened the depressed condition of agriculture which was, and is, the major industry in Wisconsin. The Farm Holiday Association, started in Iowa by Milo Reno, gained many members in Wisconsin where liquid milk was being marketed at prices ranging from 85 cents to $1.25 a hundred pounds. Farm debt delinquencies had reached alarming proportions. A rival farm organization sprang into being in the eastern and central dairying region, the Wisconsin Milk Pool. Milk Pool leadership was much more belligerent than that of the Farm Holiday group. Shortly after Governor Schmedeman's inauguration in 1933, Milk Pool farmers staged a brief strike against movement of milk into the Milwaukee and Chicago markets. The strike was called off at the request of state officials who pleaded for a little time in which to work out a solution.

The legislature failed to take any positive action and Farm Holiday leaders joined with Milk Pool leaders in declaring a strike to begin the middle of May. Foreseeing, as a result of the February strike experience, the possibility of widespread disorder and destruction of property, Governor Schmedeman requested the adjutant general of the Wisconsin National Guard, Ralph M. Immell, to submit a statement of policies to be followed in the event the announced strike might result in trouble. In view of the expense involved in mobilizing the Guard for strike duty, the adjutant general urged the governor to consider other possibilities. He suggested that the state accept the leadership and responsibility for the strike by declaring an embargo on all dairy products. In any event, the adjutant general insisted that maintenance of law and order must remain in the hands of local authorities and that National Guard troops be used only at the request of county sheriffs and under their orders.

Shortly before the middle of May, Farm Holiday leaders announced their withdrawal from the strike. Wisconsin Milk Pool members, however, struck on May 15. Roving bands of pickets stopped milk trucks, forced them to turn back or dumped the milk. In all counties save one, local law enforcement officers with the co-operation of ununiformed and unarmed National Guard troops speedily met the challenge and kept disorder at a minimum. Failure of one sheriff to take proper precautions to protect property resulted in his summary removal. That sheriff had apparently assured Milk Pool pickets that they could do as they pleased in his county. His removal broke the back of the strike and within three days it was all over. In the meantime, union members and leaders in the industrial areas expressed their sympathy with the farmers' plight and urged a joining of forces since the economic interests of both groups were much the same. The Wisconsin Federation of Labor went on record as favoring the establishment of a Farm-Labor party. It became something more than a mere organizational resolution when Thomas Amlie, a former Progressive Republican member of Congress, William T. Evjue, editor of the *Capital Times* of Madison and outspoken Progressive, Henry Ohl, Jr., president of the Wisconsin Federation of Labor, Joseph Padway, Federation attorney, and others supported the idea.

With the campaign year 1934 rapidly approaching, Stalwart Republicans were secretly hoping that the new party movement might prevail, for they saw an opportunity to elect a governor on the basis of general discontent with the Democratic administration and a split in the ranks of Progressive Republicans.

Farm leaders were incensed at the Democratic administration and felt, as one of them put it, that "the Republican party has done nothing for the farmer and hasn't a ghost of a chance in the next election." Farmers, many of whom were Progressive

Republicans, were insistent that a new party be formed. But Theodore Dammann, state secretary and the only Progressive Republican to survive the Democratic landslide of 1932, warned in public addresses that Progressive leaders, presumably the La Follettes and the Progressive Republican members of Congress, were not wholly in sympathy with the new party idea. Democrats were interested in the situation because they hoped that by forming a new party the Progressives would split the Republican vote.

In the early months of 1934 the political grapevine buzzed over Washington announcements that President Roosevelt would support Senators Norris of Nebraska and Johnson of California for re-election. Nothing was said about two other prominent members of the Progressive bloc of Senators up for re-election, Bronson Cutting of New Mexico and Robert M. La Follette, Jr., of Wisconsin. The latter two, it was pointed out, were as deserving of the presidential blessing as Norris and Johnson. Both had not only campaigned for Roosevelt in 1932, but had supported practically all the President's proposals to stem the tide of depression. Democratic National Chairman James Farley was noncommittal and permitted the impression to get out that Roosevelt would not endorse either Cutting or La Follette. The Democratic organization in Wisconsin was beginning to think of the possibility of having two Democrats in the Senate representing Wisconsin instead of but one. A Democrat, J. Ryan Duffy, had been elected to the Senate from the state in the 1932 landslide.

Summarizing the political situation facing Senator La Follette in his own state, a New York *Times* correspondent wrote:

"The two major factors in the Senator's problems are the uncertainty as to what measure of Democratic support a Progressive Republican nominee can count upon and whether to listen to one faction of La Follette adherents that wants a third party, or to the other faction that insists on capturing the nomination in the regular Republican primary, according to traditional custom and the Senator's preference."

In the latter part of February, 1934, a letter signed by Robert M. La Follette, Jr., Dammann, Herman L. Ekern, and two Progressive Republican members of the legislature was sent to county leaders announcing a Progressive conference to be held in Madison on March 3. The letter stated:

"It seems the unanimous desire of all Progressives that a conference be held . . . for consideration and discussion of matters of importance."

Newspapers throughout the state interpreted the letter to mean that plans were being laid for the formation of a new party. The conference drew a crowd of over five hundred Progressives from every part of the state. A number of county delegations were openly opposed to formation of a new party but a majority favored the step. Concerning his own feelings about the matter, Senator La Follette told conference delegates:

"We have before us one of the most momentous decisions Progressives in this state have ever been called upon to make. I appeal to you not to consider your decision on the basis of the political fortunes of any individual, but on the basis of the welfare of the Progressive movement and the people of Wisconsin. I want you to know that I would not hesitate to throw what political future I may have in this state into the hopper with your decision."

Despite the clamor among his constituents, Senator La Follette, with nearly ten years of experience in the Senate and before that as his father's private secretary, was not sure that the time had come for a new party. He could not dismiss, either, his father's intransigent stand against third parties. He had stood with his father during the 1924 campaign and saw him literally give his life in protest against the entrenched reactionism of both major parties. As the New York *Times* correspondent had reported, Senator La Follette personally leaned toward the traditional custom. Yet his statement to delegates at the Madison conference left the decision to a majority determination.

The ardor of the new party enthusiasts was considerably dampened when it was pointed out that state statutes controlling the placing of a new party column on the ballot were uncertain of interpretation and that there was a possibility that a new party could not qualify soon enough to get its name and candidates on the 1934 primary and general election ballots. The only positive action taken by the conference was to appoint a committee em-

powered to obtain a declaratory judgment from the state Supreme
Court interpreting the law and to call another conference as soon
as possible after such action.

On May 1 the court resolved doubts over interpretation of the
statutes and stated that there was nothing in the law to prevent
the inclusion of a new party on the ballot so long as individual
candidates conformed to provisions affecting the filing of nomination papers. Progressive leaders issued the call for a state convention to meet in Fond du Lac on May 19 to decide the fate of the
new party proposal. Between the announcement and the event
itself, many individuals speculated over what leading Progressives
would do. It was freely predicted by the political reporters and on
the usual "word of close associates" that both Robert and Philip
La Follette would cast their lot with the new party. No crystal
ball was needed to dredge up that tidbit because the senator had
so stated on March 3. Both men, however, had been careful to
make no definite statement revealing their personal feelings. In
the meantime county delegations were being selected, some instructed to support the new party, others instructed to oppose,
while many were uninstructed. The majority preconvention sentiment, however, was in favor of forming a new party.

The Sheboygan *Press*, of which Charles Broughton the Democratic national committeeman from Wisconsin was editor, undertook to lecture the Progressives in their own history and printed
generous quotes from Robert M. La Follette's *Autobiography* to
remind them that the founder of their movement would have remained in the Republican party. As Democratic national committeeman, Mr. Broughton was apprehensive of the effect a Progressive third party might have on the future of his own party in
the state. Wrote Broughton:

"If former Senator La Follette were alive today we feel that
he would throw his full influence with the party of Roosevelt and
Jefferson, to kill those interests which are attempting to belittle
and combat the New Deal. In 1896 he was determined to remain
in the party and fight the machine. Today the same interests that
he had to combat, or many of them, are merging their forces to
undermine and prevent the carrying out of a program by President Roosevelt. Those who are endeavoring to organize a third

party are entirely out of accord with the principles of the senior and honored late Senator Robert Marion La Follette."

While there continued to be some opposition among Progressives to formation of a new party, it became apparent as delegates arrived in Fond du Lac that formation of the new party was merely a matter for formal approval. Two questions were uppermost in the minds of the 300-odd delegates as they met on May 19; one, how large the vote would be for the new party; two, the name. Following discussion of the mechanics of securing the necessary 10,000 signatures to petitions for the new party to get on the ballot, delegates voted 252 to 44 to establish the new party.

The name of the new party was the subject of spirited debate. Farm delegates, supported by AFL leaders, were in favor of Farmer-Labor as a name. Joseph Padway, counsel for the Wisconsin Federation of Labor, declared, however, against such a name.

"I, too, am attached to the name Farmer-Labor," Padway told the convention. "But in order to promote the interests of the farmers and laborers we must ask others, not farmers or laborers, to assist. If the program is right, I say that no laborer will be ashamed to come into this movement and they will come."

Former Governor Philip La Follette clinched the argument in favor of adopting the name Progressive when he said:

"The name we choose may or may not be important. If it is a symbol, it is important. It will point to what we intend to do. We are hopeful that we are laying the cornerstone of a realignment in political life. We have had 25 years' education under the Progressive name. I am convinced that the great bulk of our people are not farmers first or laborers first—we must appeal to them as Americans, and not to them on the basis of their occupations. For whatever my judgment is worth, I think it is a fatal error, an irretrievable blunder, to launch this as a class party."

The name Progressive was adopted, with 236 delegates voting for it, 41 for the Farmer-Labor label, and scattering votes for other names.

The climax of the day's deliberations came with Senator La Follette's announcement that he would conduct his campaign for re-election as a Progressive. In a speech enthusiastically applauded by the delegates, Senator La Follette called attention to the failure of national Republican administrations to solve the many problems that helped to bring about the depressed condition of the country. He also warned that within the Democratic party and its administration there were the seeds of reaction that would further delay constructive action.

"This is a challenge to the best traditions of our citizenship," La Follette said. "We are on the threshold of the promised land where everyone may have economic security. Our resources and productivity fairly distributed can provide the farmer with an adequate return upon his capital and for his labor, the wage earner steady employment at an increasing standard of living, the business and professional man a fair return for his services.

Senator La Follette recalled his father's position with respect to the realignment of political forces in 1924 and his reasons for leading the independent movement at that time as a protest against the reactionism of the two major parties. As to his own beliefs and activities:

"It was my privilege to take an active part in the campaign to build a new party in 1924. At public conferences with Progressives in Washington, in the presidential elections of 1928 and 1932, and on the platform of every state in the northwest, I have advocated and labored for a political realignment through the election of Progressives regardless of party.

"It is my deep conviction that equal opportunity cannot become a reality, security in the enjoyment of our abundant resources cannot be attained, democratic government cannot exist, tyranny cannot be avoided, without a party free from the control of organized wealth and frankly dedicated to the interests and aspirations of the mass of the people.

"There is no magic in any political party that will insure good government. In the future, as in the past, no lasting benefit for the people can be gained without fearless and independent champions of the public interest, serving as a spearhead against entrenched reaction in the legislative branches of the government at Washington and at Madison. No party can be stronger than those who give it allegiance."

La Follette closed his address to the members of the new Progressive party by suggesting:

"Any new and enduring movement must appeal to people in every walk of life who believe in true democracy and who are determined to achieve a satisfactory and full life for every man, woman, and child in this country. It must provide opportunity for the farmer, the wage earner, the business and professional man to make common cause to solve the enigma of privation in the midst of abundance."

The reaction to formation of the party was, of course, mixed. Senators Gerald P. Nye and George W. Norris expressed approval and pledged themselves to campaign for Senator La Follette's re-election. Those two, together with Senators Edward P. Costigan of Colorado, Burton K. Wheeler of Montana, and Lynn J. Frazier of North Dakota, toured the state speaking in behalf of the Progressive party candidate for the United States Senate. Fiorello La Guardia of New York and Frank P. Walsh, chairman of the New York State Power Commission, also journeyed to Wisconsin to speak in behalf of Senator La Follette and the new Progressive party.

Wisconsin Stalwart Republicans were "relieved." Badger State Democrats declared a "fight to the finish" against Progressives, while Socialists were suspicious. The *Nation* saw "plenty of evidence that we are witnessing the development of a national third party." State secretary Theodore Dammann and other leading Progressive Republicans were still unwilling to declare allegiance to the new party. The Milwaukee *Journal* was somewhat skeptical. It asked editorially:

"Will these 'Progressives' get anywhere? The answer is a question. Is there running through the grass of this country a demand for a new political party? Or are the sister states inclined to say, 'Roosevelt is a Progressive; let's give him his chance'?

"This Wisconsin movement is an explosion of a feeling that is deep-rooted in this land. Many of us have said and say that there ought to be a new poiltical alignment. But we wait for the leader who can head such a movement.

"In Wisconsin an attempt is made. It is captained by men who have been accustomed to count upon Democratic support to win their victories. It may be as little a thing as an attempt to win a single year's elections; there is much to point that way. It may catch hold in the nation and give a name to a feeling that has grown through a quarter of a century."

The Chicago *Daily News* took a dim view of the new party by observing that "in its present stage, at least, it is but a pale imitation of the new deal, more logical, more consistent, perhaps, but far less vigorous. About all it can accomplish, it seems to us, is the splitting of the new deal vote in the Wisconsin elections."

Leaders of the Fond du Lac conference set a goal of 50,000 signatures to the petitions to put the new party on the state ballot. Three weeks after that meeting, Progressive party chieftains announced that 120,000 citizens had signed the petitions and that the new party was a reality. The drive to obtain the signatures provided the initial unifying element needed to bring into the party those leaders like Dammann and others who had opposed formation of the party.

In another direction enthusiasm for the new party was shown. Nearly two hundred individuals filed for nomination as the Progressive party candidates for the legislature. Local groups organized tickets for the county offices. For the 10 Congressional district races, 16 Progressive candidates were in the field.

The Democratic state machine was made uneasy by news stories coming from Washington indicating that President Roosevelt was interested in assuring the return of Senator La Follette. National Democratic leaders were quoted in the dispatches as viewing the situation with respect to Wisconsin as "delicate" in view of the desire of the state organization to put a candidate into the field. The President was scheduled to speak at a Democratic party rally in Green Bay during August.

Senator La Follette, meantime, worked out plans for his campaign in the state and released the platform on which he made his appeal for re-election. The platform reiterated a number of older Progressive aims and presented several new ones. La Follette's proposals centered around four major points. First was the proposition that the farmer is entitled to a profit on his investment above the cost of production. Second, La Follette insisted that labor must have the right to organize without interference from employers. He advocated shorter hours, a shorter workweek, and wages that would ensure a comfortable living. Third, the senator advocated control of credit through a government-owned central bank and, fourth, that if private employment failed, the government should step in and guarantee to every able-bodied person willing to work a job at decent wages.

The platform contained statements favoring public ownership of the power industry and railroads, encouragement of co-operatives, taxation based on ability to pay, discontinuance of tax exemption for certain securities, a restoration of civil liberties, and a plank reiterating the Progressive position for nationalization of munitions industries, restriction of power to declare war except in case of invasion by direct popular referendum.

The Oshkosh *Northwestern* stated that "some of the Senator's planks, dealing with the major economic problems, are not new. Many of them are in the direction of plans already conceived and pushed by the Roosevelt Democratic administration under the 'new deal.' Others are so strongly socialistic as to indicate they are intended to attract Socialists to the Progressive party, and interest various classes of radicals."

The Scripps-Howard newspapers characterized La Follette's platform as the "most enlightened and realistic platform we have seen."

With Philip La Follette seeking election as governor, Senator Robert M. La Follette, Jr., making a bid for re-election, and with full tickets of Progressives in nearly every county, politics zoomed in the Badger State that hot, dry summer of 1934. True to earlier predictions from Washington, President Roosevelt did, in his Green Bay address, endorse Senator La Follette's candidacy. He referred to the senator as "my good personal friend" and publicly acknowledged his indebtedness to the senator for his unrelenting efforts to get adequate relief and rehabilitation measures through Congress.

At the November general election the new Progressive party put Philip La Follette back into the governor's office with 373,000 votes, while the Democratic candidate, Governor Schmedeman, received 359,000 votes and the Republican candidate but 173,000 votes. Seventy-five Progressives were elected to the state legislature. Theodore Dammann was re-elected state secretary but Democrats won the lieutenant-governorship and the offices of state treasurer and the attorney generalship.

The biggest vote getter of the new Progressive party was Senator Robert M. La Follette, Jr. He carried 66 of the 71 counties of the state with a total vote of over 440,000—more than twice the combined total received by the Democratic and Republican candidates. Citizens of the Badger State also sent seven Progressives to the House of Representatives.

While the Progressives carried the state again in 1936, the Republican organization bit into the vote for the governorship, although Progressives won handily in other state contests.

Having served three terms as governor, as had his father, Philip La Follette ran for a fourth term in 1938. Many of the governor's policies had stirred Stalwarts and Democrats to protest. The governor had had a noisy and public dispute with the president of the University of Wisconsin, Dr. Glenn Frank. His program of relief was criticized as one which would bankrupt the state, and he was accused of playing politics with old-age pensioners. A number of Progressives looked askance at the governor's attempt to launch a national Progressive party in 1938. They were concerned, too, that the governor in public statements was sharply critical of President Roosevelt.

The political situation was further complicated early in the summer of 1938 by the emergence of a coalition of Democrats and Republicans with the announced purpose of "stopping La Follette" and returning the state to "majority rule." Democrats and Republicans joined forces to run on a coalition ticket. Theodore Dammann ruled the action legal but coalitionists finally decided to run in both Republican and Democratic primaries rather than on a separate ticket. They agreed to run, in the general election, under the label of the party that nominated them.

The coalition candidate for governor on the Democratic ticket was defeated by another Democrat, but coalitionists won the other constitutional offices in the primary. They were all nominated by Republicans and ran as such in the general election. The result was that the Democratic candidate for governor in the November election received only 78,000 votes, while the successful Republican candidate, Julius Heil, received 543,000 votes, and Governor La Follette received 353,000 votes.

Taking advantage of the Wisconsin Corrupt Practices Act by which, under a Supreme Court decision, "voluntary" political organizations are permitted to spend any amount for organizational purposes while the legally constituted State Central Committees are limited, the Republican party began to become aggressive once more. A smoothly working and well-financed full-time voluntary organization took over the functions of running the Republican party in Wisconsin.

When Senator Robert M. La Follette, Jr., conducted his campaign for re-election in 1940, he was up against a determined opposition—determined to retire the La Follettes from public life. The senator's announcement of support for President Roosevelt's bid for a third term made his work no easier. The Republican machine, stimulated by the 1938 victory, had as their candidate a manufacturer of farm machinery from Horicon. La Follette was attacked for "New Dealism" and despite the fact that the state once more, as it had in 1932 and 1936, gave heavy support to President Roosevelt, the November election returns were close. La Follette and his Republican opponent were practically even in the state. When all returns were in, Senator La Follette had been re-elected by 55,000 votes more than Mr. Clausen received. Those 55,000 votes came from Milwaukee. Six years later, in 1946, Senator La Follette lost the nomination by about 5,000 votes that Milwaukee voters gave to his successful opponent, the present Senator Joseph R. McCarthy. The Progressive candidate for the governorship in 1940, Orland S. Loomis, reecived 546,000 votes, while the Republican incumbent, Julius Heil, received 558,000 votes.

In 1942 the Progressive candidate, Orland S. Loomis, was elected governor over Mr. Heil. Well meaning but totally lacking in any understanding of governmental processes, Governor Heil had so disgusted citizens of the state that the vote for Loomis was actually a protest vote against Heil. Before he was inaugurated, Loomis died and Republican Lieutenant Governor Walter S. Goodland was named by the Supreme Court as acting governor to serve out the term to which Loomis had been elected. Goodland had been first elected lieutenant governor in 1938 as a coalition candidate.

As acting governor, Goodland attracted wide Progressive support by his success in fighting off Stalwart attempts to alter the tax laws and by his complete independence of Stalwart machine support. Despite his eighty-odd years, Goodland kept a tight rein on the legislature. His record as acting governor was sufficient to re-elect him by more than 697,000 votes. The Progressive candidate, Adolph Benz of Appleton, received a bare 76,000 votes, slightly more than the minimum required under Wisconsin law for the party to remain on the ballot.

The day after the general election in 1944, Governor Goodland took note of the poor showing Progressives had made and at an informal press conference invited, in all sincerity, the Progressives back into the Republican party.

"They used to be Republicans and that's where they belong today," Goodland said.

The governor's invitation, however, was repudiated by other Republicans, notably the chairman of the voluntary Republican committee, Thomas Coleman.

As the 1946 campaign year loomed, it was evident that Progressives, as a separate party in Wisconsin, were in a hopeless position. Senator La Follette would be up for re-election. Many Progressives openly declared for a return to the Republican party and invitations were reecived to join the Democratic party. A conference of Progressives, held at Portage on March 17, 1946, decided by a 284-to-128 vote to return to the Republican party. Of the 128 votes opposed to the move, 51 were cast to enter the Democratic party and 77 opposed any shift.

The decision was not reached without its poignant moments. Many of the delegates had attended the Fond du Lac conference twelve years before to found the party. The major question, of course, was to which of the two parties to turn. Liberal Democrats of Wisconsin were especially active in their efforts to get Progressives to join with them. They tried to get county delegations to the Portage conference instructed to vote for joining the Democratic party. They had support from national Democratic leaders including members of the Cabinet. Republican leaders in Washington hoped Wisconsin Progressives would return to the fold and heal what they considered a breach between Republicans in one of the important midwestern Republican strongholds.

Individually, Wisconsin Republicans were hopeful that the Progressives would decide to return to the party of their origin but the leadership of the voluntary group was not only cold but openly hostile to the suggestion. The reason for that hostility was largely personal, for the chairman of the group, Thomas E. Coleman, openly admitted to newspaper correspondents his personal detestation of the Progressive movement and especially the La Follettes.

In an effort to forestall a possible return of Progressives or any other group to the Republican party, Coleman had actively supported a proposal, introduced into the 1945 legislature at his request, to alter the primary law to prevent "fence jumping" by candidates for office. The proposal was recognized for what it was, an effort to "stop La Follette." Had it passed, it would have made it impossible for the senator or any other Progressive officeholder to return to the Republican party in the 1946 election campaign. To Coleman's dismay, and despite all his efforts to get the measure approved, Governor Goodland issued a bristling veto message in which he pointed out that in effect the proposed bill would return Wisconsin primary law to the era of the party convention and would prohibit free choice of candidates by the electors. Just as under the Wisconsin law the elector is free to choose his party, Governor Goodland declared that the candidate ought to be permitted to continue his free choice of party. As the governor sized up the situation:

"Parties change their complexion and sometimes do so in a short space of time. These changes occur by reason of changing leadership, and the selection of leaders is the prerogative of the voters.

"Overwhelming majorities are apt to be dangerous in government. Large majorities in the halls of Congress, and in the legislature, often become intolerant and dominating, to the detriment of the people as a whole. Sizeable and aggressive minorities are wholesome in government, just as differences within a party itself make for virility. The inevitable result is higher ideals and finer and cleaner statesmanship."

The governor's veto was sustained and the path back to the Republican party, or a shift to the Democratic party, was still open to Progressives who met at Portage to decide the fate of their party.

Senator La Follette attended the Portage conference but had no plans for active participation in the deliberations. He felt that whatever decision was to be made should be based on majority opinion and not on any desires of his own. Late in the afternoon, after delegates had threshed the matter out and it was a foregone conclusion that the conference would probably vote to return to the Republican party, the senator was asked to state his views. Conference rules limiting each speaker to five minutes were unanimously suspended and in the course of an extemporaneous 45-minute address, La Follette acknowledged that as a political entity the Progressive party was up against the fact, not a theory, that it could no longer serve as the vehicle of Progressive principles. Its position, the senator said, had been weakened by the same forces that had weakened all other minority party movements, the putting aside of domestic issues during the period of the war. He also pointed out that the Progressive party had been weakened because it had not been able, for a variety of reasons, to become national in its scope.

"The Progressive movement," Senator La Follette said, "is more than a form of political organization. It is a vital moving force that transcends personalities, politics, and parties. It is based on the fundamental principle that 'the will of the people shall be the law of the land.' . . .

"We believe strongly in our principles but we are not visionaries. We are practical idealists. The statute books of the last half century contain many laws that we have succeeded in putting there. We have doggedly stood by policies and principles when it was not popular to do so. . . . Good intentions and fine principles are meaningless if they are never put into effect.

"I cannot emphasize too strongly that the decision made here today will not compromise our position on any of the fundamental issues for which we stand."

Taking up the alternatives open to Progressives, Senator La Follette acknowledged that the Democratic party contained in its membership many able, liberal men with whom he had been proud to work during his twenty years in the Senate. He rejected the notion that Wisconsin Progressives should align themselves with the Democratic party.

"In my opinion, the Democratic party is now stalled on dead center. Although it is the party in power, with a clear majority in both houses of Congress, it has been unable to act with sufficient unity of purpose to meet the urgent problems of today. The Democratic party has become so enmeshed in bureaucratic control and intraparty wrangling that some of its leaders are resigning in disgust."

So far as the Democratic party in Wisconsin was concerned, La Follette denounced it as reactionary and declared:

"Only once in fifty years have the Democrats succeeded to power in this state. A party which can succeed only once in half a century doesn't offer much opportunity to translate progressive principles into law.

"The fact is written in past election returns that the Progressive party in the present condition cannot serve as a vehicle for the advancement of progressive principles. It is clear from the record that the Democratic party is not our hope for a liberal instrument for political action."

With respect to the Republican party in Wisconsin, Senator La Follette admitted to no illusions about some elements of the party.

"Nevertheless, I am convinced that the Republican party of Wisconsin offers us the best opportunity for the advancement of Progressive principles. Wisconsin has always been a Republican state—and by this I don't mean a reactionary state. Some of the most farseeing legislation ever enacted anywhere in America was enacted in our state when Progressives were in the Republican party . . .

"By going into the Republican party, we Progressives do not propose to be bound to support reactionary candidates any more than my father or his associates were, or we were in the period before 1934."

The decision to return to the Republican party was regretted by some sincere Progressives who had been all-out supporters of President Roosevelt and his program. The point cannot be proved by specific reference, but it seems quite likely that aside from the immediate practical problem faced by Progressives of the state running for re-election or hoping to enter the election contests, a deciding consideration was based on the fact that traditionally the movement in Wisconsin had been a part of the Republican party.

Senators Wayne Morse of Oregon and George D. Aiken of Vermont were among those who hailed the decision of Wisconsin Progressives as a step in the direction of revitalizing the Republican party. Voluntary Committee Chairman Thomas E. Coleman accused Progressives and the La Follettes of "political hypocrisy." William T. Evjue, editor of the Madison *Capital Times* and chairman of the Fond du Lac conference when the Progressive party was founded, was disappointed and annoyed at what he termed the "opportunism and expediency" of the La Follettes. Governor Goodland declared that the move "clarifies the political atmosphere." But as the Milwaukee *Journal* saw it:

"Wisconsin has for many years been a political enigma to the rest of the nation, a state of delightful confusion. But for the last 12 years we at least knew what we were voting for and what we had after we had voted. Now that short era of political clarity is past. Back we go to 'confusion worse confounded,' as Milton put it."

Senator Robert M. La Follette, Jr., opened his 1946 campaign for re-election on May 19 in an address over a state-wide radio network by announcing that "I am running for re-election to the United States Senate under the same banner that I first ran in 1925 and again in 1928—as a Progressive Republican."

The other major contender for the Republican nomination was Joseph R. McCarthy, a district court judge from Appleton who had opposed Senator Wiley in 1944. McCarthy had the support and endorsement of the voluntary committee and carried on an active, personal campaign all through the state. The Democratic candidate was Howard McMurray, former member of the House of Representatives from a Milwaukee district and a University of Wisconsin lecturer in political science on leave of absence.

Senator La Follette felt, because of the heavy pressure of

legislation at the end of the 79th Congress, that he could not be a "part-time senator and a part-time campaigner." He chose to stay in Washington and seized the opportunity to push through to passage the Congressional reorganization bill. His opponents meantime conducted their campaigns along two general lines.

The Democratic candidate, with a background of one session in the Congress, chose to attack La Follette on the basis of his so-called pre-Pearl Harbor isolationism. Himself assured of the Democratic nomination since he had no opposition, McMurray astonished everyone by in effect entering the fight for the Republican nomination with full-page advertisements in most of the daily newspapers of the state just before election in an attempt to stir up the international-isolation issues against La Follette. McMurray was motivated by the belief that of the two Republican candidates McCarthy would be easier to beat in the general election. McMurray's action, however, did result in alienating a large number of Progressives who would have supported him in the general election had he kept quiet during the primary fight.

Judge McCarthy, Marine veteran of the war who had been on active duty in the Southwest Pacific, traded heavily on his war record. He said many things in many parts of the state about matters that were being settled by Congress. The voluntary committee added its bit to McCarthy's campaign by sponsoring full-page ads attacking La Follette on the ground that his state income tax returns showed that investments he had made in a Milwaukee radio station had paid high dividends in 1944 and 1945. The inference was that the senator had been guilty of using his position and influence in Washington to secure special favors from the Federal Communications Commission. In two directions there was an ironic aftermath to the attack. The voluntary committee had done its best to cultivate the notion that without a job paid for by the taxpayers both the La Follette brothers would starve. Philip La Follette was, and is, a highly successful attorney and lecturer of national repute. So far as the revelations of enormous earnings from the radio station were concerned, it was apparent that the only sin involved was that a La Follette had made some money. The voluntary committee charges against the senator did not even suggest that there was anything wrong with the tax return itself.

Late in February, 1947, citizens of Wisconsin lifted eyebrows over a story out of the State Tax Commission office that the newly elected senator, Joseph R. McCarthy, was in tax difficulties. He had failed to declare as income profits made from the sale of securities while he was in the service and on leave of absence from his judgeship. His explanation for failing to declare such income was that he believed himself not a resident of the state during his military service. Yet he was a candidate for Republican nomination as United States senator from Wisconsin in 1944, during his military service.

It cannot be denied that such tactics hurt La Follette's chances for re-election. The charges in themselves lacked substance—in short, they were phony—but the fact that the senator was not per-sonally present in the state to meet them resulted in spreading doubt.

The shift of Progressives back into the Republican party had its effect in alienating a portion of the pro-Roosevelt labor vote. Finally, Senator La Follette had opportunity for only eight days of personal campaigning in the state before the primary election on August 13. Many citizens understood and sympathized with the senator's decision to stay in Washington until the adjournment of Congress, but many others, grown up to expect to be able to see and hear their candidate in person, felt that they were being slighted. These factors, together with the tactics of the Com-munist-dominated Milwaukee County CIO council in throwing support to the McMurray candidacy and even soliciting votes of its members for McCarthy, added up to La Follette's defeat for the Republican nomination. The reason for the CIO council's curious action in "knifing" one of the stanchest friends organized labor had in the Senate was Senator La Follette's refusal to accept the "Russia-can-do-no-wrong" line. Communist sympathizers in Milwaukee were exacting payment for the senator's foreign rela-tions address to the Senate on May 31, 1945.

The vote was light, scarcely more than 30 per cent of the registered voters cast ballots. During the short time he did have to campaign, Senator La Follette, sensing the general apathy, used what opportunity he had for public speeches to warn voters that failure to exercise their franchise meant a shriveling up of democracy. His opponents criticized the senator for "wasting his time" on such trivial matters!

CHAPTER XV

Champion of Labor

IT WAS FUNDAMENTAL, of course, that relief measures in themselves, no matter how generous, could not supply the solution to the deep-rooted problems that had caused the economic crisis. The problem was to get purchasing power back into the hands of citizens—to get factories back into production. Senator La Follette was in the forefront of the effort to help people get back to work, not on a temporary relief basis, but permanently. With business economy seemingly paralyzed or unwilling to take the venture, Senator La Follette, as has been noted, urged that it was the duty of the federal government to embark on a huge program of public works. The Hoover administration, however, paid scant courtesy to the suggestion. Such pump-priming activity was apparently beneath the dignity of the government. The Roosevelt administration came along and adopted the La Follette program.

The senator was concerned with other matters also. He noted, with mounting concern, the way business interests were using the depression as an excuse to rationalize antilabor practices in an attempt to put a stop to the growth of the organized labor movement in the United States. Until 1932, with the exception of laws relating to railroad employees, the La Follette Seamen's Act of 1915, the establishment of the Department of Labor in 1913, the federal government had not concerned itself with either the regulation or the encouragement of the labor movement. True, the Sherman antitrust law had been interpreted by the Supreme Court as restrictive of strikes when they restrained interstate commerce. But not until the passage of the Norris-La Guardia Anti-injunction Act of 1932, which freed organized labor from the restraints of the Sherman law, did the federal government give much positive encouragement to the movement.

Senator La Follette was sympathetic to the efforts of organized labor to secure what it considered its right to bargain collectively and to enjoy the same protection under the law that employers enjoyed. It had always been his contention that labor was under an unfair disadvantage when it came to bargaining with management. It was his belief that labor should be strengthened by legislative recognition of the right to bargain collectively and to be protected against the restriction used by many employers to deny that right. In the first few years he was in the Senate La Follette had forced investigations into police brutality in the Passaic textile strikes and the Pennsylvania anthracite coal situation. He had enthusiastically supported the Norris-La Guardia Act.

The first of the labor acts passed during the Roosevelt administration was the National Industrial Recovery Act of 1933. Basically the law contained three elements: a relaxation of the anti-trust laws with permission to industrialists to eliminate certain competitive practices; labor provisions that established floors under wages and hours in industry and protection of union organization; a $3,300,000,000 public works program designed to speed re-employment and recovery.

The bill was introduced into the House, where it encountered practically no difficulty. When it came to the Senate it was another matter. Senator Wagner, Administration spokesman for the bill, did his utmost to keep amendments to a minimum. Certain of the senators, however, including Borah and La Follette, were skeptical of what they considered too much relaxation of the anti-trust laws. Borah sponsored and secured adoption of an amendment to prevent combinations in restraint of trade, price fixing, and other monopolistic practices. La Follette introduced and secured adoption of an amendment providing full publicity for income tax returns. Both amendments were adopted by comfortable majorities and the bill received the approval of the Senate.

Both amendments, however, were stricken from the final form of the bill by the conference committee with no reasons stated for the action.

When the conference report came before the Senate for action, La Follette objected to what he termed a complete lack of consideration by House and Senate conferees for the purpose and intent of the Senate amendments. Other senators joined in the objections and spoke at such length that a number of seasoned Washington correspondents reported to their papers that the bloc of western senators seemed intent on filibustering the bill to death. It was one of the last of the major pieces of legislation to be considered by the special session of Congress in that period called "The Hundred Days." The measure was finally approved but by a vote of 46 to 39. As one observer commented, "antitrust policy was by no means a dead issue in American politics."

Nevertheless, Progressive senators joined with La Follette in calling the bill that hatched the Blue Eagle a progressive approach to the economic problems of the nation.

The National Industrial Recovery Act was not destined to last long although it did set the pattern of later labor legislation. As a result of the now famous Section 7 (a), which labor leaders hailed as the Magna Charta of the American labor movement, large segments of industry discovered they had to incorporate into their codes provisions for minimum wages and maximum hours. In a number of the codes, child labor was specifically limited. The act also guaranteed to workers the right to organize and bargain collectively.

Controversies raged over the labor provisions of the act and to settle them the President created a National Labor Board to administer those sections of the law. NRA was killed by the Supreme Court decision in the famous Schecter "dead chicken" case just two years after its passage and at a time when remedial legislation was under consideration.

Moving swiftly to salvage as much as possible of the labor provisions of NRA, Senator Wagner of New York introduced the National Labor Relations bill which was passed by Congress less than two months after the demise of NRA. The act restated the principles of Section 7 (a), listed unfair practices, gave specific directions as to the duties of employers in labor matters, and set up the machinery to determine employee representatives for collective bargaining.

Under NRA organized labor had attracted many new members to its banner. The American Federation of Labor added about a million members. Organized industry did not view with any kindliness this growing movement. Antiunion activities soon developed that caused serious friction and strikes. Many employers breathed a sigh of relief when the Supreme Court killed NRA. But it was only a short sigh, for the National Labor Relations Act of 1935 was much more specific in its language relating to antiunion activities.

Almost before the measure had been signed by President Roosevelt, industrial leaders were shouting that the act was unconstitutional. The most famous of the statements of opposition was the letter issued by the Liberty League which in effect dared the federal government or its agents to try to enforce the law. All the resources of organized industry were marshaled to kill off the National Labor Relations Act. Acting as a sort of Supreme Court for industry, the legal department of the National Association of Manufacturers advised its members and others that the act was unconstitutional and inapplicable to manufacturing industries.

Frequent resort to injunctions to prevent the National Labor Relations Board from putting into effect its findings was made by many industries faced with bargaining with the representatives of unions in their plants. "Independent" company-dominated unions were sponsored to wreck the legitimate labor organizations. Strikes were fomented and violence engineered to arouse a public reaction against the unions. David J. Saposs, chief economist of the Division of Economic Research of the National Labor Relations Board, observed:

"The antiunion employers are operating through a well-organized mass offensive in their fight against organized labor. Forbidden by law to interfere with their employees' right to organize, these employers and their allies have turned from open opposition to indirect, antilabor maneuvers and stratagems in order to fulfill their old objectives . . . They have concentrated their energies on creating public opinion hostile to organized labor.

The increasing skill with which these employers crystallize public opinion places in jeopardy their employees' right to organize and bargain collectively."

Senator La Follette watched with mounting apprehension the growing antiunion feeling. He compared notes with other senators. He discussed the subject with officials in the Department of Labor and especially with those connected with the National Labor Relations Board. The chairman, J. Warren Madden, told him of incidents that had been exposed in examination of cases appealed to the board. The information made Senator La Follette thoughtful.

The brutal beating of Joseph Shoemaker in Tampa, which resulted in his death, had just taken place. A reign of terror spread over Arkansas as lawless bands of men rode through the state flogging defenseless sharecroppers who had dared to assert their rights to organize for the purpose of bargaining collectively with the large landowners. A group of indignant citizens gathered at an informal supper party at the Cosmos Club in Washington to talk the situation over and try to do something about it. Senator La Follette was one of that small group. Those citizens gathered at the Cosmos Club agreed that the gang brutalities about which they were concerned were symptomatic of a serious disease. They agreed that ways and means, somehow, should be found to bring out into the light the underlying causes that resulted in the violence that had made headlines and shocked the nation into an awareness that something was wrong.

As the group discussed the issues a number of plans began to emerge by which their sponsors thought public attention could be called to the well-organized assault on civil liberties and the rights of labor. The trouble, as is so often the case, was that the majority could not agree on one particular plan of action. It began to look as though the well-meaning and earnest efforts of the group might be dissipated in several directions without accomplishing much. At this juncture Senator La Follette suggested that the group decide on nothing until he had had a chance to explore the possibilities of getting a Senate investigation. With a promise "to see what I can do" from La Follette the group agreed to wait before pursuing other plans. After talking with his colleagues and consulting with responsible government officials, Senator La Follette introduced a simple resolution late in March, 1936. That resolution read:

"Resolved, That the Committee on Education and Labor is authorized and directed to make an investigation of violations of the rights of free speech and assembly and undue interference with the right of labor to organize and bargain collectively. The committee shall report to the Senate as soon as practicable the results of its investigations, together with its recommendations for the enactment of any remedial legislation it may deem necessary."

Such was the statement—Senate Resolution 266, 74th Congress, to give its official designation—that resulted in the famous Civil Liberties investigations which lifted the lid off a Pandora's box of ugly violence, brutal and conscienceless violation of civil liberties, and evasion and violation of the law by "blue ribbon" industries that shocked the nation.

As soon as the subcommittee of the Senate Committee on Education and Labor had been appointed by chairman Hugo Black on June 6, 1936, the investigation got under way. Senator Robert M. La Follette, Jr., was named chairman, with Senators Elbert D. Thomas of Utah and Louis Murphy of Iowa as the other members. Senator Murphy died shortly afterward and no additional member was appointed.

Senator Thomas, a quiet, unassuming scholarly man internationally recognized as an expert on labor problems and international relations, and the equally quiet and unassuming Senator La Follette, who had a deep knowledge of labor matters and a broad parliamentary experience, made an ideal team to conduct the investigation. Not once during the four years of the actual hearings and gathering of the mass of evidence did either man resort to any sensational public statement concerning their findings. They were content to let the facts speak for themselves. Apparently steeled to expect sensational disclosures when the committee opened its hearings on California's industrialized agriculture in San Francisco on December 6, 1939, Arthur Eggleston of the San Francisco *Chronicle* expressed surprise and paid the committee a tribute in these words:

"Those who expected a direct, sensational and dramatic assault on men and organizations at the opening Senate civil liberties hearing in San Francisco must have been disappointed.

"This attack on California's and the nation's industrial agriculture problem as it touches labor relations and civil liberties is a sapping operation, a digging in and under and around rather than the sort of dashing storm trooper assault which makes a false front or a solid wall look even more imposing and harder to demolish.

"The hearing here was an education for those who only know congressional investigating bodies through the sort of thing that has gotten the headlines in the past year.

"Perhaps it was unusual in a way, because the committee was dealing with expert testimony and charts and statistics and research setting forth the depersonalized causes of California's most pressing problem.

"Those who have seen the La Follette committee in action, though, say that this is the normal way in which that Senate investigating body operates.

"What Senators La Follette and Thomas heard from the first witness, Dr. Paul S. Taylor, was the considered opinion of perhaps the foremost expert on the subject of industrialized agriculture and migratory farm labor in the country.

"His charts and statistics and conclusions . . . may not make any headlines, perhaps won't even interest those who have already made up their minds that California's trouble arises because there are 'good people and bad people,' 'agitators and soap box artists' and 'respectable, substantial citizens.'

"But the cold unemotional analysis of causes affords the only base upon which there can ever be a truly American solution."

Even before the subcommittee was set up, Senator La Follette and his colleagues on the Education and Labor Committee were literally deluged with letters, telephone calls, and telegrams relating incidents of unfair labor practices and violations of civil liberties they were asked to investigate. From the beginning, because of the magnitude of the job, the committee used the sampling method of getting at the facts. From preliminary surveys and volunteer information, together with the facts gathered by the

National Labor Relations Board, the committee limited itself to what it believed to be typical examples of prevailing practices.

"For example," Senator La Follette explained, "out of a known total of hundreds of detective agencies in the major industrial cities of the country, the committee chose five in its study of labor espionage and strikebreaking services. From a study of these five agencies, it was able to identify approximately 1,500 companies using one or the other of these services. Yet even this staggering total is not comprehensive."

The committee discovered, for instance, that one of the largest of the nation's industrial organizations at one time employed fourteen detective agencies in its labor espionage program. The committee did not, however, rely on complaining witnesses for its evidence of labor espionage and strikebreaking activities. It went with its subpoenas directly to the detective agencies and compelled them to appear and testify concerning their own activities and the meaning of the documents found in their files. It summoned employers, who, from the documentary evidence, utilized such antilabor services, questioned them on the basis of the evidence, and sought explanations and comment.

In investigating activities of strikeguards, company policemen, or the violent episodes occurring in strikes and industrial disputes where there was no documentary evidence, the committee brought witnesses from both sides into the same room, and set their testimony down side by side in the same record. Impartial bystanders and observers were called upon and often witnesses were confronted by photographic evidence and, in one case, a movie newsreel of the incident.

All kinds of "road blocks" were thrown into the path of the committee by those under investigation. Subpoenaed documents were destroyed. Attempts were made to intimidate witnesses. Records were altered. As Senator La Follette told the Senate in an interim report on January 5, 1938, "In various business quarters record-keeping has gone out of fashion and systems of bookkeeping seem to have given way to systematized 'book cooking.'"

Having learned that one organization under subpoena to turn over its records was destroying them, the committee subpoenaed the wastepaper taken from the organization's offices and pieced

together the torn fragments. Witnesses were unwilling and vague
in their testimony. They became victims of amnesia on the witness
stand. In some instances elected law enforcement officers and
other public officials refused point-blank to turn over requested
material. Asked during the course of his examination by the committee to explain why, in the face of evidence showing his organization had spent nearly $900,000 for labor spying and strike-
breaking purposes, there was an almost complete absence of any
records in the corporation files, the head of the labor relations
department said: "I would say the Senate resolution passed in
June would be as good an explanation as any." This official further
testified under oath that he had stripped not only his own files
but those of the president and the general manager of the corporation. Commenting on the practices to keep pertinent data
from the scrutiny of the committee, Senators La Follette and
Thomas bluntly stated:

"These are the methods, not of criminals and sadists, but of
employers high in the esteem of the nation, possessing wealth and
power over millions of men and women; these practices are not
the sporadic excesses of mismanagement, but rather the chosen
instruments of a deliberate design to thwart the concrete expression of the right of collective action by individual workers who,
without that right, have no rights."

In its investigations the committee limited itself to investigation of labor espionage, strikebreaking, industrial munitioning,
and open-shop and antiunion activities financed by industrial
management. Hearings and investigations were conducted over a
period of more than four years. From the beginning they attracted attention. The parade of agents provocateurs and individuals with past criminal records ranging all the way from rape and
murder to petty thievery who admitted doing the bidding of
respectable businessmen, and plant managers who in turn confessed to a widespread conspiracy against permitting citizens to
exercise their constitutional rights and privileges, made the nation
gasp.

The industries and names involved at first caused many to
wonder if the investigation was not merely another example of
"headline grabbing" for the sake of a sensation. Those who were

disclosed as being in the forefront of the assault on civil liberties complained that such tactics would create disrespect and shake confidence in the essential soundness of the American industrial situation. The frantic attempts to bring into question the evidence of the committee failed for the simple reason that it did not indulge in mud-slinging or smearing attacks. It stuck to the job of bringing out testimony and evidence that was unassailable. It was after the facts, not hearsay. The hearings soon took on the aspect of a continuing indictment of certain segments of industrial management such as American industry had never been subject to before.

Behind the public hearings that produced much dramatic news—typical of which was the almost casual manner by which Senator Thomas secured an admission from a Pinkerton operative that he and a number of others had been ordered to shadow and eavesdrop on the federal conciliator Edward F. McGrady, called into a strike situation in Toledo, Ohio—a staff of able people carried on field investigations, examined thousands of documents, letters, interoffice memos, and took depositions which were used as the basis of questioning in the public hearings.

Eighty-one volumes contain the results of the investigation, the most thorough of its kind ever conducted into the labor policies of industrial America. The considered judgment of the committee, after careful study of the evidence and exhibits, is contained in twenty-odd reports to the Senate. Senators La Follette and Thomas pulled no punches in their reports. In its investigations into the antiunion activities of "Little Steel" the committee was suddenly confronted with the Memorial Day, 1937, incident at the South Chicago plant of the Republic Steel Corporation. Ten strikers were killed and many others suffered from police beatings and the effects of tear gas used to dispel the "mob."

"The cause of and responsibility for the encounter has been the subject of sharp dispute by the police, the union, and the public," the committee reported. "The police have charged the demonstrators with a conspiracy to capture the Republic Steel plant by violent means and assert that the casualties were a regrettable but necessary incident to their efforts to disperse a riotous mob. The union, on the other hand, accuses the police of a brutal attack upon a group of citizens in the exercise of their constitutional right peacefully to assemble and picket."

After careful study of the evidence and hearing the testimony of the police, strikers, and onlookers, Senators La Follette and Thomas joined in the conclusion, given to the Senate on July 22, less than sixty days after the incident:

"We are of the opinion . . . that if the police had permitted the parade to pass down Burley Avenue and in front of the plant gate, and under a proper escort, the day would have passed without violence or disorder . . . From all the evidence we think it plain that the force employed by the police was far in excess of that which the occasion required. Its use must be ascribed to gross inefficiency in the performance of police duty or a deliberate effort to intimidate the strikers.

"We conclude that the consequences of the Memorial Day encounter were clearly avoidable by the police. The action of the responsible authorities in setting the seal of their approval upon the conduct of the police not only fails to place the responsibility where responsibility properly belongs but will invite the repetition of similar incidents in the future."

Equally forthright and blunt was criticism of use by industry of sickening gas and other munitions in strikes. The use of private police systems in Harlan County, Kentucky, was presented in all its naked brutality. Residents of that unhappy region were denied the rights of free speech and assembly by an open reign of terror with irresponsible bands of thugs roaming at will through the territory threatening strangers on the public highways. Citizens were denied their right to entertain in their homes guests of their own choosing. Even murder was condoned by public officials of the county with the connivance of the coal company managers.

The committee also turned its attention to the labor policies of industrialized agriculture. John Steinbeck's *Grapes of Wrath* dramatized an aspect of the problem that Senators La Follette and Thomas went to California to study. They discovered that the Associated Farmers of California, Inc., was a blind behind which operated a ruthless conspiracy to prevent the exercise of civil liberties, not only of agricultural workers but of workers in the urban centers. The committee disclosed a record of labor oppression that used every device of repression known.

"That record," the committee pointed out, "also constitutes a warning to the organized trade-union movement that the security of its rights in urban industrial areas may depend to a considerable extent upon the security of the rights of those who labor in the fields and farm factories outside the city gates. A nation cannot exist 'half slave, half free.'"

In all its previous reports the committee had been content to consider only the specific problem under examination. But in one of the final reports, on the Associated Farmers of California, Inc., published just eight years after introduction of the Senate resolution that gave life to the Civil Liberties investigations, the committee members suggested the broader implications of its findings. They said:

"Apart from the organized labor groups, those who believe in democracy and place a store by the freedom of individuals to organize and bargain collectively with their employers must recognize an old struggle in new surroundings. That struggle is the effort to protect the rights of those who work in an industrialized society, whether urban or rural, whether in the factory or on the farm, to band themselves together and bargain with their employers. Defenders of civil rights must recognize the march of economic events; wherever and whenever the 'family farm,' where employer-employee relationships were inevitably conditioned to man-to-man relationships, gives way to a system of 'industrialized agriculture,' the rights of rural workers must be treasured and protected by all who value their own freedom."

The antiunion propaganda activities of the employers' associations was scrutinized by the committee. The disclosures had the same immediate effect on the determined efforts of a powerful minority of American industry to eliminate organized labor as the throwing of a powerful floodlight would have on the safebreaking activities of a robber.

The campaign was stopped cold.

In a radio address over a Washington, D. C., station on February 14, 1938, Senator La Follette emphasized the purpose and aim of the investigation. He discussed the growth in union membership and hailed it as an indication of health for American democracy.

"Labor when well organized," he told his radio audience, "helps to advance progressive social legislation. In those communities where labor organizations are strongest we find democracy advanced and civil liberties most freely exercised.

"There are some people who regard this recent increase in union membership with feelings of alarm. Many of them are neither ultra conservative nor nonunion employers of labor but persons who, quite honestly and sincerely, feel uneasy at the prospect of growing organization among the ranks of industrial workers. In many cases this feeling is due to the fact that these people do not realize that the growth and development of unions depend upon the exercise of two of our most cherished rights—the right of free speech and the right of assembly. Those rights are in the Constitution and to fear the results of their exercise is to fear democracy itself."

In May, 1939, Senators La Follette and Thomas introduced an Oppressive Labor Practices Act to outlaw the use of labor spies and labor espionage, use of strikebreakers and strikebreaking agencies, use of privately paid armed guards off the premises of an employer, and the possession and use of industrial munitions such as tear gas and submachine guns. Representative Reuben T. Wood of Missouri introduced an identical measure in the House. Senator La Follette warned against acceptance of the apparent reform of employers and their public repudiation of the practices exposed by the Civil Liberties investigations.

"It is easy to overestimate the deterrent effects flowing from the subcommittee's investigations," he said. "Temporary publicity can never take the place of permanent and enduring legislation."

He reported that, despite the wide publicity given to the practices by the investigation, the Civil Liberties Committee was constantly receiving complaints from all parts of the country that the antiunion drive was continuing. He urged that the bill was necessary to provide for some continuing medium of safeguarding civil liberties.

La Follette outlined the course of the investigations in introducing the bill and, while not making any particular point of the matter, announced that as a result of the inquiries evidence of tax evasions had been turned over to the Bureau of Internal Revenue on which the bureau had recovered nearly a quarter of a million dollars. He called attention to the fact that the investigations had established that American industry had spent millions of dollars on oppressive labor practices. The committee had figures for the period 1933–1937 of firms who had used espionage and strikebreaking services for which they paid nearly ten million dollars.

"The money of the stockholders has made the labor spy racket and the strikebreaking racket lucrative fields for the crook and the gangster. Money paid to such characters is money spent to create industrial strife, not to prevent it." La Follette summed up the purpose of the measure in these words:

"Civil liberties are under attack. In many countries today, the black shadow of dictatorship hangs over the lives of ordinary citizens. The press is the voice of dictatorship in these countries; the radio is controlled by the censor; the right to be secure in one's home is no longer respected. Free trade unions have been abolished. The ordinary citizen lives in fear of the concentration camp and the armed police force of the dictator. The rights of free thought, free speech, free assembly have given way to the rule of autocratic force and the despoliation of civil liberties.

"But in America, democracy has gone resolutely forward. The national labor policy adopted by the Congress has extended democratic principles and procedures from the political to the economic sphere. Today millions of workers share through collective bargaining in the making of decisions that affect their lives. The ballot box is replacing the machine gun as a means of settling industrial disputes. Industrial workers are being granted the rights of free men in a free country." The Senator closed his appeal for affirmative action with this warning:

"There are forces within the country which openly clamor for the destruction of civil liberties through the perversion of governmental power. These forces are encouraged by the existence of private tyrannies maintained by private armed forces and by private gestapos. Other democracies which have permitted private armies to operate no longer exist. The price of liberty is eternal vigilance. Let us not let evils continue to flourish through our own neglect."

The Senate passed the bill on May 27, 1940, but it was never acted upon by the House. The bill was a victim of the antiunion drive that seized upon the national defense program to demand "industrial peace" in terms of restrictive labor legislation. Proposals—later incorporated into the Smith-Connally Act—were even then being made to give the President powers to take over defense plants during a strike or even the threat of a strike. Work stoppages of whatever nature and from whatever causes were being given wide publicity as "strikes against defense."

Senator La Follette, however, was not deterred by this new twist against labor. Aggressively and at every opportunity he called for the democratic solution to the problem. He knew full well that the key to opposition of the legislative statement upholding collective bargaining rights and the setting of restraints against the use of force to break unions lay in the thought he had expressed to the Senate when he had said:

"The national labor policy adopted by the Congress has extended democratic principles and procedures from the political to the economic sphere."

La Follette recognized that ingrained habits, both of action and of thought, were hard to dislodge. In the course of an address in New York on May 9, 1941, the senator took note of "a blitzkrieg against the legitimate aims of labor by a triumvirate of antiunion employers, antiunion legislators, and antiunion organs of 'public opinion'" because of the strikes in industry. He called attention to the fact that comparative figures proved that less time was lost in defense industries in 1940 because of strikes than in the last peacetime year, 1939. He pointed to the facts, as presented by the Bureau of Labor Statistics, that industrial accidents caused four times as much lost time and illness among workers caused six times as much lost time as did the strikes. He traced the fate of free trade unionism in the countries then under the heel of dictatorship and pointed out that organized unionism was the first to suffer.

"Our first concern must be to prevent this pattern from being fastened on American labor in this critical hour of decision.

"Hence, labor's rights and national defense are inseparably linked; they are mutually supporting, damage to either in a democracy may be fatal to both; the furtherance of each strengthens both.

"Those who honestly and sincerely believe that the true purpose of national defense is the preservation of democracy in the United States will be vigilant to oppose and condemn those within our borders who by private deed or public law would weaken or undermine that great citadel of modern industrial democracy—the civil rights of men and women of labor."

In blunt, forthright language, Senator La Follette condemned the antilabor movement as expressed in the legislative proposals then before Congress.

"We cannot save democracy by destroying it at home. It would be one of the tragic ironies of history if in the process of preparing for the defense of our national democracy, we blindly sacrificed it in a legislative lynching bee . . .

"The passage of these bills would be the first token of appeasement to the dictators, at home and abroad. Think of it!—the destruction of the precious civil liberties of the men and women of labor who must work unceasingly and effectively in the dark days ahead to forge the delicate instruments of national defense. The stupid folly of this proposed Congressional hari-kari would indeed be a tribute to the dictators and their philosophy; a confession that democracy cannot survive a crisis; that free men cannot outproduce slaves."

That address was heard by over five hundred citizens representing both the AFL and the CIO who were gathered to pay tribute to Senator La Follette. At that dinner the Workers Defense League presented to La Follette a bronze plaque "For Distinguished Service to Labor's Rights" as chairman of the Civil Liberties Committee.

Senator La Follette went back to the Senate, where the Selective Service Age Deferment bill was under consideration. Attempts made to incorporate a number of antiunion provisions were strenuously and successfully fought off by the senator. He warned, apropos of a provision to grant power to the President to take over defense plants where a strike existed or was threatened:

" . . . a fixed bayonet behind every worker will not increase defense production. The abrogation of inherent rights, whether of labor or management, will not produce more guns, ships, tanks and planes. It will produce only bitterness and discontent. . . ."

So successful was Senator La Follette's plea that he got Senate acceptance of an amendment to the Selective Service bill declaring that complete co-operation between government, management, and labor "can best be achieved by the wholehearted acceptance of the principles of collective bargaining and the recognition of the rights of employees to designate representatives of their own choosing, for the purpose of collective bargaining, without interference through unfair or oppressive labor practices."

All through the war years Senator La Follette led the small but active and influential group of congressmen who stood as sentinels to oppose any weakening of the broad governmental policy as enunciated in the National Labor Relations Act, the Walsh-Healy measure, wage and hour legislation, and other measures designed to provide that extension of political freedom to the economic field. As his father before him, Senator Robert M. La Follette, Jr., did not permit the exigencies of the moment to becloud the fundamental issues as he saw them. He carried on his opposition to the Hamiltonian doctrine that identified the well-being of the nation with the well-being of the business groups at the top.

In the midst of the debate on the measure that finally became known as the Smith-Connally Act, La Follette introduced a new Oppressive Labor Practices Act. He charged that antilabor interests sought "not to prevent strikes in war industries but to remove and relax the gentle restraint of the National Labor Relations Act so that union busting may proceed under cover of the war effort."

The new bill contained all the provisions of the former measure and included several classes of conspiracy by employers or employer associations to deny collective bargaining rights to employees. He reiterated his previously expressed beliefs on the subject when he told the Senate:

"This bill will symbolize as nothing else labor's stake in the democracy we are striving to defend from totalitarian aggression. I suggest that such an assurance is needed now to reassure the men who labor that the nation is not going to yield to that clamorous minority which in Congress and out for the past six years has been seeking to subvert, eliminate, or substantially weaken the federal guarantee of collective bargaining."

Despite vigorous efforts on his part, the bill was never reported out of committee.

When peace came in 1945 and industry was reconverting to a peacetime basis to meet the huge backlog of demands for consumers' goods that had built up during the war, citizens of the nation were suddenly aware that getting back to peacetime production was not an easy task. The nation seemed to be in the grip of a whole series of strikes in key industries that threatened to tie up the whole nation. One of the most notable of the strikes involved the General Motors Corporation. The number of workers affected, the plants closed down all over the United States, and the length of the dispute—over three months—were in themselves newsworthy.

"A labor strike is a symptom of industrial illness," Senator La Follette said in February, 1946. "Too many people are concerned only with the symptom." The underlying causes of the labor-management trouble were traceable to a number of causes, in La Follette's opinion. Speaking of the removal of wage controls and abolishment of the War Labor Board, the "carry-back" and "amortization" provisions of tax laws enacted to help businesses caught between the war and the time they could turn out peacetime goods once more, the relief from excess profits taxation, the Wisconsin senator characterized them as a giant subsidy to business.

"Congress has unwittingly stacked the cards heavily in favor of management," he said.

Other factors, according to La Follette, included the feeling of workingmen generally that they had been held down during the war but in the face of a vacillating policy on the part of the Administration and an almost certain increase in living costs believed that the time had come to demand more pay.

At a great rally in New York City on February 26, 1946, to

raise funds to aid General Motors strikers and their families, Senator La Follette reiterated and reaffirmed his position with respect to the interdependence of our constitutional liberties and the rights of labor. He suggested that in spite of the evidence of the Civil Liberties Committee there was still the spirit of intransigent opposition to organized labor on the part of a minority of employers. He denied the classic economic theory that identified the prosperity of the nation with the business classes when he said:

"Industrialists should recognize that it is good business to give their workers decent standards of living. The prosperity of industry, and that of farmers and service groups as well, depends largely on the prosperity of the worker. Labor is part of the mass market on which mass production rests.

"Farm prices and farm income are paid largely out of labor's share of industrial income. Historically, American industry has prospered when labor made its gains. Increased purchasing power, often very reluctantly given or wrested from industry, has been the life blood of our economic system."

La Follette warned his New York audience that punitive and restrictive measures enacted against labor were not the answer to the current unrest.

"Strike down the rights of labor and you have struck a major blow in wrecking the freedom of speech, and all the other liberties we cherish. . . .

"These self-evident truths should give warning to those who would extend the federal power to curb alleged abuses of labor. A temporary victory resulting in a curtailment of labor's fundamental rights will pave the way for governmental encroachment on the rights of management. Permanent regulation of salaries, profits, and prices will be a logical outcome of federal policies that place labor in a strait-jacket. . . .

"The only real answer is full and free collective bargaining, in an atmosphere permeated with mutual confidence instead of mistrust. The spotlight of public opinion must be turned on those who refuse to bargain in good faith."

The progressive position on labor legislation, which Senator Robert M. La Follette, Jr., symbolized for so many people, rests in the final analysis on two propositions. The first is the proposition that, as the senator believes with an unshakable and fierce sincerity, the American democratic way of life can be made to work —that it can provide political freedom, religious liberty, and equal economic opportunity to all citizens. The second proposition, already noted in this discussion of labor, is the progressive denial of the Hamiltonian theory of national industrial prosperity and the aggressive espousal of the view that economic stability is based on the welfare of the broad base of industrial workers, small businessmen, and farmers.

Those tenets, supported by facts and inferences logically drawn from the facts, sustained Senator La Follette throughout his public career. They were not just a set of convenient and pretty-sounding phrases to be trotted out on occasion. They were a refinement and application of the same principles for which his father had fought throughout his career. They were, and are, the present-day expression of the Wisconsin Idea which the elder La Follette hammered out in his fight against the bosses, the railroads, the trusts. Civil liberties, unemployment, collective bargaining, equal economic opportunity, are the names of the issues Young Bob has faced. And with the new issues came a restatement of the principles that have come to be so closely linked with progressivism.

CHAPTER XVI

Taxes, Business, and Agriculture

ONE OF THE VITAL ASPECTS of a democratic form of government is its pragmatic approach in searching for the solutions to problems of society. True, there are times when the purely practical aspects of a given problem seem to outweigh social factors and sometimes the solutions arrived at and incorporated in the statute books favor one group at the expense of another.

The method is slow at times and there have been, and no doubt will be in the future, occasions when our system has seemed to falter. Certain dictators of recent memory made the fatal mistake of assuming this characteristic to be a weakness, a sign of decadence, a crack in our armor that would make it simple for those dictators to overwhelm democracy and give them the world to play with just as the movie actor Charlie Chaplin did in an unforgettable bit of ironic pantomime in *The Dictator.* The method of democracy at times makes individual reformers impatient. They see and feel an immediate need and are willing to compromise the fundamental basis of our government just to meet an immediate felt want.

These observations are commonplace yet they are important in understanding the significance of the motivation of those men and women in our public life who have come to be known as Progressives. In the first place, the true Progressives have an unquenchable faith in democracy as a way of life. They are not the "yes, but—" sort of individuals who pay lip service to democracy yet, for fear of sacrificing some privilege which they have come to look upon as a "property right," refuse to grant that political freedom also means freedom to enjoy equal economic opportunity. The Progressive is a firm believer in, and defender of, the doctrine of freedom as expressed in the Constitution which, as he or she interprets it, means economic as well as political freedom together with the unquestioned right to the full personal exercise of the civil rights of free speech, petition, assembly, and religious liberty.

True Progressives have a deep respect for the lessons of history but waste no time in nostalgic murmurings about "the good old days." They are practical and realistic. They know that we live in a present and look to a better future for ourselves and our children. The Progressive is a practical idealist. He is not content with things as they are but realizes that even modest suggestions for improvement arouse antagonisms that take patience to overcome. Thus, one of the functions of the Progressive is to keep reminding us of the problem of the democratic state. That problem, the one of keeping democracy alive and working, has so many facets that the constant Progressive reiteration of the same fundamental concepts applied to every matter calling for legislative action has caused shortsighted individuals to dismiss Progressives as scolding bores. They lose battles but bounce right back into the fray.

The reason they keep coming back is to be found in what they fight for. Their battles are over practical matters—taxes levied on the basis of ability to pay, the right of labor to bargain collectively with employers, the principle that government has a responsibility for the economic welfare of the country, public ownership where it can accomplish social objectives that lie beyond the power of private initiative, fostering those elements in our economy which make for healthy business competition, to mention only a few—those matters which in the last analysis are fundamental if the dreams of the Founding Fathers for a truly working democracy are to be realized. There is no tortured use of language in the Progressive's platform. He borrows from no foreign ideology to give his position an intellectual aura. His position and outlook is as American as baseball and

U.S. Highway 40. The Progressive goes all the way in applying his program.

The goal for America, as the Progressive sees it, was set long years ago by the men who established this nation. He has accepted the challenge of helping all of us to achieve that goal.

It must be kept in mind, as has already been pointed out, that progressivism as such is not a program that is the exclusive property of one political party. It is true that the country has made notable social and economic gains in recent years under Democratic leadership. The nation also underwent progressive changes under President Woodrow Wilson. Both Wilson and Roosevelt made tremendous contributions and left great heritages to American democracy. Yet, without detracting one bit from their positive contributions, it cannot be denied that they came to leadership at times when the progressive viewpoint was in the ascendancy. They possessed the imagination to take advantage of the solid groundwork already laid down by other Progressives.

Progressive concepts and programs become accepted without being recognized as the "radical" principles over which long and bitter battles have been waged in the past. The leadership of a Republican-dominated 80th Congress, faced with the problems of world leadership as well as mapping the course of domestic affairs that led to peacetime pursuits, discovered that what it thought was a mandate to "turn back" was nothing of the kind. The exuberant, postelection promises of Republican leaders for a 20 per cent "across the board" reduction in income taxes, for instance, had to be considerably toned down. The heaviest opposition to such a program was expressed in the Progressive principle of taxation on ability to pay which the Knutson proposal frankly ignored. Further, Republican leaders learned, what Progressives had long been contending, that the economic and political well-being of the nation is inseparably linked to a sound policy of taxation.

Representative Albert J. Engel of Michigan warned his fellow Republicans against the policy of giving tax relief only at the top and emphasized his point by quoting Treasury reports that over 53,000,000 persons in the nation had incomes of $2,500 or under. He told Republican members of Congress that they were wrong in the theory that "if you will only give tax relief to the man on top the benefits will trickle or percolate down to the little fellow." Representative Engel, by no means a radical or even accused of mild progressive leanings, declared that increased purchasing power must be in the hands of the lower income groups in order to be effective. "No profit system can survive without profits," he said, and there is no profit in a pair of overalls, a suit or a dress that the low income group does not buy."

That was exactly the argument Senator Robert M. La Follette, Jr., and the other "radical" Progressives were using before 1929. Throughout his senatorial career, La Follette never once deviated from that position. Even during his fight to secure adequate federal assistance for the unemployed, he fought for a tax program that would more adequately and more fairly spread the costs of government. He never ceased preaching the doctrine that a comprehensive overhauling of the federal tax structure was long overdue. He constantly objected to the unseen taxes, which hit the lower income groups hardest. Taxes, in his judgment, should be "visible" and based on ability to pay, not on the ease with which they might be collected. He frankly advocated a broadening of the income tax base to include more citizens.

Careful study of the voluminous record of Senator La Follette's activities in behalf of an adequate, modern tax structure indicates that the Progressive economic position, as expressed by La Follette, was to keep capital flowing in a stable, orderly manner and not permit it to be siphoned off into nonproductive, speculative ventures that led ultimately to the paralysis of depression. Basic in La Follette's economic thinking was that the changing emphasis of national life demanded a new outlook. The frontier was no longer available to offer the individual a chance for a new start or to offer new economic opportunities for capital. As he stated in an address in Washington, D.C., on March 8, 1937, at a meeting of Labor's Non-Partisan League:

"The frontier is gone. When a man steals or exploits property rights today he is sinning not only against nature and the principle of Christianity but against his neighbor as well. This Nation is no longer a loose-jointed, overgrown agricultural community made up of more or less self-sufficient, independent units. America of this day is a complex, interdependent society in which the production and distribution of wealth is a very complex business."

La Follette and the Progressives have stanchly supported the concept of the American free enterprise system. If democracy is to survive, competition must be fostered. The independent, small businessman must have the same opportunity for goods and markets as the larger units of business and industry. The monopolistic practices of marketing restrictions, price fixing, control of patents, licensing agreements which artificially restricted production and kept prices high, must be prohibited.

The farmer must receive a far greater share of the wealth he creates.

There must be greater purchasing power for the lower income groups, to provide which there must be jobs at decent wages.

That set of principles, an extension into the realm of economics of the same fundamental concepts that motivated Senator La Follette in his struggles to get aid for the unemployed during the depression and to get a fair deal for organized labor, naturally did not go unchallenged, even in the friendly atmosphere of the Roosevelt administration.

The "knockdown, drag-out" aspect of the fight put up by the progressive group led by Senator La Follette reached the pitched-battle stage with the debate on the 1940 Revenue Act. As submitted to the Senate, the bill carried no excess profits tax provision. Senator La Follette offered an amendment assessing an excess profits tax based on the provisions of the 1918 act. He called attention to the fact that during the years of the first World War the Treasury collected about 45 per cent of its revenues from the excess profits tax. La Follette reminded the the Senate that he had long advocated the broadening of the income tax base and had carried on a continuing fight for revision of the tax structure on the basis of ability to pay. Without an adequate excess profits tax provision, the bill, according to the Wisconsin Progressive, was both inadequate and unfair. It hit the wrong people.

"I cannot see how Congress can justify in this emergency reaching the long arm of the Federal Treasury into the pockets of the lower income groups by broadening the tax base. I do not see how Congress can justify reaching the long arm of the Treasury into the pockets of the people who pay the excise taxes and at the same time refuse to increase the taxes upon those corporations which, directly and indirectly, will profit by the very expenditures which are made possible in part by the taxes which these low-income group families are required to pay."

La Follette urged the Senate that the time had come to put into effect, as a permanent part of the tax structure, an excess profits tax. Profits were large and getting larger. He recalled that every time such a proposal had been made during the time he was a member of the Senate, refusal to act was based on the excuse that it was a complex subject and could wait for the general revision of the law. The Senate approved La Follette's amendment providing for an excess profits tax but it was rejected by the conference committee with the promise that an excess profits tax law would be enacted as a separate measure. La Follette characterized the measure as passed as a sham and a delusion. "The taxes it imposes, as well as those it failed to enact, mark it as one of the most unjust and ill-advised measures put on the statute books in a long time."

An excess profits tax was passed by Congress in September, 1940, which Senator La Follette characterized as "a two-headed monstrosity that ought to be put in a Believe It or Not Odditorium rather than on the statute books." He objected to the option given corporations under the bill by which they could pay according to a plan based on profits in relation to invested capital or on a plan based on earnings in excess of the average net earnings for the years 1936 to 1939 inclusive.

In a stinging minority report submitted to the Senate during debate on the measure, La Follette called attention to the fact that in hearings on the bill much of the testimony brought out the fact that a majority of corporations were willing to pay their just taxes but objected to a measure that gave undue advantage to competitors. He presented statistics and examples showing conclusively that the optional provisions for figuring excess profits taxes gave to the older, well-established corporations a distinct advantage over newer concerns. On this point La Follette wrote:

"One can agree that it is not the purpose of a tax bill to equalize competitive conditions. But it is undeniable that tax bills should not distort existing competitive conditions and place unwarranted tax handicaps upon one class of corporations as opposed to another, thereby creating an indefensible competitive advantage in favor of the latter. The objection to the committee amendment is not that it does not equalize existing competitive conditions. Rather, the objection is that the committee amendment in and of itself creates new and far reaching competitive advantages."

Senator La Follette's fight to secure a sound taxation program, not only for the war emergency but for the future, reached a climax in the debate on the Revenue Act of 1941. That measure combined in one package all the defects against which La Follette had fought. Even Administration leaders responsible for the bill were apologetic and rationalized their support on the ground that the need for revenues was critical. Senator George, chairman of the Senate Finance Committee, admitted in opening the debate on the measure that "it is not a perfect measure." As a member of the Finance Committee, Senator Vandenberg submitted his own minority report on the bill.

"I shall reluctantly support the bill, if at all," the Michigan senator reported, "only because any bill could not possibly be worse than no bill at all, in view of the truly desperate fiscal emergency which the Federal Treasury confronts."

After comment on the necessity for additional revenues and admitting that it could not be denied that there were dangerous and discriminatory taxes included in the bill, Senator Vandenberg declared:

"My complaint against this pending measure is its failure to go to fundamentals in meeting this emergency . . . We have only started to pay in this pending bill. And we have started in the same old, familiar, habitual way—namely, by picking out the easiest and most convenient tax targets and giving them another blast."

Senator Bennett Champ Clark of Missouri could not find it in his heart to praise the bill although he announced his intention of voting for it. Almost sadly he characterized the bill "as unscientific, haphazard and patchwork a measure as it would have been possible to devise in this time of great national crisis."

It remained for Senator La Follette to give the bare-knuckles treatment to the bill. He minced no words.

"The pending revenue bill is a vicious assault on the rank-and-file taxpayer. It is inadequate, inequitable, and in my opinion, indefensible. It conforms to no standards of justice or fairness. It 'soaks' the poor while confirming, protecting, and entrenching the corporate wealth and power engendered by the defense program. It levies the major share of the costs of 'all-out' defense on those who have the least property to protect and those who have the least ability to pay.

"The bill is a hodgepodge of inconsistencies, with no underlying principle of taxation whatsoever, except that, like many previous tax bills, it 'plucks the goose that squawks the least.' Unfortunately, the small individual taxpayer who will dig deep in his pockets to pay these bills has not made himself heard."

With that opening blast, Senator La Follette confined the major part of his opposition to three aspects of the bill—the excess profits tax, estate and gift taxes, and the lowering of personal income tax exemptions. In his opinion, the most serious defect of the bill was failure to tax excess profits adequately or fairly.

"The government is pumping billions of defense dollars into our industrial structure. Huge profits are accruing to industry. Generally speaking, the initial and primary beneficiaries are the corporations. It is not punitive taxation—it is just good common-sense fiscal policy supported by expert economic, as well as layman, logic—that a lion's share of all excess and defense profits be siphoned back into the government Treasury. To the extent that such profits are diverted from the general income stream, the dangers of inflation are accordingly reduced. The excess profits tax should be a major item of our tax structure."

La Follette called attention to his arguments of the year

before regarding the necessity for a truly adequate excess profits tax. He read into the record table after table of figures to support his contention that not only was there a tremendous profit being taken by American industry as the result of defense and war activity, but that it was well able to pay a much larger share of the tax burden than was being proposed.

During the debate, Senator Lister Hill of Alabama asked La Follette if he was going to introduce an amendment to provide for adequate excess profits taxes. Hill reminded the Senate of the "able argument" the Wisconsin senator had presented the year before and expressed the hope that an amendment would be offered. La Follette, however, told Senator Hill that it was not his intention to offer such an amendment because he was convinced that it would not be accepted.

On the basis that estate and gift taxes were not bearing their fair share of the burden since the personal income tax deductions were being lowered, La Follette submitted an amendment which reduced exemptions on estates and gifts and at the same time increased the taxes. His amendment was defeated.

Senator La Follette coupled his opposition to lowered personal income exemptions to the increases made in the excise taxes. His previous position favoring reduction of personal income tax deductions, he reminded the Senate, had been predicated on the desirability of reducing the indirect excise taxes that bore heavily on low-income groups. In this instance, however, he vigorously opposed such action because Congress had seen fit to increase the excise taxes. He said:

"When we go down into these income levels we are taxing persons who are already paying substantial sums in the form of excise taxes, sales taxes, and state and local taxes. We are taxing them at the expense of their standard of living.

"Taxes which mean a reduction of an already unconscionably low standard of living are proposed to be levied, while fat profits from defense spending get off with only a relatively minor share of the total burden . . .

"It is my firm conviction that the pending bill, which makes an intolerable tax structure infinitely worse, should be rejected and thoroughgoing revision of the tax structure based on the sound principle of ability to pay should be immediately undertaken," La Follette concluded.

At the close of the two-day debate and with Senate approval a foregone conclusion, Senator La Follette once more gained the floor and said:

"Mr. President, I find myself in such a position that I cannot support this bill, and therefore, although I would naturally be afforded a position on the conference committee, being of such rank in the minority representation on the Finance Committee, I beg to be relieved of such duty, since I cannot support the bill, nor can I support the amendments adopted by the majority of the committee and the amendments adopted by the Senate. In justification for this extraordinary position, I ask unanimous consent that the individual minority views which I filed on the bill be printed in the *Record* at this point in body type as a part of my remarks."

The Revenue Act of 1941 was passed by a vote of 67 to 5. La Follette was joined by Senators Langer, McCarran, Nye, and Clark of Idaho.

During the war years Senator La Follette continued his efforts to obtain a sound tax program. He warned that failure to tax war profits would provide the basis for a dangerous inflation. As he expressed the idea in the course of the debate on the tax bill before the Senate on May 14, 1943:

"It is a blind man, Mr. President, who cannot see that one of the principal factors that produced totalitarianism in this world was the uncontrolled inflation that accompanied certain events in Europe . . . There is no nation in all history that has preserved the liberties of the people under a condition of runaway, uncontrolled inflation.

"In my opinion, we do not discharge our full responsibility to the men who are fighting on all the far-flung battlefronts if we do not have the courage to tax heavily enough to maintain a sound economy."

Joining with other members of the Senate Finance Committee, Senator La Follette took an active part in the framing of the law for renegotiation of war contracts. His active participation in the conference committee to which the bill was referred insured the inclusion of provisions by which the government ultimately saved billions of dollars.

The same economic philosophy that had sustained Senator La Follette in his fighting efforts to secure fairer and more adequate tax legislation gave him his basic arguments in his enthusiastic support of President Roosevelt over the struggle with the Supreme Court in 1937. As the Supreme Court in decision after decision struck down as unconstitutional the legislation passed by Congress to establish a better economic balance, and by that action brought the efforts of the government to alleviate the depression to a standstill, President Roosevelt suggested legislation increasing the number of Supreme Court justices to fifteen. Pointing out that it had been only in recent years that the court had used to any extent its presumed power to declare legislation unconstitutional, Senator La Follette declared in a radio address on February 13, 1937:

"Our Founding Fathers never intended the Supreme Court to be the dictator of this nation. Not a word in the Constitution sanctions it. But when the court substitutes for the will of the people of this country its own will; when it supplants the prevailing economic theory with its own smug theory of days gone by; when it decrees that it is beyond the power of the people to meet the national needs—then it has become a dictator and we have succumbed to a fascist system of control which is inconsistent with fundamental principles upon which our government is founded."

The central issue raised by the President in his proposal, La Follette continued, was between special vested interests represented by an outmoded economic theory, on the one hand, and the will of the people to govern themselves, on the other. In a two-fisted discussion of the Supreme Court issue at the convention of Labor's Non-Partisan League in Washington on March 8, 1937, Senator La Follette highlighted the issue by bluntly stating:

"President Roosevelt during the past four years courageously launched the federal government upon a program designed to stimulate the forces of economic recovery and to restore harmony to an economic system which had been allowed to run itself into the ditch under the do-nothing administrations that preceded him. . . . The American people have solemnly expressed their approval of the President's general program at the ballot box. They know that government is the only instrumentality which can bring order out of the chaos produced by the laissez-faire doctrine of economics; they know that the federal government is the only agency which can solve the pressing problems of our day and generation.

"But although the people who sense the problems that face them today realize this, the councils of the older generation, schooled in the thought of a bygone day, do not. . . .

"When a majority of the highest court in the land, one of the three co-ordinate branches of the federal government, stubbornly cling to an outmoded philosophy which the people of the country have emphatically repudiated it is a threat to a functioning democracy. These judges are the lame ducks of our courts today."

La Follette reviewed the action of the court against the legislation designed to correct economic maladjustments. In the long run more was at stake than theory, the senator pointed out.

"The collapse of the democratic governments in other countries should serve as a solemn warning to those who really believe in that form of government," La Follette said. "These governments were discarded because for one reason or another they were impotent. If a majority of the court is permitted indefinitely to throttle the legislative branch of the government, and thus block all effective means of meeting the grave economic problems of today, I say it can happen here. Conscientious and intelligent statesmanship demands that we find ways and means to make our form of government work, so that it can solve the problems of minimum wages, collective bargaining, social security, crop insurance, soil erosion, unemployment relief, housing, flood prevention, conservation of our natural resources, and a more equitable distribution of our annual wealth as it is produced from year to year in this country. As long as a majority of the Supreme Court stands athwart the will of the people and obstructs the working of democratic government, it is inviting the breakdown of our economic system and the ultimate destruction of our form of government by revolutionary changes."

Senator La Follette recalled that his father had been pilloried
by reactionary forces during the 1924 campaign for his support
of a platform plank that called for a constitutional amendment
providing for Congressional review of laws declared unconstitutional by the court. The younger La Follette was scornful of
the current proposals made to amend the Constitution and con-
tended that if the problem was critical in 1924, action should
have been taken then. But to wait until the nation was faced
with a crisis, a crisis that threw doubt on every act of Congress
to lessen the weight of depression on individual citizens, was
merely an effort to delay by "reactionaries who were licked to a
frazzle at the polls last November."

"Our task at the present time," La Follette concluded, "is to
make sure that the voice of the masses of the people on the farms,
in the factories, in the shops, and in the small businesses of this
country is not lost in the tumult raised by the well-financed propaganda of organized minorities. Special interests are protesting
to Congress against President Roosevelt's plan for judicial reorganization. They come with the hands of Esau but the voice
of Jacob. They claim to represent the sentiment of the people,
but be not deceived. We must not confuse noise and activity
with numbers. The special interests are both very noisy and
exceedingly active at this time, but the people have the numbers
and the people want to retain control of their government."

Over the years, Progressives have waged a constant battle
against monopoly control of business. In the early days the fight
was against the trusts and was motivated primarily by individual-
istic reaction against forces that operated to deny to individuals
their right to conduct businesses. It developed, as time went on,
into a more pointed program of protest against the railroads
inspired by men who, like the elder Senator La Follette, agreed
that they did not fully understand the economics involved but
who felt intuitively and saw with their own eyes the results of
many manifestations of corporate practices that to them augured
no good for the future of the country.

The fight against the "trusts," the "special interests," "Wall
Street," and "monopolies" provided the basis for much political
oratory and the mixing of much potent political medicine. Many

politicians interested only in attracting votes adopted the words of the Progressive fight for equal economic opportunity but they were not interested in making the program a reality. The honestly conceived but possibly too indignant exposure of the evils of the "trusts" by the Ray Stannard Bakers, the Ida Tarbells, the Lincoln Steffenses, and others may have helped to discredit the steady sincere program of economic reform. As the journalists reported it, the truth was too shockingly brutal. Furthermore, as a result of the pressure brought by Progressive elements, the federal government had taken some action. The Sherman antitrust law was on the statute books; legislation favorable to organized labor was beginning to be adopted; an Interstate Commerce Commission to regulate railroad rates was established, as was the Federal Trade Commission.

When the elder Senator La Follette made regulation of big business and antitrust legislation one of the major issues of his 1924 campaign for the presidency, he was pooh-poohed by his opposition as fighting against windmills. Yet in 1933, during the debate on the National Recovery Act, Progressives were apprehensive of the ultimate economic effect of any relaxing of the antitrust laws.

The older generation of Progressives recognized intuitively what the unregulated development of big business meant for the future. The newer generation of Progressives were better grounded in economic theory and understood why the business monopoly was a threat to the democratic ideal of equal economic opportunity and how it might ultimately threaten or destroy the constitutionally guaranteed civil liberties.

Briefly, the older Progressives considered monopoly an economic evil in itself. So long as it could be kept in check and there was still the opportunity of the frontier there was a chance for the individual. The elder La Follette recognized that the disappearance of the frontier had complicated the problem and his position that it was the responsibility of government to provide equal economic opportunity by close regulation of monopoly shocked the laissez-faire Old Guard of his day.

The newer generation of Progressives had the advantage of an economic scholarship that began to question many of the conclusions of the classical economists. To the newer and questioning economists, economic behavior was not something to be considered as apart from the social and political behavior but an important aspect of the trinity of society, politics, and economics. These considerations were the basis for the insistence of Senator Robert M. La Follette, Jr., that the Hoover administration acknowledge the responsibility of the federal government and provide the leadership for fighting the depression. It was the basis of his support of Senator Borah's amendment to the National Recovery Act limiting any relaxation of the antitrust provisions of past legislation. It was the basis of his continuing interest in and insistence upon long-range planning by government to control or offset possible future depressions. Senator La Follette gave all-out support to the establishment of the Temporary National Economic Committee, which during the latter part of the 1930's investigated and reported on the manner by which the nation was subject to monopoly and monopolistic practices.

Senator La Follette was indignant at the way the defense program was administered by government officials. He believed that so far as practicable government contracts for defense materials should be spread in order that both large and small business enterprises be benefited. He warned, in December, 1940:

"Frenzied grabbing of all defense contracts by the giants of industry is not only depriving smaller plants of their share of defense production, but is seriously stalling the entire rearmament program."

La Follette cracked down upon administrators responsible for the uneven distribution of defense contracts in an editorial in the *Progressive*:

"Most of the critical economic problems which this country has faced during the past decade can be traced directly to the distortions of our national economy during the last war. That experience has been a costly lesson. It is a tragic fact, therefore, that some of the administrators of the present program are ignoring that lesson . . . One of the factors that is unnecessarily aggravating the industrial pattern is the uneven allocation of defense contracts. Ten cities in the country have received almost

40 per cent of the total value of contracts awarded. Thirty industrial counties have received over 75 per cent."

During that same period the Department of Justice asked Congress for increased appropriations to carry on antitrust investigations and prosecution of cases already filed. Senator La Follette led the fight to obtain the increased appropriation. He did so because, he informed the Senate on May 19, 1941:

"It is highly important that the Antitrust Division be given sufficient appropriations so that it may proceed against those monopolies in control of the vital products of defense metals, drugs, and other articles. I make my appeal secondly because it is the only hope of the independent business men in this country."

La Follette reviewed the situation as it pertained to specific products like aluminum and lashed out against permitting the defense program to be bogged down in these words:

"Various notorious industrial combinations, national and international, have schemed and preyed upon our economic system for a score of years. Both in depression and prosperity years, sordid parasitic profits have been exacted successfully by price fixing and production control, legally and illegally.

"The monopolistic practices have been screened to the general public by ingenious trade agreements, intercorporate managements, complex patent assignments, and a score of economic devices to circumvent antitrust laws. Government prosecution in the past has been only partially successful, due to a lack of sufficient Congressional appropriations to finance a government legal fight against the powerful monopoly giants.

"A long-smoldering resentment against the existence of this cancer in our economy resulted a few years ago, in June, 1938, in the establishment of the well-known Temporary National Economic Committee empowered by Congress to investigate monopoly and the concentration of economic power.

"The committee's voluminous hearings established indisputable evidence of various industrial combinations that were stifling the activities of the small businessman and independent concerns; squeezing an unreasonable distributive share from both the farmer's and the consumer's dollars, and in general preventing a normal functioning of a competitive economy.

"More recently the so-called Truman Committee, investigating defense expenditures, disclosed the shocking story of how the monopolists have hindered the defense program, and the even more serious disclosure that the Office of Production Management condoned policies which would have the effect of fostering a 'bigger and better' monopoly in the production of aluminum."

La Follette and the Progressives got the appropriation for the Antitrust Division.

On numerous occasions Senator La Follette pointed out that it was a shortsighted economic policy of government to squeeze the small independent businessman out of the picture. He called attention to the fact that the government itself was doing what no combination of monopolies would have dared to do—reduce the competition of small business by its program of priorities and in its letting of war contracts. The government was "sacrificing on the altar of national defense" an important part of the national economy.

When the Senate bill to establish the Smaller War Plants Corporation was debated in March, 1942, La Follette warned his colleagues that mere passing of a bill would not of itself correct the problem. He called attention to the numerous but ineffective plans that had already been set up and discarded for the purpose, presumably, of helping small, independent business.

"Unless there is a change in the policy of those who are letting the contracts, unless there is a change in the policy of the executive branch of the government, it will not remedy the situation which has prevailed up to this time.

"If we do not save the segment of our economy which is made up of so-called small business, we shall change entirely the whole economic structure of the United States and we shall come out of the war in such a situation that there will be left in the country practically no competition whatsoever."

As one of the last of his acts in the closing days of the 79th Congress, in June, 1946, Senator La Follette conducted a one-man campaign to restore $200,000 to an appropriation for the Antitrust Division. In his speech asking reinstatement of the amount, La Follette criticized what he termed a dangerous curtailment of the government's antitrust drive and declared that failure to prosecute a "continued growth of monopoly" would block widespread use of plastics and light metals.

La Follette suggested that small business enterprises could easily be deprived of war-born techniques and materials, developed often through government-sponsored research. He insisted that such wartime advances must be made to small businessmen and independent producers. The plastics and light metals industries, he told the Senate, were the brightest hope for industrial expansion and greater employment.

"We have to open up new enterprises in this country for full employment, and to make our economy function, we must do something to check the trend of concentration of economic power."

His amendment to restore the $200,000 to the Antitrust Division was adopted.

The constant reiteration of that doctrine, not only by Senator La Follette but by other Progressives in the Congress was largely responsible for the policy followed in the disposal of surplus properties built with federal funds during the war. At the beginning of the defense program in 1940 the Aluminum Company of America, to cite but one example, controlled 100 per cent of the output of the light metal and controlled all the processes involved in the reduction of aluminum ores. In February, 1947, it was reported by the War Assets Administration that 50 per cent of the production of new aluminum in the United States was accounted for by plants and processes made available to independent producers.

Finally, but certainly not the least important of his activities in behalf of a more stable economy for the nation, came Senator La Follette's efforts to secure for the farmer his share of the profits which accrued from the products of the land. Senator La Follette did not look on agriculture as such as a separate and distinct element of the national economy. He recognized it as a highly important and interdependent aspect. His efforts to assist the farmer and his continued interest in agricultural problems made him the spokesman of the farmer.

Just as La Follette performed an outstanding service for the organized workingmen and -women of the nation by his championship of their hopes and aspirations and the positive contribution he made to secure their rights in the Civil Liberties investigations, so too did he aid constructively in helping to work out the solutions to the problems of the farmer. As one of the outstanding exponents of the conservation of national resources, La Follette was concerned with the fate of the soil of the farm. Soil-erosion and flood-control programs that had made possible cheap electricity, Senators La Follette, Norris, and other Progressives visioned as an aid to make farm life richer by bringing to the rural areas many of the conveniences of urban living. Rural electrification programs found in Senator La Follette an able and stanch supporter. He was concerned over the financial plight of many farmers and helped to establish improved credit facilities and to help marginal farmers buy their own land.

Basic in his thinking on the problems of agriculture was the belief that the farmer must receive a far greater share of the wealth he creates. La Follette, together with economists of the Department of Agriculture, worked out plans to ensure that the farmer received his costs of production plus a fair profit for his products.

Despite his interest in other aspects of the defense program beginning in 1940, Senator La Follette did not overlook the importance of food and the ability of the farmers of the country to produce it. Early in February, 1941, he outlined the plight of agriculture in the defense economy and pointed out:

"Industrial production, construction contracts, freight loadings, electric power production, income payments, factory employment, department store sales, and all other important business indicators have been at record levels in recent months. Corporation profits have soared beyond all expectations. And all the trends are sharply upward.

"But one segment of our economy is not sharing the upward spiral: agriculture. The long-suffering farmer, whose income has been 20 billion dollars short of parity in the last ten years, has again become 'the forgotten man.'

"Not in two decades has agriculture got its fair share of the national income. Although agricultural workers constitute more than 20 per cent of all gainful workers in the United States, in past years agricultural income has constituted less than 10 per cent of the national net income, and this despite government payments of three-fourths of a billion dollars in each of the last two years, and lesser amounts in previous years.

"The agricultural outlook is now ominous. The European war and the defense program are affecting agriculture very adversely. Unless the government takes prompt action, all signs point to a harder road ahead for the farmer. Export recovery is not in sight. Foreign buyers have shifted their demands from farm products to munitions.

"On the domestic front, the defense program has diverted all attention from the plight of the farmer. While government money is pumped into industry to further our national defense, manufacturers are driving hard bargains—and even refusing to bargain—to obtain handsome profits from government defense contracts.

"Even labor is receiving a measure of protection in the government assurances that past gains will not be jeopardized, but agriculture thus far has received no equivalent attention. In the face of this gloomy outlook, the new budget proposes to cut agricultural aid by about 45 million dollars.

"The need existed before this present crisis, but now, more than ever before. Congress should take decisive action to protect agriculture as a way of life. One phase of the long-range problem that should be tackled immediately by Congress is farm debt adjustment.

"An avenue through which the immediate price crisis in certain products can be effectively handled is through the highly popular stamp plan.

"The stamp plan, school lunch program, the low-cost milk program, and all the allied programs of surplus commodities disposal were expanded last year. According to the Department of Agriculture, more than three billion pounds of price-depressing surpluses of forty different farm products were bought and distributed through these programs to an average of eleven million persons in three million low-income families throughout the nation."

Government plans to aid the farmer in getting rid of surpluses were, however, not enough, according to Senator La Follette. He called attention to the fact that low farm incomes, despite favorable conditions in other economic activity throughout the country, were the cause of an increase in farm mortgage foreclosures and for the fact that nearly 23 per cent of farm borrowers were in arrears in their payments.

"There is every indication that unless Congress acts with boldness and vision the American farmer will be the first—although not the last—economic casualty of this war," he warned.

CHAPTER XVII

Foreign Relations

JUST BEFORE THE OPENING sessions of the 70th Congress were called to order in December, 1927, Hearst newspapers throughout the nation announced the forthcoming publication of documents "proving" that President Calles of Mexico was the center of a Communist plot to overthrow the established government of the United States. The Hearst papers also charged that certain highly respected publications, their editors, and other citizens had probably accepted bribes to influence the policy of the United States toward Mexico.

The series of sensational exposures started out with an attempt to show that Dr. Ernest Gruening, editor of the Portland (Me.) *Evening News,* acted as go-between for President Calles with striking British coal miners. Dr. Gruening promptly brought suit for libel against Hearst's New York *American.* Next came revelations of an alleged secret treaty between Mexico and Japan that provided, among other things, for large colonies of Japanese citizens on Mexican territory. Then came accusations that American business interests were linked to Mexican efforts to ship arms and munitions to Nicaraguan rebels engaged in guerrilla warfare against American forces sent there to maintain order.

On December 9, 1927, readers of the Washington *Herald* were duly astonished by this headline:

$1,215,000 ORDERED PAID TO FOUR SENATORS BY MEXICO

The story purported to tell of a secret order of the President of Mexico to pay to certain United States senators huge sums for pro-Mexican propaganda. The facsimile document reproduced as part of the story had the names of the senators blacked out. The Senate immediately ordered a special investigation into the allegations. The first witness was William Randolph Hearst.

Hearst readily admitted that one of his motives in publishing the series was to force a Congressional investigation but complained that no action had been taken until his papers had published the material charging certain senators with having received large sums of money. The four senators alluded to without name in the Hearst articles and named by the investigating committee were Thomas Heflin of Alabama, William Borah of Idaho, chairman of the Senate Foreign Relations Committee, George W. Norris of Nebraska, and Robert M. La Follette, Jr., of Wisconsin.

All four senators denied any knowledge of such action on the part of the Mexican government or its agents and declared that none of them had been approached nor had they received a cent of the amounts they were reported to have received.

"The attempt to link my name with the charges before this committee is an infamous and cowardly fraud," Senator La Follette told the committee. "I have never been approached directly or indirectly . . . by any persons in connection with the relations between the United States and Mexico . . .

"I am not unmindful that I have been one of those who, in the Senate, on the public platform, and in the magazine of which I am editor and publisher, have resisted to the utmost the policy which was pursued by this Administration with regard to Mexico; and the dastardly attempt to link my name with the charges pending before this committee will not cause me to deviate so much as a hairsbreadth from the course which I have marked out for myself with regard to the attitude of this country toward Mexico or any other power."

The investigation that followed uncovered a traffic in forged Mexican documents that had all the trappings of an E. Phillips Oppenheim international spy thriller. Admitting that he had paid at least $15,000 for the "documents" on which his editors and writers had based their stories, Hearst finally acknowledged that he had no reason to believe any of the senators had received or accepted any money from the Mexican government. He testified that none of the accused senators had been interviewed before publication of the charges. His chief reasons for believing the documents authentic were based on a reported statement by American Ambassador Sheffield, to whom they were shown, that they "looked" authentic and his trust in the individuals who had secured them. Miguel Avila, the principal, who "received" the materials from governmental employees in Mexico City, according to his story, proved an evasive witness. Of him, an American engineer with a long background of experience in Mexico told the committee:

"This traffic in documents is a business in Mexico City. You can get any kind of document you want. Avila is one of the purveyors of those documents . . . He is notoriously known for that thing in Mexico City."

John Page, the Hearst correspondent in Mexico City who helped bring the documents to the United States, also proved to be vague in some of his testimony and, as Senator La Follette informed the committee, had had previous experience with forged or false documents. A free-lance correspondent who had done some work for the Philadelphia *Public Ledger,* Page thought he had a big story when early in 1926 he had been given the Spanish translation of a letter purportedly in the files of President Calles. The alleged letter was "signed" by Senator Robert M. La Follette, Jr., and supposedly assured the Mexican President that he and three or four other senators were sympathetic to Mexico and that Calles could be assured of their continued pro-Mexican support.

Page translated the Spanish version into English and sent it to the *Public Ledger* with the suggestion that the original was available at a price. In the meantime the *Public Ledger's* Washington correspondent, Robert Barry, was asked to check with both Senator La Follette and the State Department on the authenticity of what looked like a scoop. Barry reported to his superiors that La Follette had pronounced the letter a forgery and had pointed to the fact that, while it appeared to have been written on the stationery of the Senate Foreign Relations Com-

mittee, he was not a member of that committee and possessed
none of its letterheads.

"I never expect to be as smart as my father was about such
matters, but I never expect to be such a damned fool as that
letter makes me out to be," La Follette told Barry.

Informed that La Follette had denounced the letter as a forgery, Page protested that showing it to La Follette had made it
impossible to secure the original.

Arturo Elias, Mexican consul general in New York, had been
prominently mentioned in the Hearst articles with the plot to
bribe the United States senators. It was allegedly through his
office that arrangements were made for payment. He waived
diplomatic immunity to testify before the committee and requested the committee to investigate his bank accounts. He
offered to present anything his office might have to assist in
clearing up of the matter. He unhesitatingly pronounced as fakes
the documents supposed to have come from files in his office.

Senator Joseph T. Robinson of Arkansas announced on the
floor of the Senate on December 19 that the evidence showed
without a shadow of a doubt that the charges against the four
senators were utterly without foundation. He and Senator Hiram
Johnson of California had been the two members of the investigating committee most active in questioning witnesses and in
trying to run to earth the source of the documents.

Handwriting experts representing both Mr. Hearst and the
committee were unanimous in agreeing that the documents had
been forged. Language experts reported that the documents could
not have been part of the government files. The language used
was not typical of official Mexican documents. Even the paper
used for the documents was not the kind, nor did it bear the
characteristic watermarks, generally used by the Mexican government.

The Senate committee reported all the Hearst documents to
be nothing more than crude forgeries and cleared the four senators of any guilt in the matter. The incident was, however, but
one in a series of false alarms about the political situation in
Mexico. From the moment he had been elected president of
Mexico, Elias Plutarco Calles had been the target against which

the charge of "Bolshevist" was hurled with an almost monotonous regularity by certain business interests in this country. They yelled bloody murder when in 1926 Calles by presidential decree ruled that the subsoil of Mexico belonged to the nation and its people.

The United States Department of State, with an assist from the Associated Press, was guilty of helping to spread the alarm against the "specter of a Mexico-fostered Bolshevist hegemony intervening between the United States and the Panama Canal." The material on which the Associated Press based its story was furnished by Assistant Secretary Robert E. Olds on November 17, 1926. The other major news services, the United Press and Hearst's own International News Service, had rejected the story because Olds refused to be quoted and refused to permit the reporters to indicate that the material came from the State Department.

The story was exposed as a propaganda fake by the St. Louis *Post-Dispatch*. When denied by Secretary of State Frank Kellogg, Senator Burton Wheeler introduced a resolution for an investigation. It was killed by the Committee on Foreign Relations. Senator Frank Willis of Ohio is reported to have explained that the *Post-Dispatch* story was correct, that "Kellogg's denial is a diplomatic denial and we would be foolish to start an investigation."

The efforts of the Calles government to bring to Mexico a greater degree of peace and tranquillity caused many owners of oil and mining concessions in that country a lot of unhappiness. They helped spread the anti-Mexican propaganda. Mr. Hearst was evidently hypnotized by his own propaganda, for on January 4, 1928, in a long explanation for having published the false accusations against the four senators, he said they were made public "because we believed they supported the declarations of Assistant Secretary of State Olds . . . he gave to the Associated Press for general distribution on November 17, 1926." The Socialist Milwaukee *Leader* summed the matter up as "a fight between different American business camps. The Morgan camp can get along with Calles and Obregon, Hearst and others cannot."

Those incidents in themselves were not, perhaps, of great importance but they did indicate the trend of American policy in foreign relations. Senator Robert M. La Follette, Jr., early took his stand against the apparent policy of exploitation—dollar diplomacy, as it has been characterized. He criticized the Coolidge administration for its use of armed intervention in the Central American and Caribbean areas and warned that such a policy could only result in bad relations and misunderstandings with the other republics of the Western Hemisphere.

No doubt one of the reasons La Follette's name, or, rather, his initials, appeared on the forged Mexican documents was that he was one of the outspoken defenders of the sovereign right of Mexico to work out her own domestic policy. He, as his father had before him, rejected the argument that American arms necessarily followed American investments abroad. La Follette, Jr., early adopted the view that an imperialistic policy was not the way to keep the peace. As time went on, he extended that view to embrace his opposition to all commitments with other nations which in effect supported any form of imperialism or was designed to maintain the exploitative status quo.

This facet of Senator La Follette's views on American foreign relations is illustrated by two incidents from many that might be chosen. Mention has already been made of his opposition to the loan to Great Britain negotiated in 1946. He based his opposition chiefly on economic reasons but pointed out that Great Britain's natural desire to hold the empire together and be a dominant power in world trade were also important in considering the effects of the loan.

La Follette insisted that those long-term considerations were being underestimated and declared that by granting the loan America would be embarking on a program that "enmeshes us in long-range problems that we cannot blithely assume without risking not only this loan but also whatever loan follows this in pouring good money after bad.

"There is absolutely no justification to underwrite the British Empire nor a dominant place in world trade for the United Kingdom." La Follette stated quite frankly that it would be far less expensive in the long run if the United States were to make an outright gift of the money to Great Britain.

Extended to its logical conclusion, this tenet of Senator La Follette's philosophy included the championship of subject peoples wherever they were. La Follette did not shrink from the implications of that conclusion but always spoke out. He did not hesitate to criticize the British government for its failure to live up to the promises of the Atlantic Charter or to its expressed commitments with respect to the subject peoples under its domination.

In an address in Toledo on April 15, 1946, Senator La Follette bluntly charged the British government with a violation of international law and morals in its handling of Palestine. And because the United States had not, up to that time, officially protested British action in the Holy Land, the senator said that the United States was giving indirect support to those violations.

"Palestine," La Follette told his Toledo audience, "is not a proposition of finding a solution to a problem. The solution was found and agreed to many years ago in the adoption of a basic policy to permit Jewish migration to Palestine with the view toward ultimately establishing a Jewish national home. It is now a proposition of abiding by a formal promise and policy . . .

"Political wisdom, justice, humanity, and plain respect for the letter of the law—all point to a course of action that was honorably promulgated but then drastically altered by unilateral action of the British government."

La Follette's opposition to imperialism in all its forms and his criticism of whatever nation was embarked on such a program was a corollary to his basic philosophy that the American democratic way of life could be made to work—that it should provide political freedom, religious liberty, and equal economic opportunity to all citizens. Those being the principles for which the government of the United States was established to provide, as La Follette insisted, American foreign policy must have the same basis. The United States, to be consistent and true to its fundamental principles, could not adopt any policy that compromised them. In the mouths of many men such doctrine would sound flamboyant and demagogic. Such was not the case when Senator Robert M. La Follette, Jr., spoke. He commanded respect and often slowed or stopped precipitate action he could not condone.

In vigorous and often blunt language La Follette urged his point of view, not by cheap histrionics, but by a careful review of unassailable background facts.

Another factor that gave strength to Senator La Follette's position was that he never emphasized one of his principles at the expense of the others. They all went together, for it was his belief that without one none of the rest could survive for long. These views were criticized as having nothing to do with the "realities" of international relations. The only trouble was that those who presumed to criticize did not appreciate or understand the basic propositions on which his position rested. Senator Robert M. La Follette, Jr., was given the tag of "isolationist"— a term, it will be recalled, that carried a highly emotional content between 1936 and 1941. In an address delivered in Chicago, April 25, 1938, La Follette said:

"I am not an isolationist except in the sense of the President's speech at Chatauqua in 1936 when he said: 'We are not isolationists except in so far as we seek to isolate ourselves completely from war.'

"International co-operation is of course essential, and I have supported every form of co-operation which I believed would advance the cause of peace and welfare among the nations."

La Follette could have gone into some detail about his support of the reciprocal trade agreements put into effect by Secretary of State Cordell Hull. He could have pointed to his record of support and encouragement of the Good Neighbor policy and hemispheric solidarity. Yet Professor Kenneth Colegrove of Northwestern University, using the shotgun technique of blasting at all who did not agree with a particular point of view, characterized Senator La Follette as one of the "outspoken opponents of American participation in a co-operative peace system." It was Senator La Follette who hailed the results of the Inter-American Havana Conference in 1940:

". . . a great step forward . . . to buttress the military defense of the hemisphere by strengthening the economic preparations of the member nations of the Pan-American conference to deal with economic warfare from any quarter now or in the future. Notice has been served upon the Old World that the

Monroe Doctrine's enforcement has the support of twenty other nations.

"There are great opportunities to build a dynamic expanding economy in this hemisphere.

"It must not be done on the basis of exploitation, but every effort should be made to increase the economic ties between nations in this hemisphere.

"We should take the lead in development of strategic materials such as tin and rubber, fostering the production of noncompetitive agricultural products and stabilizing the banking and foreign exchange systems of our neighbors to the south of us.

"Thus we can make this hemisphere invulnerable against economic or military aggression by any nation or group of nations."

What incensed the interventionists and made Senator La Follette the target of much of their vitriol from the time war started in Europe until the United States was attacked at Pearl Harbor was his disconcerting habit of meeting their emotionalized arguments with the plain, hard facts. He caused serious alarm, for instance, among Administration supporters of the proposal to dispose of fifty obsolete destroyers to Great Britain when he pointed out:

"The interventionists are shouting for the sale of fifty destroyers from our Navy to Great Britain. They refer to them as 'obsolete.' They argue that they are of little use to us but that they may be the difference between victory and defeat for Britain. These vessels are not 'obsolete' in the sense that they are no longer useful for our own defense.

"On March 1 of this year [1940] 150 of the 301 combatant vessels in commission in the U.S. Navy were listed as over-age or obsolete. All of these ships are a vital part of the naval strength of the United States. If we can sell fifty destroyers on this ground we can sell one-half of the combat strength of the Navy . . . Congress has been told three different times this year that we must increase our navy.

"Since the first of January, 1940, Congress has approved the following: (1) expansion of combat ships by 11 per cent and aircraft 50 per cent; (2) expansion of aircraft and aviation shore facilities 100 per cent; (3) increase of combat ships 70 per cent and another increase in aircraft of 50 per cent.

"Now, there is something screwy in this argument that we do not need these destroyers when our naval experts have made such tremendous demands for increases of naval strength on the ground that rapid expansion of the Navy is vital to the defense of our country. It will take two years at least to build new destroyers to take the place of these fifty it is now proposed to sell."

During these discussions on foreign policy Senator La Follette found himself more than once in an embarrassing position. The *Progressive,* successor to *La Follette's Magazine,* which had been established in 1928 with the senator as president of the publishing company, often appeared with editorial comment on foreign policies that was widely divergent from the senator's views.

The *Progressive,* beginning with 1928, was a joint publishing venture with the La Follette family and the *Capital Times* of Madison whose editor was, and is, William T. Evjue. Senator La Follette was president of the publishing company with his brother Philip as secretary and Mr. Evjue as editor of the *Progressive.* As editor of the *Progressive,* Mr. Evjue reprinted editorials from his *Capital Times* supporting interventionist foreign policies of the Roosevelt administration. Some of the editorials which appeared as the expression of the *Progressive* appeared at the same time both the senator and his brother Philip were fighting against the very policies that the editorials endorsed. And yet their names appeared on the masthead as principal officers of the paper that was opposing their views!

This state of affairs, which was widely recognized and widely commented upon, reached a climax in May, 1940. Mr. Evjue took the initiative in steps to resolve the matter. The La Follettes welcomed the opportunity to reach an amicable adjustment and an agreement was worked out by which the brothers regained full control of the paper founded by their father. In the issue of June 29, 1940, over their joint signatures, the La Follettes announced:

"The *Progressive* refuses to join those pessimists who see disaster lurking around every corner. Man created the paradox of privation and lack of opportunity in the midst of potential plenty and man can solve it. We have nothing to fear except blind and unreasoning fear. But we must not fiddle away our chance. Time and events press.

"Any program of national defense that does not give each citizen a faith and conviction for which he will give his all will prove a sham and delusion.

"The *Progressive* will fight for a sound program of rearmament to defend this hemisphere from the Arctic Circle to Cape Horn against all comers. It will fight for a tax program to prevent fat profits from being made from our new defense program.

"The *Progressive* will fight to the last ditch any effort to involve the United States in fighting an overseas, foreign war.

"The *Progressive* will fight to drive the Money-Changers from our temples.

"The *Progressives* will fight for the genuine political realignment essential to the solution of our basic problems and for the preservation of democracy.

"The *Progressive* will fight to give the American farmer a decent living for producing the nation's food, a readjustment of his crushing debt burden and for a restoration of farming as a way of life.

"The *Progressive* will fight for a program to provide the opportunity to those who work in shop, store, office and factory to earn a decent and secure living by assuring to every able-bodied American a real opportunity for useful and productive employment at a living wage.

"The *Progressive* will fight to end the crime, for which there can be no pardon, of denying opportunity to the nation's most precious asset—its youth.

"The *Progressive* will fight for a national program to assure a generous, adequate and self-respecting security for those who because of age, or other disability, are unable to provide for themselves. But it will oppose the policy which slams the door of opportunity in the face of able-bodied Americans solely because they are past middle age.

"The *Progressive* will fight for the holy doctrine that 'it is more blessed to give than receive.' It will seek to restore to our national life the concept that every American is a national asset and not a public liability.

"These are essential to our national morale and the efficient use of our economic and social resources. These are our internal defenses against the enemies of democracy.

"There is no time to waste in meeting the challenge of our day and generation. To guard America effectively against the fifth columns of communism and fascism we must have a contented and united people. We must banish the discouragement and dissatisfaction that breed in the dead atmosphere of idleness and poverty on which ruthless dictators have risen to power."

On September 1, 1939, German armies invaded Poland. World War II was a fact. One of the first matters to engage the attention of Congress was an Administration request to repeal the provisions of the Neutrality Act regarding the embargo on sales abroad of arms and ammunition. Senator La Follette raised serious objections to the proposal on the ground that sudden and huge orders for the materials of war would have a disastrous effect upon American economy. He questioned the ability of nations to pay for the implements of war ordered from this country and pointed to the fact that nation after nation had defaulted in its promises to the United States after World War I.

"Repeal of the embargo, in the present circumstances, and the sale of arms, ammunition, and implements of war is a significant step toward participation in the European war," La Follette told the Senate during the debate on the repeal measure. "It is not in the best interest of American democracy to gamble everything of value which we possess in return for some temporary profits together with a permanent participation in a postwar chaos most certainly to be revolutionary in character."

La Follette ridiculed the idea that the American economic system needed the impetus of war contracts to take up the slack of nearly a decade of depression. He suggested that the problems then faced were due to the economic distortion produced by World War I.

"I repudiate the idea that we cannot solve our problems here at home without resort to the stimulus to business brought about by the wholesale slaughter of human beings in Europe," La Follette said with some heat.

"Our great opportunity for service to the cause of civilization is to stay out of this war. Thus we can preserve in this hemisphere a haven of sanity in a world where madness now prevails.

"We can then concentrate on our own problems and prove that democracy can work in a modern economic environment. When the war is over we will then indeed be in a position to give the world succor and leadership.

"We will have kept the light of democracy and tolerance alight. We will have demonstrated the soundness of our way of life. War-weary and disillusioned people will see in our example the way to rehabilitate civilization in their own lands."

Senator La Follette proposed that, instead of entertaining a dangerous war boom, the government of the United States take the lead in building a hemispheric economy that would help raise the levels of living all through Central and South America and keep our own industrial machinery going. With European markets gone as the result of the war, La Follette insisted that new opportunities and new responsibilities were opened up that would benefit every nation in the Western Hemisphere. He offered it as a constructive alternative to "a policy of partisanship and adventuring in Europe's perpetual quarrels with their self-interested ramifications throughout the seven seas."

In this same address Senator La Follette rebuked the Administration for its efforts to secure the power to decide which nations were considered to be belligerents and which nations were to be favored with permission to buy arms and munitions in the United States. He criticized the Administration for attempting to short-circuit the constitutional functions of Congress. To emphasize his point La Follette introduced an amendment to the neutrality bill under debate which provided for an advisory referendum on the question of an overseas war. It was similar to the one his father had introduced in 1916.

Two points troubled Senator La Follette—and a large group of citizens for whom he spoke—in all the debate over how far the United States could or should go in helping certain of the belligerent nations. The first was the absence of any aims to be accomplished by the war specifically and officially expressed by the nations fighting the Axis powers. There were, of course, general statements of a propagandistic nature which appealed to most citizens of democratic nations, but Senator La Follette was of the opinion that the various governments would be on much more solid ground in their appeals to the United States for aid if they officially and specifically enumerated their war aims. He reminded the Senate often that World War II had its roots in the peace treaties of World War I and that those treaties were the result of secret agreements, imperialism, and other baser motives that shaped the foreign policies of the Allied nations. He did not want the United States to have any part in a repetition of the dismal results of the Paris Peace Conference.

His second concern was for democracy itself. As he expressed it on many occasions and in almost exactly the same words:

"Modern war poisons democracy. Men cannot speak, think, or write freely. No longer do they participate as citizens of a free state. They become subjects of war dictatorship. They become objects under the control of the war machine. There is censorship of the press and radio.

"The last war struck staggering blows to our democracy. It created and intensified economic problems which brought this nation to the brink of disaster. Unemployment, idle money and machines, huge debts, economic dislocation of agriculture—all these are the tragic reminders of our last mad adventure into war abroad."

Senator La Follette was bitterly critical of the Administration for sponsoring and pushing through Congress the Lend-Lease law. He characterized the measure as one which permitted the President to get us into the war by the back door. He declared that it gave the Chief Executive sweeping dictatorial powers that took from Congress its own constitutional powers. During the course of the Senate debate on the measure, La Follette called attention to its effect on American relations with Latin America. He said:

"We made progress toward hemisphere solidarity last summer at the Inter-American conference in Havana. Our representatives conducted themselves with honor and distinction. Out of that conference came the foundation for a truly enlightened hemisphere program. But the foundations remain almost untouched.

"Measured in terms of the billions we have spent and are to spend for aid to the nations in the Old World, there is little money, time, or energy to build our own edifice in this hemisphere. We are too busy trying to put out fires all over the rest of the world.

"The spirit of the Havana and Panama agreements calls for the nations of the hemisphere to consult on matters affecting their defense and foreign intercourse.

"Yet I do not know that this government has consulted with our southern neighbors on this most far-reaching bill which intimately affects our entire foreign policy and theirs also. . . .

"It has been reported that protests against this bill have been lodged by several Latin-American ambassadors to the United States. If this be true, we are weakening our incompleted foundations for hemisphere solidarity in favor of foreign adventures in the Old World.

"The opportunities which lie to the south of us, opportunities for the mutual advancement of both ourselves and our neighbors, staggers the imagination. The realization of these opportunities calls for the same kind of courage, energy, and resourcefulness that our forebears showed when they pressed ever westward against the peril-ridden frontier. But in our time, we can achieve by friendly co-operation and mutual understanding what they took by force of arms or by courageous pioneering."

Despite his seeming preoccupation with ways and means of keeping the United States out of the war, Senator La Follette was not blind to the plight millions of people found themselves in as a result of the war. Early in 1941 he suggested that humanitarian motives alone required that the United States help supply food to starving Europeans. He admitted that there were formidable problems to be solved in putting such a program into effect but felt that they were not insuperable. La Follette proposed that our agricultural surpluses could well be utilized and said:

"Terrible as is the bombing of hospitals and homes and the maiming of innocent civilians in the lightning aerial activities of modern war—the slow persistent starvation of millions of men, women, and children is more terrible, more tragic, more brutal. The long-range results in social, economic and political upheaval are more catastrophic. Thirty-seven million people in Europe— 15,000,000 of them children—are doomed to the gnawing agony of inadequate nourishment unless the United States acts immediately to supply food and effective safeguards."

But when Japan attacked the United States on December 7, 1941, Senator Robert M. La Follette, Jr., put aside his opposition to Administration policies of assisting the Allies in all ways "short of war" and bent every effort to support of the war program. It was not a sudden shift in attitude or the easy acceptance of the inevitable on the senator's part. His support of the war program was based on exactly the same grounds as his hitherto strong opposition to what he believed to be war-breeding policies of the government.

La Follette's concern was in utilizing to the best possible advantage all the nation's vast resources to bring the war to a successful conclusion. He was still concerned with the impact of the war on American democracy and warned against delegation of powers that unduly limited the exercise of our freedoms. He saw no reason, despite the war crisis, for the restrictive legislation proposed against labor. He strongly opposed the Smith-Connally labor law and the Case bill. He was one of the leaders in the Congressional fight to secure a federal fair employment practices act.

As had his father before him, Senator La Follette pleaded with the Administration to adopt a fair and adequate revenue policy by which every citizen could be taxed on the basis of ability to pay. He advocated heavy excess profits taxes and fought efforts to lower income tax exemptions without at the same time increasing the taxes on those well able to pay. La Follette was one of the authors of the legislation providing for renegotiation of war contracts that saved billions of dollars to the government.

A persistent foe of monopoly and a consistent friend of small business and free enterprise, Senator La Follette made every possible effort during the war to obtain a more equitable distribution of war contracts and to secure for small business some voice in the war program.

La Follette championed the cause of the GI during the war. As ranking minority member of both the Senate Education and Labor and the Finance committee, which handled veterans' legislation, La Follette was in a position to make his views count. He fought to eliminate the "caste system" in the armed forces as a situation unworthy of a great democratic nation. He turned his attention to the plight of the families of men drafted into the Army and Navy and initiated much legislation that eased the burdens of the men called to the fighting fronts.

Even in the stress and strains of fighting a global war, Senator La Follette always insisted that we must not lose sight of the principles of democracy for which this nation stands; to keep our economy, despite the exigencies of the period, on an even keel in order to be able to help effectively in leading the world to a more democratic basis following the war.

Peace-loving citizens of the whole world watched anxiously as delegates to the United Nations Organization met in San Francisco during May and June of 1945. They were hopeful that the nations could find among themselves a solution to the accelerated problems that within a generation had resulted in the costliest wars of civilization. Preliminary blueprints for the new world organization had been prepared at Dumbarton Oaks. For the moment the city behind the Golden Gate was the city of golden promise for the future.

Senator Robert M. La Follette, Jr., had followed the development of the Dumbarton Oaks proposals with keen interest. In an important statement of progressive thinking about international affairs, he told the Senate on May 31, 1945, that, if the world was to survive, the United States must join in an effective world organization to ensure the peace.

"I believe that we should face the new responsibilities that our decisive role in the war has brought upon us. I believe we should strive to create a realistic international organization which will actually work, and to create a peace settlement which will endure. Past experience teaches us that to achieve this purpose both the peace settlement and the world organization must be rooted in principles of justice.

"I am profoundly convinced that the United States should throw her moral strength into the international balance to tip the scales on the side of justice and liberty, just as America threw her military strength into the balance that tipped the scales against nazism, fascism, and militarism," La Follette said at the outset of his address.

He warned, however, that if the nations forgot the lessons of the past any new international organization would suffer the same fate the League of Nations had. "We must constantly remember that no permanent peace can be based on wrong and that no world organization can be formed strong enough to maintain a bad peace."

Instead of emphasizing the mechanics of enforcement of the peace terms, Senator La Follette urged that:

"Any enduring peace must ultimately depend upon the decisions as to what finally happens in Poland, Italy, Greece, Burma, Malay, the Philippines, and in other areas liberated from the yoke of Axis tyranny. It also depends on what is done with conquered Germany and Japan. It depends, too, upon how the urgent problems of imperialism, competitive armaments, world trade, natural resources, and slave labor are determined."

The League of Nations failed, in La Follette's opinion, because the treaties on which it was based did not eliminate the basic causes of war. The treaties were based on revenge, imperialism, territorial aggrandizement, and trade grabbing and not on reconstruction, democracy, self-determination or equal opportunity for all nations.

"If we are to engage in international co-operation for enduring peace," La Follette suggested, "America should use all her power to uphold a standard which expresses the aspirations of the peoples of all creeds and colors for political freedom and economic opportunity—a standard which would proclaim to the entire world America's aspirations in that peacemaking and in continued international co-operation."

Dispassionately and forcefully the Wisconsin senator cited chapter and verse from the history of peacemaking during the years since World War I in support of his position. Part of his argument was based on the proposition that the United States had failed to push its advantage in securing a declaration of democratic principles from the Allied nations in the first World War when it was possible to do so and that secret treaties and agreements among them had sabotaged the high purposes, enunciated by President Wilson in his Fourteen Points, for which this nation had gone to war.

La Follette believed the same mistake had occurred again. In biting words he denounced the record, up to that time, of Russia's failure to abide by the agreements made at the Yalta conference, the failure to abide by the spirit of the Atlantic Charter, and pledges against territorial changes.

"I have watched Soviet Russia's activities in the field of world politics with grave apprehension," the Senator said. "I am deeply concerned about her policies in world affairs, for here her conduct has a direct and perhaps decisive impact on all our hopes for a just and enduring peace.

"Russia's policies in Europe have constituted a direct violation of the pledges of the Atlantic Charter, to which she subscribed. Her arbitrary policies toward Poland constitute clear-cut violations of the United Nations' pledges against territorial changes which do not accord with the freely expressed wishes of the people concerned.

"Russia's insistence on establishing the made-in-Moscow Lublin regime as the government of Poland not only violates the Atlantic Charter, but is clearly a violation of the terms of the Yalta agreement to which Marshal Stalin subscribed. . . .

"Russia has also violated the Atlantic Charter and Yalta agreements in other areas liberated from the Nazi yoke: in Rumania, Bulgaria, Hungary, and Austria. . . . In some of these areas there is double talk about elections in the future. But plebiscites held after purges, liquidations, and deportations of liberal and democratic forces are a hollow mockery of the very tenets of democracy as practiced in the world prior to the advent of totalitarianism."

La Follette ironically recalled that it had been the new revolutionary government of Russia that had caused embarrassment at the Paris Peace Conference by publishing the texts of numerous secret agreements among the powers and in suggesting that peace terms be drawn up without regard to previous secret commitments. Now, La Follette said, "the Soviet Union has proceeded unilaterally, and without in any way consulting her two partners, the United States and Great Britain, to set up in country after country governments which are made in Moscow, and which do not fulfill any of the basic requirements agreed to at Yalta."

La Follette's censure was not reserved for the postwar activities of Russia alone. "I am convinced that Mr. Churchill's dogmatic, and at times arrogant, refusal to discuss any definite plans for freedom for subject peoples of the British Empire deserves the greatest censure if we are seeking a lasting peace. I am no more prepared to commit the United States to enforcing British rule over India, Burma, or Malta than I am to commit my country to enforcing Russian domination over Poland, Rumania, Austria, the Balkans, or any nations in the Baltic States. . . .

"We must make it clear that, although we are firmly resolved to participate actively in world affairs and meet to the full our responsibilities, we are equally determined that the power and influence of the United States shall never be lent to policing unjust peace terms and perpetuating an unjust status quo."

La Follette pleaded with his fellow Americans not to put too much faith in vague, general statements of idealistic purposes. "Verbal idealism does not cost anyone anything. Practical idealism comes high, for it demands mutual sacrifices and constant co-operation in the achievement of a common purpose. It is harder to achieve this practical idealism in peace than in war. If we are to be committed to deep-going international co-operation, we must be on the alert in behalf of true democracy and justice. . . .

"Too many of us forget that the death of Hitler has not removed a single cause of Hitlerism. Too many of us find it easy to hope that a package marked Peace, postmarked San Francisco, will be delivered to us some day soon, free of charge. Too many of us overlook the simple fact that there must be sweat and toil in peacemaking if we are to escape the blood and tears of war. There are no easy answers to peace. . . .

"America has a great constructive role to play at this critical juncture," Senator La Follette concluded. "America's role is to prove that economic abundance can be attained without sacrificing political freedom and human liberty. Here in the United States we can demonstrate that both are attainable if we have the courage, the vision, and the perseverance to plan and work for them. . . .

"Let us join with the other nations to preserve peace, but let us never give our consent or support to any extension of slavery, great power domination, or imperialism.

"Let us co-operate to extend freedom, democracy, and equality of opportunity to all men, regardless of race, color, or creed."

That address was the complete summing up, as Senator La Follette interpreted it, of the progressive view of the peace and the problems connected with it. While he found fault with a number of the provisions in the proposed United Nations Organization, and believed that certain improvements could be made, he nevertheless expressed it as his opinion that much good to humanity would come out of the plan if we applied, as he stated, the lessons of history to avoid the proved pitfalls and work toward the goal of human betterment throughout the world.

A not altogether unexpected result of the speech was the crystallization of an antagonism to everything for which Senator La Follette stood by that group of individuals characterized as "the Russia-can-do-no-wrong crowd." The party-liners and fellow travelers had accepted La Follette as one of them during the time he supported American neutrality and nonintervention in the late 1930's. They applauded his opposition to the making of any commitments by this country that would tend to draw us into foreign conflicts. Just as so many of their activities and views seemed inexplicable to the outsider, this acceptance of La Follette by Soviet sympathizers had its ironical side.

Overnight, it will be remembered, the party line changed when Mother Russia was attacked by Hitler. To the dismay of the party-liners and fellow travelers La Follette did not alter his position of nonintervention. They realized that his views might stand in the way of possible American aid to Russia. Their dismay gave way to suspicion and finally, as a consequence of the address to the Senate just discussed, to implacable hatred.

As a matter of fact American Communists and their fellow travelers always had had reason to look with suspicion on Senator La Follette. Despite their temporary acceptance of him for his so-called isolationist policy, which had no similarity whatever to the ideology of the party line, La Follette had never by so much as a word indicated approval of their tactics. On the contrary, it was often he who was instrumental in uncovering and calling attention to their divisive ways.

Prefacing his blunt criticism of Russia's recent foreign policy in his address to the Senate in May, 1945, La Follette told his colleagues that "I have no doubt some of my words will be misinterpreted and distorted by the smear bund. It has become virtually impossible to criticize the activities of Soviet Russia—however constructively—without bringing down about one's head a storm of smearing vilification and misrepresentation by a tightly organized minority in the United States.

"The very tactics which Adolf Hitler embraced as his own in *Mein Kampf*—the big lie, the big smear, and the wholesale impugning of motives and character—have been taken over by this Russia-can-do-no-wrong chorus in the United States."

La Follette reminded his listeners that he had been one of the earliest advocates of recognition of Russia. He also could have reminded them that he helped his father draft the letter the elder La Follette sent to the organizers of the 1924 Farmer-Labor convention in St. Paul in which the warning was given that there must not be any Communist domination of such a movement. The elder La Follette, because of the Communist tactics involving that convention, refused to have anything to do with it.

Senator Robert M. La Follette, Jr., underscored his steady opposition to Russia's apparent policy of expansion and imperialism in an article published in the *Progressive* on September 23, 1946. The article was a sharp rejoinder to Henry Wallace's Madison Square Garden address. He charged the former secretary of commerce with abandoning American ideals and principles in his appeal to let Russia have her way where she would.

"Modern war settles nothing," La Follette wrote. "One set of nations is vanquished on the field of battle, but the other set—the victors—hobbles away from the carnage, nurses its wounds, and quarrels over the spoils until a new alignment develops for a new and always more destructive war.

"It is criminal folly to think of war with Russia. But it is criminal folly, too, to underwrite and approve actions by the Soviet Union which must end in a world collision."

Senator La Follette concluded his remarks by terming as "totalitarian liberals" those who prostitute the real meaning of our language and counterfeit the coin of democratic, free-speaking, freedom-loving people.

"I for one intend to go on fighting until we get an American foreign policy which strikes at the very causes of war—which are imperialism, spheres of influence, power politics, dictatorships, social and economic dislocations, and racial and religious antagonisms.

"I for one will never lend my support to any group, organization, party, or candidate that endorses, accepts, or harbors policies or persons whose philosophy is destructive of the democracy which is the very heart and soul of everything I believe in."

The Communist-dominated Milwaukee County CIO Council marked their account against Senator Robert M. La Follette, Jr., "paid in full" on August 13, 1946, when the senator was defeated in the primary. The Milwaukee County CIO-PAC group succeeded in splitting that county's normal heavy labor support for La Follette and swung enough votes to La Follette's Republican opponent and to the Democratic candidate to help defeat him. In turn, the "Commie" element that had ruled the Milwaukee County Council and the state organization was thrown out of office within a month after the general election.

First appointed to the Senate Foreign Relations Committee in 1929, Senator La Follette's views on international matters were not fully appreciated at first. At the time of his appointment foreign affairs had not assumed a particularly important place in national affairs. As a matter of fact, after the historic debates of 1919–1920 on the League of Nations, American citizens were happy to follow President Harding back to "normalcy." Throughout the world there was a growing nationalism. True, the League of Nations was established in Geneva and there were slight flutterings of interest when Germany was permitted to join the international councils but we were chiefly interested in "keeping cool with Coolidge" as the decade wore on. When the economic crash came in 1929 we were still myopic in our world vision. We were hectically trying, with President Hoover, to find those two chickens and that corner around which prosperity was shyly hiding.

As our national economy gradually dragged itself out of the mire and it dawned on thinking Americans that international relations were a part of the whole situation, Senator La Follette began to be heard. Even though his was a minority membership on the Foreign Relations Committee, he was one of the few who had developed a working philosophy to bring to bear on the problems of foreign policy. Many individuals did not agree with La Follette. As the dictatorships gained ground in Europe and he refused to go along on certain matters that at the moment seemed important in efforts to halt, even temporarily, the totalitarian movement, Senator La Follette was branded as an isolationist. It was a nice smear word and short-circuited the thinking of many citizens who should have known better. Few, indeed, realized that he was one of the men in high elective office who possessed a truly broad viewpoint; that he was truly an American citizen, loyal to the principles of democracy that everyone at least paid lip service to but few related to problems and their solution. Senator La Follette was a practicing democrat and as such, like the Seekers mentioned in the introductory chapter, sought to spread democratic doctrine in a democratic way.

His view that we in this country must make democracy live and work, not only for our own good but as a vitalizing example for the rest of the world, was looked upon by the feverish internationalists and interventionists as isolation. The only trouble was that Senator Robert M. La Follette, Jr., stood for and urged a practical, workable idealism. Those who would have none of him were so busy chasing the will-o'-the-wisp of international brotherhood and good will that they never stopped long enough to define what they were after. It was the difference between those persons who were so impatient for reform that they accepted anything and those persons who sought reform but realized that its achievement is a painfully slow evolutionary process.

In terms of his position on foreign policy, *Life* regarded Senator La Follette as "the conscience of America." On June 5, 1944, the editors of the magazine contrasted the cynical power politics of Winston Churchill and the progressive American viewpoint as expounded by La Follette. While Franco seemed to have little to fear from the Churchillian policy and the British prime minister stood as the symbol of British exploitation, *Life* editors concluded:

"Neither Franco, nor Britain's rule in India, nor our own many shortcomings, nor any form of tyranny is permanently safe so long as America harbors her La Follettes, her democracy and her beliefs."

CHAPTER XVIII

Reorganization of Congress

On may 21, 1929, the United Press sent over its news wires from Washington a story telling of the confirmation of former Senator Irvine Lenroot as judge of the United States Court of Customs Claims. The story, written by Paul R. Mallon, contained the voting record of the senators in approving the nomination. It was not an unusual story of its kind. Previous stories of such action had carried roll-call votes and no one thought much about it.

But on this occasion the Old Guard senators were incensed. Senators Moses of New Hampshire, Reed of Pennsylvania, and Bingham of Connecticut decided that violations of the secrecy of executive sessions had to stop. The Rules Committee was persuaded to "withdraw" the floor privileges of the offending reporter. Senator Robert M. La Follette, Jr., rose during the course of the debate on the resolution to point out that, according to Senate rules and precedents, reporters were not among those listed as having the privilege of access to the floor of the Senate.

Senator La Follette ended his discussion with the observation that, since the Rules Committee was offering a resolution for which there were no grounds, it amounted simply to a resolution of censure and that Paul R. Mallon had done nothing more than many other correspondents had done in the past. The resolution was lost.

Senator Reed then initiated a move to punish the offending reporter by citation for contempt of the Senate if he refused to reveal the source of his information. Senator La Follette again rose and denounced the rule of secrecy. He declared that he had always believed it his right to tell how he had voted on any matter in any secret session.

"To this extent I have refused to place a Senate rule above the interest of the American people in their own public business. And if that is ground for my expulsion, I welcome submission of that issue to the electorate of Wisconsin."

La Follette then read a Washington dispatch written some time previously by Theodore Huntley, then correspondent for the Pittsburgh *Post-Gazette*. It gave full details about a Senate executive session at which Senator Reed and others tried to secure confirmation of John J. Esch as member of the Interstate Commerce Commission. La Follette carefully pointed out that part of the article was a quotation from Senator Reed himself, the man who, as the speaker said, "is so sedulous about preserving the complete secrecy of these executive sessions."

At that juncture Senator Burton K. Wheeler asked La Follette if he could tell the Senate what position the writer of that *Post-Gazette* article held at that moment.

"Why," replied La Follette, "he is now the secretary of the senator from Pennsylvania [Reed]. The senator hardly needs to subpoena reporters to find out how news of secret sessions is obtained; he can get it right in his own office."

With calm good humor Senator La Follette then read several other stories of secret executive sessions until even the Old Guard senators who were most determined to stop the leaks had to laugh. As a result, the Rules Committee reported for consideration and approval a new rule that eliminated the secrecy of voting in executive sessions of the Senate. This action was characterized by a Washington correspondent of long standing as "one of the really historic events" of the decade of the twenties.

This fight over the right of the Senate of the United States to conduct the public business in secret and its outcome were precedent shaking and probably would have been much longer in being decided in favor of the public had not Robert M. La Follette, Jr., seized the opportunity to carry on the campaign for a legislative branch of the government that would be more responsive to the public. But what he accomplished in the early summer of 1929 was nothing to what he finally brought to fulfillment on July 25, 1946, when the House of Representatives finally adopted Senate Bill 2177, 79th Congress, 2nd Session—a measure better known as the Congressional Reorganization Act of 1946.

The history of the reorganization of the machinery of Congress has been one of the development of the committee system. In the House, occasional reaction against a lack of centralized authority over the course of legislation through Congress or against overdictatorial powers of the speaker of the House had resulted in some rule and procedural changes.

One of the most spectacular revolts of the House membership against the powers of the speaker as they had developed through the years was the successful fight against Cannonism which took place in March, 1910. A coalition of Democrats and progressive Republicans under the leadership of Representative George W. Norris put through the rule that stripped the speaker of powers to appoint committees and set up the Committee on Committees.

The Budget and Accounting Act of 1921 had a profound effect upon House organization. Provisions of that measure forced the House to place all responsibility for appropriation measures in the Committee on Appropriations. Prior to that time, no less than eight committees acting independently had divided the work of determining appropriations.

It was also in 1921 that the Senate adopted a resolution offered by Senator Brandegee which reduced the number of standing committees of the Senate from 74 to 34. The Senate, as a continuing body, was not faced with the job of having to organize for every new session of Congress. Changes in the Senate were accomplished through changes in rules and procedure. Occasionally, as a result of heavy public pressure, a new rule might be approved. Such was the case when at the beginning of the special session in April, 1917, the Senate adopted the rule of cloture to limit debate. Public reaction to the famous filibuster by the Senate opposition to the Armed Ship bill forced the new rule on the Senate.

Earlier, as has been mentioned, the elder Senator La Follette watched the methods used by the Senate majority to secure passage of pet measures he thought inimical to the best interests of the nation and on several occasions forced modification in applications of the rules by himself using the rules to make some changes. He had earlier fathered bills to provide for a Legislative Reference Service and in 1919 had urged changes in the conference system of reconciling differences between Senate and House versions of bills.

An important factor motivating the appeals for a thoroughgoing reorganization, aside from the growing complexity of government itself, had been the shift in emphasis from the purely legislative branch to the executive branch, which had at times seemed to take over the functions of determining what legislation should be considered. There was also involved a drift away from the policy-making functions of the legislative branch toward an emphasis on administrative agencies responsible to the executive. Discussing this issue, Senator Robert M. La Follette, Jr., said:

"The phrase delegating to the President or some one of his · recognized agents the power to 'issue such regulations and orders as he may deem necessary or proper in order to carry out the purposes and provisions of this act, is now one of the indispensable and most significant portions of most policy legislation adopted by Congress.

"The constantly growing body of executive or administrative law has become both a necessity to the operation of modern government and a threat to the constitutional function of Congress as the legislative policy-making branch of the government.

"As the function of government has become more and more technical, the administrative problems have become more significant in the formulation of legislation. Consequently there has been a growing tendency for Congress to turn to the Executive for guidance in drawing new legislation—not out of any lazy desire to avoid its responsibility, but rather out of conscientious effort to frame good legislation that will prove workable. The administrators of the government are for the most part responsible to the Executive, and as a result the Executive's function in proposing and drawing new legislation has been tremendously enlarged.

"With this growing emphasis upon the day-to-day application

of laws, the policy-making functions of government are drifting away from the point at which the laws were passed.

"Basically, the present weakness of Congress lies in its failure to meet this problem. To check on an administrative agency's appropriation after it is spent is a crude discipline at best—a negative approach, capable of crippling an agency and its offending program, but incapable of putting something positive and constructive in its place.

"If the control of governmental policy is to remain with the people's elected representatives, as the framers of the Constitution intended it should, and not drift into the hands of a relatively irresponsible bureaucracy, Congress will have to streamline its organization. At the same time it will have to devise new instrumentalities and methods which will afford a positive, constructive liaison and high-policy relationship with the administrative arm of the national government."

Taking note of a growing tendency to criticize Congress for every kind and degree of irritation felt by citizens against government, Senator La Follette warned in an article in the July, 1943, *Atlantic Monthly* that there was danger of complete loss of influence if Congress did not take stock of the situation and get to work on reorganization to meet the needs of the present day. He pointed out that, contrary to general assumption, the membership of Congress was on as high a level as it ever had been but that they were enmeshed in a system of committees, rules, and precedents that made it difficult, if not almost impossible, to operate efficiently.

Without mincing words La Follette took sharp issue with "the despicable misrepresentation" of Congressional activities and even called President Roosevelt to task for charging in his Labor Day address that Congress, by its inaction, had brought the nation perilously close to a dangerous inflation for approving certain legislative restrictions in the price-control law. Senator La Follette pointed out that the provision to which the President had taken such exception had been enacted with the full approval of the secretary of agriculture.

As Senator La Follette analyzed the matter, the criticisms of Congress, whether justified or not, did indicate a growing belief that Congress was not adequate to "the needs of modern government." He suggested a regrouping of committees, greater collaboration between the two Houses of Congress through the instrument of the joint committee, tighter control over appropriation and revenue measures, and means for closer liaison between the legislative and executive branches of the government.

The July issue of *Atlantic Monthly* had scarcely hit the newsstands when Senator Harry S. Truman rose and asked that the article be inserted in the *Congressional Record*. "It is a most interesting article," Senator Truman said in asking the privilege. "I hope all members of this body will read it."

Following up his suggestions in the *Atlantic* article, Senator La Follette introduced on July 5, 1943, a resolution to amend the rules of the Senate to provide a reorganization of the committee structure of that body. La Follette proposed to cut the number of Senate committees from 33 to 13. Members were to be limited in the memberships they could hold, and jurisdiction of all thirteen committees was carefully outlined. Stating that the proposal was merely suggestive and submitted in all humility for the consideration of his colleagues, Senator La Follette said:

"I have not served in this body for these many years without realizing the grave difficulties involved in any attempt to reorganize its committee structure, but I do say that, in the face of the enormous problems and the complex subject with which the Congress is now confronted, and with which it will be confronted in the postwar period, I think no person familiar with the situation in the Senate today can deny that there is a pressing need for committee reorganization and for the streamlining of the legislative branch of the government if it is to survive in the struggle for power which is bound to continue.

"I realize that the moment it is suggested that one committee shall be combined with another immediately the question of the chairmanship is involved, and also other matters; but, Mr. President, it is my considered judgment that there is no more important problem before the Congress of the United States than the question of trying to reorganize its procedure and to strengthen its committee structure in order that it may stand on a more equal footing with the executive arm of the government."

Following La Follette's explanation of the resolution, Senator Francis Maloney arose to agree with him and said:

"I do not know that I would approve of his suggested plan in its entirety, but rather than to do nothing about it, I would, on the basis of the explanation he has made, accept his plan without seeing it. He has wisely recognized the fact that as such a plan is considered, senators will be confronted with the necessity of giving up chairmanships of important committees, and that that presents a kind of sacrifice. I have not been a member of the Senate for so long a time as has the senator from Wisconsin, but I have been here for a longer period of time than most members of the Senate now on the floor, and so strongly feel the need for such a step that I would sacrifice whatever seniority positions I hold on committees and start over again on any or all of them."

In the meantime members of both Houses of Congress became interested in the subject but nothing definite resulted until late in December, 1944, when, without a dissenting vote in either House, a joint committee composed of six senators and six representatives was set up under the chairmanship of Senator Maloney. Maloney, however, died before anything could be started. The original resolution had been sponsored jointly by Senator Maloney and Representative A. S. Mike Monroney.

Authority for the joint committee was renewed early in February, 1945, at which time the committee organization was completed with Senator La Follette as chairman and Representative Monroney as vice-chairman.

The committee held thirty-nine public hearings and four executive sessions between March 13 and June 29, 1945. The testimony of 102 witnesses was taken, 45 of whom were members of Congress. In addition, 37 members and many interested private citizens submitted written statements. The testimony heard by the committee fills nearly 1,200 printed pages and the index lists every possible subject on Congress from "Absenteeism" to "Witnesses, treatment of." In addition, both Senator La Follette and Representative Monroney made every effort, through personal letters to members of Congress and by telephone calls, to get as many as possible to submit their ideas on reorganization to the committee.

The unanimous committee report submitted to both Houses on March 4, 1946, reported:

"A review of the testimony received reveals a wide area of agreement among the witnesses with respect to both the conditions that handicap Congress in the efficient performance of its proper functions and as to many appropriate remedies for these defects."

Shortly after the report had been submitted, Senator La Follette and Representative Monroney discussed it in addresses before the annual meeting of the American Political Science Association. Said La Follette:

"After long and careful deliberation last fall and winter, the Joint Committee reached almost unanimous agreement upon its final report. All things considered, I think you will agree with me that this was a notable achievement. Considering the scope and complexity of the undertaking, the complexion of the committee in representing diverse viewpoints, and the sweeping character of the proposals, I had hardly dared hope that we could obtain such general agreement upon a program of positive action. In a real sense, therefore, the report of the committee is a consensus report."

That modest statement, however, failed to tell the whole story. Members of the committee, anxious to present a report on which they all could agree in substance, finally worked out a simple procedure. During those "long and careful deliberations" mentioned by Senator La Follette, the chairman would read portions of the proposed report. Those matters about which there was some division of opinion were passed over as committee members found portions on which they could agree. At the next meeting the passed-over sections were reread and after careful discussion members discovered areas of agreement with still some points in dispute. Persuasion and debate continued until there were but four points on which three committee members could not agree with the rest. And each of the three members disagreed over different matters! Finally, in order to circumvent that difficulty, the report was prepared with footnotes indicating the recommendations on which the three could not agree.

The report recommended action on eight general topics:

1. *Committee Structure and Operation.* The major recommendations included reorganization and reduction in the number of Senate and House committees, their jurisdiction, and providing expert staffs for the committees.

2. *Majority and Minority Policy Committees.* This section recommended establishment of formal committees for determination and expression of majority and minority party policies. Also recommended was a Joint Legislative-Executive Council composed of the majority policy committees of both Houses to meet with the Executive to facilitate formulation and carrying out of national policy.

3. *Research and Staff Facilities.* The major recommendations of this section suggested enlargement of the Legislative Reference Service, an administrative assistant for each member of Congress, and establishment of a Congressional Personnel Office.

4. *Strengthening Fiscal Control.* This section suggested that by joint action of the Revenue and Appropriations committees of both Houses submit to Congress within sixty days after the beginning of a new session a concurrent resolution setting over-all estimated federal receipts and expenditures and setting the debt limitation; that the practice of holding Appropriations Committee hearings in secret or executive session cease; that legislative "riders" to appropriation bills be discontinued.

5. *More Efficient Use of Congressional Time.* The committee recommended that Congress stop serving as a common council for the District of Columbia and provide for self-rule of the district; that Congress delegate authority for settlement of claims against the federal government and to handle matters that had been the subject of private bills; that regular recess be taken at the end of the fiscal year.

6. *Registration of Organized Groups.* A recommendation that Congress enact legislation for the regulation of lobbying.

7. *Congressional Pay and Retirement.* This section recommended the salary increase to $15,000 annually and that members of Congress be permitted to join the Federal Retirement System on a contributory basis.

8. *Other Recommendations.* Under this subject, the committee

made a number of suggestions regarding improvement of the physical arrangements in the Capitol and the transfer of inactive records to the National Archives. It also made suggestions regarding the *Congressional Record*.

"These proposals," an enthusiastic editorial in *Life* for March 11, 1946, declared, "add up to the best horse sense that Congress has spoken to itself in several decades. If adopted, as they certainly should be, and *in toto*, Congress can become a more effective body, well on the path to retrieved success."

Such a sketch of the far-reaching, precedent-shattering proposals made by the Joint Committee on the Organization of Congress admittedly does violence to the carefully detailed blueprint for the streamlining of Congress. Probably no member of Congress was more aware of the almost revolutionary character of the proposals than was the committee chairman, Senator Robert M. La Follette, Jr. Over the many years he had had intimate knowledge of Senate affairs, first as his father's secretary and then as senator, La Follette had achieved distinction among his colleagues as the outstanding parliamentarian. It was to him that members from both sides turned when they needed the answer to a particularly knotty problem about legislative matters. Correspondents representing the major newspapers and press services of the nation had named him the outstanding parliamentarian and hardest working senator.

To Senator La Follette the work of the Joint Committee was of supreme importance. It was a major contribution of his philosophy of a free, representative government. "Representative government is at stake," he had told members of the American Political Science Association. "Either the Congress will become an efficient lawmaking body, or it will perish in the welter of government bureaucracy and confusion. Upon a stronger and more effective Congress depends the preservation of freedom in the United States."

While the report itself was an achievement, La Follette and his colleagues knew that the next step would perhaps be the toughest. The committee decided to present its recommendations in the form of a unified bill to avoid "splintering" and possibly losing, through obstructive legislative tactics, important parts of the plan. In fact, there were criticisms that the proposed bill contained too many different matters.

On May 13, 1946, Senator La Follette introduced a bill "to provide for increased efficiency in the legislative branch of the government." The bill was referred to the Special Committee on the Organization of Congress. Planning ahead and foreseeing all possible contingencies, La Follette, with strong bipartisan support, got the Senate to approve the naming of the senatorial members of the Joint Committee as a special Senate committee to handle the bill.

In the Senate debate on the bill, Senator Forrest Donnell of Missouri objected to elimination of the power to create special committees. It was his opinion that such a change might create a situation in which the Senate would be unable to provide proper machinery to consider special problems. Donnell called attention to the fact that the bill under debate had been reported by a special committee of which La Follette was chairman.

"I think the senator's own committee illustrates the fact that under some circumstances . . . a special committee can render distinguished and valuable services to the Congress," Donnell said.

"The reason why it was necessary to create a special committee to study the pending measure," Senator La Follette replied, "was in order to escape from the archaic committee system we are trying to remedy. I think the Senate will find that if it will go along with the recommendations regarding committee reorganization that situation will disappear in the future."

The bill reported by the committee presented in legislative form the recommendations of the Joint Committee with the proposal for self-government for the District of Columbia eliminated. A separate bill providing for the same thing had been introduced and was pending. In its report asking favorable consideration the committee stated:

"Congressional reform will not solve all the problems that beset us. That will require good men, good will, and good policies as well as good governmental machinery. But modernized machinery will greatly increase the efficiency of Congress. By revising our antiquated rules and improving our facilities, we can at once revitalize our National Legislature, expedite the adjustment of our postwar problems, and renew popular faith in American democracy. The time has come for Congress to reform itself. The time to act is now."

The summer of 1946 was undoubtedly a bad time to introduce legislation of such consequence. Congressional elections were coming up and all members of the House were anxious to get back to their constituencies. A third of the Senate membership, including Senator La Follette, was in the same situation. On top of the pressure of politics was the heavy pressure of important legislation. Bills pertaining to housing, the knotty problem of what to do with OPA and price-control extension, disposition of the question of control of atomic energy, legislation respecting participation in the United Nations and UNRRA, not to mention the appropriations bills and extension of the draft, all conspired to produce an almost unprecedented legislative log jam. Early in June the Senate had caught up with the House on legislative matters and it seemed there might be a short lull in its activities.

Several Senate bills were pending, but Senator La Follette persuaded the majority Senate leader, Senator Barkley, to allot four days for consideration of the reorganization bill. Taking no chances that consideration might be blocked on the plea of senators that they had not received copies of either the committee report or the bill, La Follette sent the material by special messenger to each senator's home.

When debate on the bill opened on June 5, few people thought La Follette had a chance even to get the measure to a vote. He had bipartisan support for the bill. Both the majority and minority floor leaders favored the bill, but opponents, mostly southern Democrats, were sure they could kill it by filibuster. The burden of piloting the bill through the debate fell almost entirely on La Follette. Both Republican and Democratic leaders were hesitant to enter into the debate for the simple reason that none of them wanted it to be considered a purely partisan measure.

On the third day of the debate the opposition unexpectedly chose a comparatively minor provision of the measure as the center of their attack and La Follette just as vigorously supported the provision which had set up the office of director of Congressional personnel. Senator Kenneth McKellar started the ball rolling for the opposition by characterizing the proposed director as a "supersenator" and said:

"I am against this bill on principle. I am against it on constitutional grounds. If our forefathers had thought that the Senate of the United States ought to have a general administrator over it, to operate the Senate as he thought best, they would have so provided. That is substantially what the bill would do, in my judgment. I have not read it with the care which it deserves because I have not had the time. But as I understand it, the bill provides for a superlord over the Senate.

". . . I believe that this is the kind of bill which ought not to be hurried through. It is a revolutionary measure. It tears down all the landmarks and would substitute entirely new ones. The bill would change the whole purpose of the Senate. . . . It would entirely revolutionize the Senate."

Senator John Overton of Louisiana also was unhappy about the bill. He objected to reorganizing the committees and believed "it is a situation which in all probability ought to have been let alone to start with."

It remained for Senator Tom Connally of Texas to put the finishing touches to the agonized cries of the opposition.

"This bill is so abhorrent to my concept of the duties and responsibilities of the Senate that I simply cannot support it," Connally told his colleagues. "We are discrediting ourselves before the country by telling that we have been operating the Senate in such a slipshod way that it must be reformed and streamlined, and we must get some people with sense to tell us what to do—some experts."

Senator Barkley, however, joined with Senator Wallace White, Jr., of Maine, the minority floor leader, in pledging support of the bill. "I am for the bill, and shall vote for it, even with what may be regarded as its imperfections, because I think we must make a start," Barkley told the Senate. "The country expects us to do so."

On June 10, the last day allotted for consideration of the bill, a full-blown filibuster against the measure got started, with Senator John McClellan of Arkansas devoting more than two hours to a defense of his right to appoint page boys from his state and denouncing the very notion of a director of Congressional personnel who might have something to say about the matter. Senator Styles Bridges of New Hampshire finally obtained the floor and launched into a full-scale defense of the bill and the reasons for its proposal at that particular time. It gave Senator La Follette an opportunity to confer with other supporters and the floor leaders to work out a plan for breaking the filibuster and getting a final vote on the bill. After Bridges had spoken about forty-five minutes, and in order to hold the floor until La Follette's return, the senator from New Hampshire suggested the absence of a quorum.

At that juncture Senator La Follette returned to the floor and announced that if he could get a unanimous-consent agreement to bring the bill to a final vote by five o'clock, he was prepared to offer an amendment eliminating the entire section referring to the director of Congressional personnel and to increase the membership of the Appropriations Committee from 13 to 21. Senator Clyde Hoey of North Carolina was in the chair as presiding officer. Following agreement as to division of the time until the final vote, Senator Hoey put the question on the unanimous-consent agreement, against which he heard no objection. La Follette then offered the proposed amendments, which were accepted.

Senator Theodore Bilbo had just arrived on the floor and stated that he wished to object to the unanimous-consent agreement. The presiding officer, however, informed the senator from Mississippi that it had already been agreed to. Bilbo complained that he had told the floor leader that he wanted to speak on the bill and that he would not get through before five o'clock. Bilbo tried unsuccessfully on another occasion to obtain the floor but was again ruled out of order. Senator Harry Byrd of Virginia finally did yield the floor to Bilbo for about ten minutes. He announced his opposition to the measure and with almost disarming candor gave expression to the real reason for the opposition that had developed. He said:

"I love the Republicans but I do not like to surrender so many chairmanships while the Democratic party is in power. We have 33 committees and most of them have plenty of business to attend to. I believe that that business can be much better attended to under the present system than under a system which would undertake to consolidate so much business in the hands of 15 or 16 committees. I think that would be a mistake governmentally. It certainly would be a mistake politically."

Shortly thereafter the final vote was taken and the Legislative Reorganization bill of 1946 was approved by the astonishing vote of 49 to 16. That his colleagues considered it a personal triumph for Senator La Follette and the manner in which he managed the whole debate was attested to by the fact that immediately after the vote senators from both sides of the floor crowded around La Follette's desk to congratulate him.

The Washington *Post's* veteran Senate correspondent, Robert C. Albright, wrote of the passage of the bill:

"Washington has just witnessed a legislative miracle.

"While all the world gasped, the hidebound U.S. Senate voted 49 to 16 to streamline its antiquated committees and lift its wrinkled face.

"The man behind the miracle was Wisconsin's quiet, 51-year-old Robert M. La Follette, Jr., and a story as intriguing as the miracle itself.

"The tool he used to do the job was the rarest commodity in Washington today—the 'know-how' of a legislative craftsman.

"In a Capitol famed for its fumbles and failures—for its false starts and makeshift compromises—for its political stumblebums as well—the Senate cleanly finished a job of work. . . .

"None watched the performance with more interest than the press gallery itself. There—since before this reporter's time—there has been a La Follette legend. Newsmen who disagreed with his international views—even a few who found fault with his progressive policies—were agreed on the legend. It was this: In legislative statecraft, there was no better craftsman.

"They watched with the respect men everywhere show for a skilled workman. On Monday, June 10, La Follette lived up to the legend. In fact, he built a new one.

"At 12 noon of that day, the refurbishing he proposed to give Congress seemed far from realization. A filibuster was in full swing. Colleagues were bent on killing off any reform. By five, La Follette had broken the filibuster, and the bill was on its way to the House. . . . The Senate actually voted to go modern. The press gallery labeled the miracle: 'Operation La Follette.'"

Sent to the House, the La Follette-Monroney reorganization bill lay on the speaker's table for nearly six weeks. The end of the session was approaching and prospects for considering the measure looked hopeless. Both Representatives Mike Monroney and Everett Dirksen made every effort to get the bill before the House but Speaker Sam Rayburn did not like the bill as it had passed the Senate.

As one of the group of Democratic leaders of Congress, the so-called "Big Four," who met with President Truman every Monday morning to discuss and plan legislative matters, Speaker Rayburn did not like the provision for the Joint Legislative-Executive Council. Neither did he like any lessening of his power that might result from establishment of the proposed seven-man majority policy committee. An agreement was finally made to submit a substitute for the Senate-approved measure. It eliminated the provisions Speaker Rayburn did not like. Two other concessions had to be made to get the bill before the House. The provision of the original bill for an administrative assistant for each member of Congress was withdrawn, as was the provision for making effective the legislative budget ceilings.

The substitute measure was considered by the House on July 25. After eight hours of debate led by Representatives Monroney and Dirksen the reorganization bill was approved by a 229-to-61 vote.

An interested and concerned onlooker during that day of debate was Senator Robert M. La Follette, Jr. La Follette had to leave before the final vote to deliver an address which was to be broadcast over a Milwaukee radio station. His campaign for nomination to succeed himself as senator was in full swing and La Follette had not been able to get back to Wisconsin because of the pressure of legislative business. Stopping in the House restaurant to get a bite to eat before his radio talk, La Follette was informed that the bill had finally passed. His listeners in Wisconsin that evening got the first word of the passage of the reorganization bill when La Follette announced the fact during the course of his speech.

The next day Senator La Follette moved Senate concurrence on the bill as amended by the House. The motion was agreed to and the bill providing for the first major reorganization of Congress in many years became law. La Follette had considered carefully whether to ask for a conference between the Senate and House to compose the differences between the measures but finally decided against it on the ground that agreement could not be reached before adjournment.

On August 1, with the approval of the Senate majority and minority leaders, Senator La Follette introduced an amendment to a pending deficiency appropriation measure providing funds for an administrative assistant for each senator. The provision had been eliminated by the House when the original bill was up for passage. Senator Barkley explained to his colleagues that the amendment was merely a revival of the provision that had already passed the Senate. He announced that an agreement had been reached with House members that if the Senate wanted the funds for the administrative assistants, the House would agree to the addition to the deficiency appropriation bill. The amendment was agreed to. Thus, again because of his expert knowledge of parliamentary procedure, Senator La Follette was able to salvage another part of the reorganization measure.

Almost as soon as Congress had adjourned, opponents of the measure began to urge changes. The changes centered around suggestions that the committee structure revert to its old form. But the shift from a Democratic majority to Republican domination of Congress as a result of the November elections changed the situation. The Republican Steering Committee meeting in Washington soon after the election issued a statement that it would support the reorganization act to the full.

Without debate or opposition the House of Representatives of the new 80th Congress adopted the rule changes prescribed by the reorganization act. Committees in the House were reduced from 48 to 19 and in the Senate from 33 to 15. The new Senate committee reorganization and structure followed the pattern suggested by Senator La Follette in 1943. The reorganized House committees followed a plan given to the Joint Committee by Representative James W. Wadsworth of New York.

Former Speaker Sam Rayburn, now House minority leader, soon discovered the virtues of at least two of the provisions he had been instrumental in pruning out of the original bill. He had objected to the majority and minority policy committees but as minority leader he began to see the value of party responsibility.

On January 14, 1947, Representative Rayburn announced, after conferring with President Truman, that the President had decided to call Congressional leaders in for frequent consultation on legislative matters. The announcement was tacit admission of the value of the Joint Legislative-Executive Council that had been taken out of the bill at Rayburn's request!

According to Capitol observers, the Reorganization Act would probably play an important role in still another direction. President Truman had proposed merging the War and Navy Departments into a single Department of the Armed Forces. Under the rules adopted as a result of the Reorganization Act, the old committees on Military Affairs and the Navy were merged into single committees on the Armed Forces in both Houses of Congress. The reorganized committees provided for closer scrutiny of military matters and made possible easier co-ordination of Army and Navy affairs. It added impetus to President Truman's program for merging the two departments.

In April, 1947, a committee of twenty-three distinguished American citizens named by *Collier's Magazine* to select one member of the Senate and one member of the House of Representatives as recipients of that magazine's award for distinguished Congressional service, chose Robert M. La Follette, Jr., as the senator who in 1946 had made the greatest contribution "to direct thoughtful attention to the fundamental role of Congress to point up the fact that representative lawmaking bodies are the symbol and basis essential for freedom."

In announcing the selection of Senator La Follette, the editors of *Collier's* wrote:

". . . his defeat, in the opinion of Collier's Congressional Awards Committee, subtracted nothing from the great service he rendered our country last year, when he became the key figure in efforts to modernize Congressional rules and organization. The Congress had suffered in popular respect because it stumbled over its own feet as it attempted to operate in the 1940s with methods and organization developed in the 1890s.

"It was the definite opinion of all those consulted by the Congressional Awards Committee that La Follette is entitled to credit for passage of the Congressional reorganization plan. 'The executive branch of the government had been taking over,' said a Washington news writer consulted by the Committee, 'and the Congress, rattled by criticism and confused by the rush of events, did not seem to realize fully where its legislation was leading. The Congressional Reorganization Act, which La Follette put through, is the first well-directed effort to enable the Congress to recapture and to exercise the powers reposed in it by our Constitution and our political system.'"

Silver plaques were given to Senator La Follette and Representative Jesse P. Wolcott of Michigan in a White House ceremony presided over by President Harry S. Truman. La Follette designated the University of Wisconsin as the beneficiary of a $10,000 gift by *Collier's* that was part of the award. He asked that the regents of the university set up a graduate scholarship "to promote the study of government reorganization, to the end that the instrumentalities of government at all levels may function more efficiently and be more responsive to the will of the people."

In its comment on the honor bestowed on Bob La Follette, the Washington *Daily News* said:

"His splendid leadership in the move to reform the organization and procedures of Congress entitles him to national gratitude. But that was only one of his many contributions to the country in a long and brilliant senatorial career. The voters of Wisconsin made what we think they will come to regret as a mistake when they defeated him for reelection last November.

"We are delighted that the many Washington correspondents, editors, and political scientists who nominated him for the *Collier's* award, and the national committee of distinguished citizens which named him to receive it, placed a truer, fairer value on Senator La Follette's services to the American people."

CHAPTER XIX

An Appraisal

INDIGNANT WORKERS on the Wisconsin branch of the Underground Railroad supplied the immediate impetus that gave to the state and the nation the Republican party. Strangely enough, citizens of the new Badger State were motivated by exactly the same theory on which South Carolina a few years later based her secession—states' rights. Ardent abolitionists, Wisconsinites were angry over enforcement of the Fugitive Slave law which had been incorporated in the Compromise of 1850. They were literally up in arms, and aided by decisions of the State Supreme Court, defied the federal government. At a Lincoln Day dinner of the National Republican Club at the Waldorf-Astoria Hotel in New York on February 12, 1938, the governor of Vermont, now Senator George D. Aiken, sharply reminded his fellow Republicans of the humble origins of their party. He called to the attention of the well-fed banqueters that the strength of the Republican party had depended upon attracting men "whose families slept on beds of straw, which were renewed each year at threshing time; men who rose before daylight to cradle buckwheat while the dew was on so that it would not shell and waste the precious grain; men who wielded the ax or followed the plow until darkness fell and who, after supper, by the dim light of a candle lantern, did the chores and made preparation for the morrow, until weariness overcame them. . . .

"They were the strength of America, and the greatness of

the nation is ever dependent on such as they. Forever the rise
and fall of a political party must depend on its ability to attract
those who spin and those who toil."

Governor Aiken stated exactly one of the major factors that
elevated Robert M. La Follette to a position of political leadership in Wisconsin. In Wisconsin the Republican party had become a captive of the dominant economic interests when La
Follette came onto the scene. At that time, in the early 1880's,
the United States senatorships "belonged" to the lumber and
railroad interests, one Wisconsin senator representing each
whether Republicans or Democrats controlled the legislature.
The political rulers of Wisconsin were quite comfortable in their
unquestioned control until one of their representatives, the Republican boss of Dane County, refused to sanction Robert M.
La Follette's candidacy for the district attorneyship. It took
nearly twenty years to bring home to the Republican bosses the
disastrous effects of that refusal. In that time Robert M. La Follette had led a successful fight within the party to break the
domination of the bosses and had been elected governor. In
another five years the traditional control over the senatorships
was broken when the legislature elected La Follette as senator
from Wisconsin.

From the time that the La Follette name became prominently
connected with Wisconsin politics the state attracted the atten-
ion of interested people throughout the country. The political
reforms that came in the wake of the Wisconsin Progressive movement beginning with La Follette's election to the governorship
might have been adopted and the Wisconsin Idea developed
without much notice. The very nature of the situation, together
with the personality of the man who led the movement, pre-
cluded that. In the first place, the leadership that had been entrenched in power for so many years had been overthrown. The
same effort was being made in other states but without the same
success. In the second place was the personality of Robert M.
La Follette. One of the top-ranking public speakers of a day
when there were many accomplished speakers, La Follette used
his abilities as an orator to get his ideas and message to the
people. To him every speech was a chapter in a determined cam-

paign of adult education. As a popular lecturer on the Chautauqua circuit, La Follette spread the story of what he was trying to accomplish in Wisconsin.

It was inevitable, of course, that as he achieved political power and leadership La Follette should be accused of the very kind of bossism against which he constantly fought. He did dominate the state politically. Yet that domination did not go unchallenged. Stalwart Republicans battled to regain the control they had lost. They did not regain the governorship, though, until the Progressive Republicanism that La Follette sponsored had had an opportunity—the opportunity of fourteen years in the executive office of the state—to put its principles into practice and on the statute books.

In two other respects Robert M. La Follette did not qualify as a boss. He had done what no boss of the old school would consciously have done—he eliminated the power of patronage by having the legislature put practically all salaried positions under civil service. Nor did he possess a machine in the well-established meaning of that term. His appeal for support was to the intelligence and moral sensitivity of the people of Wisconsin.

One of the factors that made the Wisconsin situation of interest was the widely accepted notion that La Follette had succeeded in establishing a new third party. The practical political effect of the movement in Wisconsin was undoubtedly that of a new third party. "Progressive" and "Stalwart" were generally thought of as the names of different parties. Actually they were adjectives attached to members of the same party with different points of view. To confuse the unknowing further, both factions campaigned as if they were separate parties.

This gave rise to the easy explanation in some quarters that to understand Wisconsin politics one need only to keep in mind that the Badger State, like so many of the southern states, was a one-party state. It is true that Wisconsin had a long record of Republicanism with but short Democratic interludes. In the 87 years of its statehood, from 1848 to 1935, Wisconsin had had 6 Democratic governors, who served a total of 14 years, one Whig, who served 2 years, and 21 Republican governors, who served a total of 71 years. After the establishment of the Progressive party in 1934, Wisconsin has been served by one Progressive, Governor Philip La Follette, who was in office four years—he had previously served one term as a Republican—another Progressive was elected but died before his inauguration, and two Republicans.

Wisconsin Stalwarts insist, however, that of the governors serving up to 1935 at least five should be classified as "Progressive." Of one, Fred R. Zimmerman, neither faction was sure. Yet, until the Progressive party was formed in 1934, those five campaigned and were elected as Republicans. The intransigent opposition of Stalwarts to the efforts of the La Follette faction to make the party the vehicle of progressivism created the conditions that were so confusing to citizens of other states. Both factions laid claim to the same label. The intraparty strife that resulted produced, for all practical purposes, two parties. This internal strife made the primary campaigns particularly important. Progressives and Stalwarts slugged it out for the party nomination. Because of lack of contests in their own parties, both Democrats and Socialists often entered the Republican primary elections to support Progressive candidates. This situation led to many bitter arguments as to the actual numerical strength of the Progressives.

Not until 1926 were the Progressives able to send two of their number to the Senate. The Wisconsin delegation to the national Republican conventions included both Stalwarts and Progressives. From 1908 up to and including the 1928 convention, Progressives always submitted a minority report to the report of the resolutions committee. That minority report, setting forth the Progressive position, always caused discussion and sometimes no little embarrassment to the conservative leadership of the party.

At the 1928 national Republican convention in Kansas City, Senator Robert M. La Follette, Jr., presented the minority report of the Wisconsin delegation. Since 1908, the appearance of the Wisconsin delegate to present the minority report had been a regular event. It was the time for jeering and loud booing. With calm self-assurance, Young Bob reminded the delegates that of the 35 planks offered by the Wisconsin delegation since 1908,

32 had been written into law. The booing stopped momentarily and some of the delegates cheered approval. The senator appeared to be grateful.

"It is so unusual for a Wisconsin delegate to receive applause from a Republican convention," he laughed good-naturedly, "that I pause to thank you."

So far as the party label was concerned, the elder La Follette never considered himself as anything but a Republican, certainly until the 1924 campaign for the presidency. Up to and including the 1908 campaign, La Follette was regular in his support of the Republican presidential candidates. His regularity, however, was not so constant after the emergence of the Progressive Republican group in 1910. La Follette's left-handed support of Wilson in the 1912 campaign was undoubtedly a factor in placing the state, for the first time in its history, in the Democratic column in a presidential year. Although Wisconsin citizens gave the Democratic candidate for president a plurality of votes that year, they elected Republicans to the governorship and other state offices. In 1916 and 1920 La Follette refused to become active in support of the Republican candidates. The state returned to the Republican column, but in 1924 cast its electoral vote for La Follette.

One of the more important differences between Progressives and Stalwarts, despite all the campaign oratory, charges and countercharges, was the difference in attitude toward party regularity and party responsibility. In the Progressive view, the integrity of the principles that made for working democracy counted most; party was merely a means to an end. To the Stalwarts, party organization and responsibility were uppermost; principles might have to be compromised or sacrificed to preserve the party.

It is quite likely one of those interesting coincidences, but it is worth recalling that Frederick Jackson Turner wrote his monumental essay on "The Significance of the American Frontier" at the same time Robert M. La Follette was launching his campaign against the bosses in the early 1890's. Turner wrote that the frontier had done much to promote democracy but that the democracy born of free land had its dangers as well as its benefits. The individualism born of frontier democracy, the noted historian pointed out, allowed a laxity in regard to governmental affairs which made possible the spoils system and all the evils that flowed from the lack of a well-developed civic spirit.

Robert M. La Follette had been born on the frontier of parents whose forebears settled first in New Jersey but crossed the Alleghenies and moved on west in search of economic opportunity. But events held him to one spot long enough for him to realize that something was wrong with the democracy he took for granted. His brush with the political boss of Dane County over his right to run for office made him aware of a situation he, as a self-respecting citizen, could not accept. La Follette's service in the House of Representatives gave him a realization of the interconnection between political and economic domination and how the one was used to secure the other for the benefit of a few.

His experiences led to the belief that political and economic democracy—freedom of opportunity for all—would not long survive if the tendencies toward concentration of power were not checked. Being an individualist, Robert M. La Follette accepted the challenge of the political bosses and eventually put them to rout. He learned, instinctively and probably because he was not afraid to pass moral judgment on political and economic activities, that political freedom was effective only in proportion to the way it was used. Robert M. La Follette stirred an entire state into an awareness of what he knew and got the citizens to act. In effect, his was an attempt to re-create an equality of opportunity that had been lost sight of as American society turned inward upon itself when the frontier disappeared.

In the early days of the struggle the program to achieve that equality could be outlined in terms of regulating the trusts, enactment of direct primary laws, setting up programs of conservation of the natural resources of the nation, limiting some of the excessive abuses by employers of the laboring man and woman. It was and is a fundamental Progressive article of faith that democracy—equal opportunity for all—begins at home.

But Robert M. La Follette was not entirely alone in his struggle to bring to full flower the Progressive program. Democrats, Socialists, Republicans, agnostics—all in their individual way, in the true spirit of the Seekers and sometimes seemingly at cross-purposes—worked toward the same goal. The list is long and full of distinguished Americans—Eugene Debs, Jane Addams, George W. Norris, William E. Borah, Albert J. Beveridge, Louis D. Brandeis, Thorstein Veblen, Peter Altgeld, Hiram Johnson, Herbert Croly, Oswald Garrison Villard, Theodore Roosevelt, Samuel Gompers—to name only a few.

Those men and women helped to fashion the pioneering legislation designed to control and regulate the great economic monopolies. They laid the groundwork for public ownership and operation of the great electric power developments. They furnished the impetus that resulted in legislation designed to protect the democratic civil rights of the laborer.

As a younger group of Progressives stepped into prominence, the earlier battles presumably had been won. Senator Robert M. La Follette, Jr., discovered, however, that the gains already made had to be constantly defended. Besides, since there was no longer a frontier to absorb new people or to offer a new opportunity when the economy of the stable, settled regions faltered, the problem of providing equal opportunity became more acute and complex. It was no accident that Congressional Progressives were demanding that the federal government look ahead and plan and set up the machinery to combat a general depression before 1929. Those Progressives, La Follette Jr., Burton K. Wheeler, Edward Costigan, Bronson Cutting, Gerald P. Nye, Smith Brookhart, Hendrik Shipstead, James Couzens, Clarence C. Dill, and others —the "Sons of the Wild Jackass"—represented a great area in which depression had almost become endemic. Agriculture had never recovered from the dislocations caused by World War I. These men fought heartbreaking battles for Progressive principles, and when the political climate in the national government changed with the election of Franklin D. Roosevelt as president these men supplied much of the legislative ammunition used to combat the depression.

They were concerned not only with the general effects of economic dislocation, but with extending democratic rights. The rights of labor were established, the resources of the federal government were drawn upon to help the farmer and the distressed small property owner, steps were taken to make living conditions in the cities happier and more healthful for great groups of underprivileged citizens. Slum-clearance and housing programs began to appear. The blueprints for the economic development of whole regions were drawn up. TVA and rural electrification programs became a reality. Other large-scale reclamation projects and watershed authorities were planned.

As the world began to feel the effects of the lust for power and aggression of dictators, Progressives as a group were condemned for their lack of enthusiasm in embracing policies of intervention. Some of them, it is true, were out-and-out isolationists. Others, like Robert M. La Follette, Jr., had raised their sights, so to speak, and were willing to help in every effort to isolate the germ of dictatorship to keep it from spreading. They were not willing to take the "steps short of war" that meant intervention in European affairs. Senator La Follette, among others, did everything in his power to promote the Good Neighbor policy with Latin America. He supported and voted for Secretary of State Cordell Hull's reciprocal trade program. He insisted, however, that before the United States government could properly intervene in the affairs of other nations there were serious problems at home to be solved. Few denied the Progressive contention but there seemed to be more glamour in beating the drums for democracy abroad than working to make it a reality at home.

All through the years Progressives have been tempted from time to time to break away from their party affiliations to form a new party group. American history is strewn with the bones of such movements. The La Follettes, father and sons, were interested in such movements. The years 1912 and 1924 were significant years in the political life of the elder Senator La Follette. He was persuaded, however, that third-party movements did not develop because a small group of leaders broke away from established parties and set up new ones. They properly came after the election of Progressives. The elder La Follette thought in terms of the national political scene. His sons, Robert Jr. and Philip, in 1934 seemed by their participation in the forming of the Progressive party in Wisconsin to deny the tenets of their father. Conditions in the state, coupled with the political position of the La Follettes and other Progressive Republicans as a result of the New Deal, were such that a break was inevitable.

Final judgment regarding the third-party experiment of the Progressives in Wisconsin must be left to history. Tentatively, at least, it can be said that the Progressive party of Wisconsin failed to gain a foothold for the same reasons that third-party movements elsewhere failed. First and foremost is the inescapable fact that the American form of government fosters and strengthens the two-party system. Americans possess a traditional respect for bigness, for the black-and-white dichotomy on the scale of social, economic, political, and moral values. Nationally the climate of opinion toward third, or minority, parties is cold. As political beings we think in terms of Republican or Democrat, and the balance of political power has been generally with one or the other of the major parties. The exigencies of politics and economics has not forced us to think in terms of pluralities and combinations of minority groups to gain or maintain power. Ours has been a government, generally speaking, of majorities. Stalwart Republicans in Wisconsin expressed delight at the withdrawal of Progressive forces in 1934 and many newspaper editors wrote that with the Progressives in their own party, issues and elections would be on a clear-cut basis. Yet those same individuals and newspapers, after the first election under the three-party system, complained that Wisconsin was governed by a minority vote!

In the second place, American political history validates the proposition that unless a third party can gain national acceptance it is doomed to an uncertain existence. In this connection one is reminded of the National Progressive party launched in 1912. But the National Progressive party failed largely because it was imposed from on top. There was a grass-roots Progressive movement in a number of states but most of the leaders, with the notable exception of the elder Senator La Follette, achieved their progressivism after they had gone to Congress. True, their progressivism was approved by the voters back home. The elder La Follette told fellow Progressives that, until the time arrived when an irresistible demand came from the people for a new party alignment, progressivism had its best chance of survival and influence within the framework of the traditional two-party system. The effort to give the Wisconsin Progressive party a national base failed because of political reverses at home in 1938 and because, one suspects, some of the leaders misread the political temper of the times.

Thirdly, the Progressive party of Wisconsin came to an end, as Senator Robert M. La Follette, Jr., himself pointed out to delegates at the Portage conference, partly because government at the local level in Wisconsin is in spirit nonpartisan. The party had difficulty, after the first flush of enthusiasm, putting county tickets together in order to stimulate interest and activity. The war, too, supplied further reasons for the decline of the party.

One other point is pertinent in an examination of why the Progressive party of Wisconsin failed. Progressivism as the basis of a political or economic or social program, does not lend itself to being a part of the inflexible pattern of political or organizational machinery. The point has already been made that in Wisconsin one of the chief differences between Stalwart and Progressive Republicans was the differing concept between the two groups over party regularity and responsibility. Senator La Follette himself summarized the matter in his address at the Portage conference. He said:

"The Progressive movement is more than a form of political organization. It is the vital moving force that transcends personalities, politics, and parties. . . .

"Organizations are merely the instruments through which social and political ideas must be implemented. The form of organization through which we can work may change from time to time. But whatever organization we work through our ideals remain the same."

Over the years this attitude developed a contempt for party organization as such. Thus, when the Progressives were faced with the necessity of putting together a political organization they were not sufficiently schooled in such matters to do a successful job. They discovered, as time went on, that what they had been preaching was literally true. As between principle and party, for instance, many of the Progressives in Wisconsin followed principle instead of party in the 1944 state election when they gave heavy support to Governor Goodland and their own party candidate received barely enough votes to keep the name of the party on the ballot. Glenn D. Roberts, chairman of the Progressive State Central Committee, criticized his own party members in this respect at the Portage conference when he said that many of the Progressives who wanted to continue the party were the same ones who never gave any support to the party during campaigns and never put up any candidates.

From the point of view of political party machinery, the Progressive party of Wisconsin is dead. It cannot be assumed, however, that spiritually the movement is moribund. The broad social and political principles enunciated by the elder La Follette many years ago have become so much a part of thinking in Wisconsin that automatically proposals are judged in terms of those principles. Progressivism will continue to serve as a guide and provide a scale by which the promises and accomplishments of the Wisconsin politician, be he Republican, Progressive Republican, or Democrat, will be measured. In it is combined the protest against exploitation by whatever group of other groups, the simple demand for fair dealing and exact justice between man and man, and the positive expression of faith in democracy, not as an unattainable ideal but as a practical way of life—the American way.

At the national level, the two Senators La Follette—and at the state level, the son and brother, Philip—helped to keep alive and contributed to the nineteenth century midwestern American agrarian protest against the economic and political inequalities that threatened the kind of democracy that Thomas Jefferson, Andrew Jackson, Abraham Lincoln, and other great American citizens dreamed and planned for this nation. But what of the future of Progressivism?

The La Follettes at the moment are inactive politically. Robert M. La Follette, Jr., set up an office in Washington as economic consultant. After literally a lifetime spent in public life and politics, Bob La Follette was anxious to spend some time as a private citizen. Shortly after the August, 1946, primary, he laughingly told a friend that "it feels good to be my own boss for a change instead of having about three million bosses."

Bob La Follette's retirement from public life did not, however, prevent his being considered for a number of important administrative posts in the government. President Truman made several offers but he stuck by his decision to be plain Mr. Robert M. La Follette, Jr., private citizen.

To others fell the task of carrying the Progressive banner in a Congress dominated by conservative Republicans. It looked for a time as though possibly Congress had turned back to the days of 1910 when almost literally the Progressive membership could be counted on the fingers of both hands. There seemed, as the 80th Congress convened and organized, to be a swinging of the political pendulum to straight conservatism. But there were straws in the wind.

In the spring of 1947 members of the Republican majority in the 80th Congress began to complain about the "unfair" treatment they thought they were getting at the hands of newsmen who reported the day-to-day events of Congress. Basis of the complaint was the fact that the public opinion polls indicated that the Republican party and its program had slipped in public esteem. Many members of Congress were smarting under the impact of critical letters from people back home.

The Republican party had won a notable victory in the elections of the preceding November and party leaders believed their program of tax cutting, budget slicing, and labor regulation was just what the voters had ordered in electing a Republican Congress. Leaders of the Republican majority were chagrined to discover that a majority of the citizens of the nation did not think so. In their dismay at the fickle turn of events, Congressional leaders accused individual members of the Washington press corps with deliberate distortion or at least giving their stories a New Deal slant.

In their search for a whipping boy and a rationalization of their loss of popular esteem, majority leaders of Congress evidently overlooked the fact that Progressive doctrines such as "taxation based on ability to pay," fair dealing, and exact justice between man and man as they applied to relations between management and labor, and the principle of a government responsive to the needs of citizens had taken root in people's thinking. Legislative proposals and efforts to turn the clock back to the period of the 1920's met stiff resistance by the public. Republican Congressional leaders were learning that when the voters put them in office in November, 1946, they were not given carte blanche to renounce the Progressive doctrine that the resources and production potential of the nation can support a high standard of living with opportunity for all to enjoy the fruits of labor—including the laboring man himself.

Even though Progressive sentiment in the nation, and especially in Congress, seemed politically weak in 1947, there were indications that it was by no means to be discounted. Conservative Republicans in the Senate of the United States, attempting to put through laws that would put new restrictions on labor legislation already on the statute books, learned to their embarrassment that Progressives under the leadership of Senators Wayne Morse of Oregon, George D. Aiken of Vermont, and others could muster enough votes to hamper their plans.

Senators Morse, Aiken, Langer of North Dakota, and Tobey of New Hampshire, joined on occasion by Ralph Flanders of Vermont, Ives of New York, Young of North Dakota, Knowland of California, and Cooper of Kentucky—all Republicans—laid down a steady and telling barrage of opposition to their party leadership on a wide variety of subjects. They objected to indiscriminate budget cutting, labor law changes, scuttling of OPA; they opposed their party leadership in voting for major presidential appointments.

As the debate on the Greek-Turkish aid bill was drawing to a close the latter part of April, 1947, Senator George D. Aiken rose and told the Senate:

"There are some members of Congress who will vote for the aid to Greece and Turkey in the belief that this will serve the best interest of our country, but who will oppose important domestic legislation designed and urgently needed for the growth and strengthening of our nation.

"As a matter of fact, the surest way to fortify our foreign affairs is to strengthen and expand our own economy here at

home. We cannot achieve this unless we are willing to continue
to make a reasonable investment in our present and future well-
being."

The nation, Aiken said, must initiate new programs or re-
invigorate old ones for the development of our human and
natural resources. He called for positive Congressional action
on federal aid to health and education, the St. Lawrence seaway
and power project and similar public works, the rural electrification program, soil conservation, and on "other matters directly
affecting the welfare and security of our own people here in the
United States of America."

"We face the choice," Aiken told the Senate, "of taking bold,
progressive action now in matters relating to the development of
our human and natural resources, or the alternative of defaulting
now and suffering the consequences of a stagnant economy; a
disillusioned, restless people; a nation stalemated and withering
on the vine—all because we lacked the courage to go forward,
or because we were too shortsighted to invest in the future of
our own country.

"Let us strive toward racial peace and economic democracy,
and stamp out bigotry and intolerance.

"The best foundations for unity here at home are jobs, education, comfortable homes, better health, productive land, and developed resources. . . .

"We have shown in the past what can be accomplished by a
free people. We cherish our form of government, based on the
dignity and freedom of the individual.

"The best defense of our American way of life lies in the spirit
of the nation. That spirit is the bulwark of our democracy . . .
We cannot destroy communism by military might alone. An
ideology can filter through the strongest military defense.

"In this atomic age, requiring enormous expenditures for the
establishment of military defense, we can impoverish our nation
and break the morale of our people if the burden of war proves
excessive. If that comes to pass, then communism is more likely
to seep through and find fertile ground behind our lines."

Senator Aiken was not opposing aid to Greece and Turkey—
he voted for the funds—he was trying to call attention, as the

two Senators La Follette so often did, to the Progressive tenet that democracy, like charity, begins at home.

The Progressive fight continues. The conscience of America is not yet dead.

Index

Adams, Charles K., 14
Adamson Act, 82
Addams, Jane, 99, 289
Administrative assistance, senatorial, 279
Advisory referendum on war, 251
Agriculture, assistance to, 174
  Department of, 236
  industrialized, 203
  plight of in defense economy, 236
Aiken, George D., 194, 283, 284, 295, 296
Albright, Robert C., 278
Aldrich, Nelson B., 43, 51, 54, 55, 56
Allied War Debts, 114, 140
Allison, William B., 43, 52
Altgeld, Peter, 289
Aluminum Company of America, 235
American Aid to Russia, 260
American Debt Commission, 114
American Federation of Labor, 103, 121, 201
American Magazine, 66
American Political Science Association, 271, 273
Amlie, Thomas, 179
Anderson, Paul Y., 111
Antilabor practices, 198
Antitrust Division, Department of Justice, 233, 234
Antitrust investigations, 233

Appeals, District of Columbia Court of, 133
Appropriations bill, Naval, 1909, 47
Appropriations, Senate Committee on, 277
Argyle, Wis., 109
Armed Forces, Department of, 281
Armed intervention, 244
Armed Ship bill, 84, 85, 266
Armistice, 1918, 90, 94
Arnall, Ellis, 5
Associated Farmers of California, Inc., 208, 209
Associated Press, 67, 87, 90, 243
Atlantic Charter, 245, 257
Atlantic Monthly, 268, 269
Atomic energy, 275
Authier, George F., 130
Avila, Miguel, 241

Baker, Alfred L., 65
Baker, Ray Stannard, 63, 231
Ballard, John, 114
Bancroft, Levi, 59
Baltimore *Sun*, 112, 118, 146
Barkley, Alben W., 275, 276, 280
Barry, Robert, 241
Barton, Albert O., 50
Beard, Charles, 166
Beck, Joseph D., 6
Bennett school law, 23
Benz, Adolph, 190